The Leadership of George Bush

The Leadership of
GEORGE BUSH

AN INSIDER'S VIEW OF THE
FORTY-FIRST PRESIDENT

Roman Popadiuk

Best wishes,
Roman Popadiuk

TEXAS A&M UNIVERSITY PRESS
College Station

This paper meets the requirements of ANSI/NISO z39.48-1992
(Permanence of Paper).
Binding materials have been chosen for durability.

Library of Congress Cataloging-in-Publication Data

Popadiuk, Roman.
The leadership of George Bush : an insider's view of the forty-first president /
Roman Popadiuk. — 1st ed.
p.   cm. — (Joseph V. Hughes Jr., and Holly O. Hughes series on the
presidency and leadership studies)
"All photographs courtesy George Bush Presidential Library and
Museum."—ECIP galley.
Includes bibliographical references and index.
ISBN-13: 978-1-60344-112-4 (cloth : alk. paper)
ISBN-10: 1-60344-112-3 (cloth : alk. paper) 1. Bush, George, 1924– 2. Presidents—United
States—Biography. 3. United States—Politics and government—1989–1993—Decision
making. 4. United States—Foreign relations—1989–1993—Decision making.
5. Political leadership—United States—Case studies. 6. Political planning—United
States—Case studies. I. George Bush Presidential Library and Museum. II. Title.
III. Series: Joseph V. Hughes Jr., and Holly O. Hughes series in the presidency
and leadership studies.
E882.P67   2009
973.928092—dc22
2008050660

For my wife, Judith, and our children,

Gregory, Matthew, Catherine, and Mary,

who, in many ways, are part of this story

CONTENTS

PREFACE AND ACKNOWLEDGMENTS

George Bush sat straight up, his back rigid but his chest heaving slightly as he sought to hold back the tears. Barbara Bush sat quietly, unmovable, a glint of satisfaction and pride sparkling in her eyes. George Bush's eyes welled and his face tightened as he continued to stare at the television screen. Before him, his son George W. Bush, governor of Texas, was announcing the creation of an exploratory committee for a run for the presidency. The mixed emotions of pride, happiness, and history showed clearly in the elder Bush's expressions.

For George W. Bush, it was the beginning of an extraordinary journey that would lead to his ultimate victory in the November 2000 election, making it only the second time in U.S. history that a father and son had both held the presidency.[1]

The tears glistened in Bush's eyes, but the firm resolve and self-discipline held back any onrush of open, raw emotion. By his own admission, George Bush is prone to tears in emotional situations. He and his daughter, Doro, he readily admits, lead the family in the sport of "bawling."

This March day in 1999, however, sitting in the living room of his apartment at the George Bush Presidential Library Center at Texas A&M University, George Bush only came to the edge; a tight hold on the arms of the chair appeared to help him through the moment. One was struck by the frailty and humanity that Bush exhibited. Even the aura of the Bush Presidential Library Center could not mask the emotion and feelings that were rushing through him. Indeed, the moment appeared to overshadow the trappings of the presidency and highlighted what to George Bush is more important—family and friends.

Bush's display of emotion that day was not a private, momentary lapse. He is prone to showing his feelings publicly as well. It is a characteristic that has endeared him to family and friends. The American public is typically intrigued by the personal lives and character of its leaders. Beyond the questions of policy, of challenges faced and electoral strategies, one of the favorite questions regarding presidents is what kind of persons they are. Numerous presidential studies delve into the subject of presidential character, such elements as the strengths, weaknesses, beliefs, and other personal attributes that mark individuals and their behavior. From such an analysis one is able not only to glimpse the makeup of the individual but also to gain meaningful insights into the style and quality of leadership the president exhibited. This is such a study. It is the contention of this book that leadership stems first and foremost from the makeup of the individual. It seeks to examine the character of George Bush and position it in the context of his administration's policies. It examines how character influenced his leadership style, the strengths and weaknesses exhibited in that style, and it seeks to explain the rationale behind some of the actions and policies of his administration. In many ways, this is an easy task. Bush's personality is open and unvarnished; his character is easily discernible and has an impact on those he meets. It leaves lasting impressions.

This book is not intended to be a definitive analysis or history of the Bush administration. The book does, however, paint a broad picture, touching on many aspects of White House and presidential life. The aim is to present a detailed picture of the milieu in which presidents and their staffs operate and the pressures and responsibilities they face. This milieu both reflects and is affected by a president's leadership qualities.

In large measure, however, this book is a personal reminiscence. During that part of my career spent at the White House, first in President Reagan's second term and then with President Bush, I had an opportunity to view and interact with Bush while he was vice president and then president. From the Oval Office to his stay at Bethesda Naval Hospital in 1991 for an irregular heartbeat, I was able to view him up close in both official and personal situations. From Washington to California, to China, to Chile, to Egypt, to the Soviet Union, I was able to travel with the president and witness Bush's handling of the historic events that touched his administration.

I served as deputy assistant to President Bush and deputy press secretary for foreign affairs, the same position I held toward the end of the Reagan presidency. In this capacity I enjoyed a close working relationship with Press Secretary Marlin Fitzwater and National Security Adviser Brent Scowcroft. The White House Press Office afforded a unique perspective. It was involved in all issues, domestic and foreign, because of its responsibility for explaining administration policy to the media. It was not subject to compartmentaliza-

tion as was the case on the policy side; there, for example, if you dealt with
African affairs at the National Security Council, you did not get involved in
Latin American issues, or if you dealt with foreign issues, you did not get
involved in domestic affairs. The Press Office dealt with it all. Press officers,
no matter their area of expertise, needed to have some understanding of issues across the board. In addition, the Press Office had ready access to the
president; a press officer always traveled with Bush. Also, one could count
on getting direction, if needed, directly from the president on the important
questions of the day that the press was chasing. The Press Office thus provided
a special vantage point from which to observe Bush up close in both informal
and formal situations. I also had an opportunity to experience the evolution
of U.S. policy as the Soviet Union came to an end, and as ambassador to
Ukraine from 1992 to 1993, I witnessed the development of the administration's policy toward the newly emergent states.

I witnessed or participated in many of the events this book recounts. This
firsthand experience posed a particular challenge when I was deciding how to
approach the writing of the book. Since the purpose is to present a portrait
of George Bush, I decided against making this a first-person memoir in order
not to detract from its focus. I believe that the third-person approach I chose
makes the text more readable and places it in a more historical context.

The American presidency is probably the most studied and analyzed political office in world history. Presidents are judged in many areas: their ability
to pass or block legislation, to conduct foreign policy, and to communicate
their goals and policies, to name just a few. Political pundits, scholars, and the
media constantly evaluate presidents to define any strengths or weaknesses in
their effort to accomplish their goals. Woven throughout this whole process
is that ephemeral yet very important thread referred to as presidential leadership, the engine that helps propel a president's success. Ultimately, a president's leadership can be effectively judged only from the perspective of history, which provides distance and the opportunity to sift information that can
provide a more balanced evaluation of presidential actions and decisions.

Yet presidents, when they come into office, are immediately held accountable and are evaluated by other politicians, the press, and the public; they do
not have the luxury of awaiting history's judgment. Presidential leadership
is not just a dimension of a president's effectiveness that gets measured and
reported; it also becomes a catchall term employed by political opponents

of the president. Leadership—or a lack of it—is often used with a negative connotation by partisan critics and opponents, who may complain about the purported lack of presidential leadership when criticizing a president over certain policies and actions.

President Bush left office in January 1993. The almost two decades that have passed since then are not sufficient time to bring forth many comprehensive evaluations of his overall accomplishments. However, his leadership skills can easily be evaluated to determine his effectiveness and skill as a leader. Such an evaluation will also help shed some light on his accomplishments.

Leadership is probably one of the most analyzed and studied concepts in our society. Various scholars have delineated numerous elements that constitute leadership, and others have offered a variety of paradigms by which to judge the effectiveness of leadership. An increasing number of books, seminars, lectures, and retreats are devoted to the subject, and the issue is a staple in college courses on business and politics. In addition, both the private sector and government and military bureaucracies at various levels have applied considerable energies to determine what constitutes effective leadership and how to develop better leaders, all for the purpose of providing a more efficient and motivated work force. In those public and private arenas, various mechanisms of leadership, including communication, negotiating skills, and personal charisma, among others, are examined on the individual level, and group dynamics are studied on the organizational level.

It is debatable whether or not leadership can be taught. Many believe it is an innate quality or somehow a combination of natural ability and conscious development. Irrespective of the debate, one can learn much from observing the qualities and characteristics of successful leaders in whatever field they occupy. This is particularly true of George Bush, whose style and personal demeanor serve to underscore that leadership is a fusion of character and experience, with personal character being at the forefront.

Speaking about U.S. leadership in a changing world during a visit to West Point in January 1993, Bush offered the following, which can just as easily be ascribed to individual leadership: "Leadership cannot be simply asserted or demanded. It must be demonstrated. Leadership requires formulating worthy goals, persuading others of their virtue, and contributing one's share of the common effort and then some. Leadership takes time. It takes patience. It takes work."

In addition, Bush has a number of other criteria for sound leadership. "Leadership involves giving the other guy credit," Bush believes. "It means working hard. It means defining the issues clearly so that people know what to do and then do it."

Ultimately, however, he views individual characteristics as the underpinning of leadership. "Leadership also has to do with character," he states in this regard. "If people do not respect the values of a person, then you cannot be a leader. Leadership is treating people with respect. My mother always reminded us not to talk about ourselves. Not bragging is leadership also." In the 1997 Gauer Distinguished Lecture in Law and Public Policy for the American Enterprise Institute in Washington, D.C., Bush stated, "Whether you're a president, or a student, or a businessman, or a public servant, or a journalist, remember this: character matters. Scoops, words, and pictures are important, but character is what remains."

On the practical level, Bush's own concept of leadership is simple and to the point. For Bush, a leader is someone who "can bring people together to get things done." This pragmatic view is devoid of any grandiose rhetoric or rules, reflecting his own unassuming style and his belief in getting the job done. Studying George Bush will not reveal any rules of management or a formula of steps to be taken but will reveal that strength of character may be the cornerstone of successful leadership. Film star and California governor Arnold Schwarzenegger once listed several things that he had learned from George Bush: Be a good father; Be a good citizen; Be a good man; Be a dedicated and selfless public servant. The emphasis was on what George Bush as a person stood for and what he had to offer.

During a presentation to the Whitehall Breakfast Club in Houston in 2003, Chase Untermeyer, a longtime associate who first served Bush as head of presidential personnel at the White House and then headed the Voice of America, gave examples of actions and behaviors that he considers characteristic of Bush's leadership style: writing short, handwritten notes; cleaning out the in-box; answering all telephone calls by the end of the day; showing loyalty up and down; presuming competence and loyalty in subordinates and letting only their actions persuade you otherwise; being friendly and polite to everyone; letting your people pursue their own goals but keeping them in the circle; and believing that defeats can become victories. For example, in 1980, although Bush lost the race for the presidential nomination, he did get the vice-presidential spot on the Reagan ticket. Other Bush behaviors that Untermeyer pointed out include taking the hand you've been dealt without complaining and making the most of it; believing that nice guys can finish first; being on time; making the other person feel as if he or she is the only person in the room; not holding grudges or otherwise dwelling on the past; and not making personal attacks. The emphasis, once again, is on the personal characteristics that Bush exhibits. "His sense of honor, duty, hard work, and caring are extraordinary," says Tom Collamore, a longtime associate who worked for Bush in various capacities, including as assistant secretary of commerce, and his qualities "are a continuing model and inspiration."

This book focuses on a number of points. First, it examines the experiences and values that have marked Bush's life and have given him strength in terms of his political and other leadership roles. Second, it examines the specific principles that underlay his leadership style. Third, it reviews Bush's own views of leadership and his guiding philosophy. Fourth, it outlines Bush's actual management style and how he acted in certain situations. The examination of Bush's management style is covered in six chapters. One chapter examines the actual policy process and corresponding bureaucratic structure that Bush set up in the White House. That chapter also reviews how Bush viewed his management role, how he conducted himself, and how he worked with his staff, all of which helps shed some light on Bush's leadership style as well as on the internal workings of the White House. Another chapter presents an overall view of the White House environment, its glamour and daily difficulties, in order to underscore the type of atmosphere in which presidents operate and how they react to it. The next chapter examines Bush's role as a communicator. Communication is probably one of the most potent tools in a president's leadership arsenal, and it is important to gauge Bush's success in this area. A chapter on foreign policy then examines Bush's role in the international arena, with a focus on the Soviet Union. Part of this examination involves Bush's views of his roles in domestic and foreign policy. The next chapter is devoted to examining Bush's relationship with Congress. Relations with Congress are critical to the success of the legislative program of a president and thus have an impact on the president's legacy. The chapter examines how Bush applied his leadership qualities, what his goals were, and what obstacles he faced on Capitol Hill and how or why he was unable to overcome those obstacles. The last chapter looks at Bush's handling of the economy and the presidential campaign of 1992, two issues that greatly affected his management and leadership skills. In a postscript, I try to place Bush's presidency in a historical context by comparing his effectiveness and leadership to those of other presidents. With such a comparison one can form an early judgment of Bush's place among his peers and thus gain an added understanding of his presidency.

Writing this book has been a pleasant task. It has brought back many fond memories and led to many conversations with colleagues who have kindly shared their recollections and views. There are many personal remembrances. After the election in 1992, while I was still serving as ambassador to Ukraine, my younger son, Matthew, then ten years old, wrote to the president. He sought to reassure him: when he was in the fourth grade he lost a bid to be the class president. The president wrote back—now they were just a couple of guys who lost an election to be president. When my older son, Gregory, needed to collect signatures for a class project on individuals whose name started with "G," George Bush promptly obliged. Years later, after Bush left office, my daughters, Catherine and Mary, visited Kennebunkport with me. We were promptly bundled off in the president's boat in a high-speed race across the bay for lunch at a local restaurant. That is George Bush.

I want to thank my wife, Judith, for her encouragement in this project. She was an inspiration and most helpful with her assistance and editorial advice. Our children, Gregory, Matthew, Catherine, and Mary, were also of great assistance in helping to shape the outline of the book.

I also wish to acknowledge David Abshire, Jackie Adams, Lud Ashley, James Baker III, David Bates, Jean Becker, David Beckwith, Brad Blakeman, Michael Boskin, Phil Brady, Ann Brock, Andy Card, Jim Cicconi, Tom Collamore, Julie Cooke, B. Jay Cooper, Jim Dyer, Tom DeFrank, Michael DeLand, David Demarest, George Edwards, Stephen Farrar, Laurie Firestone, Marlin Fitzwater, Bob Gates, Gene Gibbons, Jon Glassman, Bob Grady, C. Boyden Gray, Shirley Green, Bill Harlow, Stephen Hart, Betsy Heminway, Kaki Hockersmith, Michael Jackson, Admiral David Jeremiah, USN (Retired), David Jones, Jack Kemp, Ron Kaufman, Bobbie Kilberg, General Charles Krulak, USMC (Retired), Terri Lacy, Gary Laughlin, Fred Malek, Katie Maness, Tim McBride, Fred McClure, Jim McGrath, Doug Menarchik, Lawrence C. Mohr, M.D., Bob Mosbacher, Virginia Lampley Mulberger, Bonnie Newman, Mark Paoletta, Linda Casey Peopsil, Gregg Petersmeyer, Dale Petroskey, Richard (Digger) Phelps, Roger Porter, Patty Presock, Dan Quayle, Don Rhodes, Dennis Ross, Brent Scowcroft, Bill Sittmann, Curt Smith, Dorrance Smith, Tony Snow, Joni Stevens, John Sununu, Ginny Thornburgh, Chase Untermeyer, Gene Van Dyke, Ken Walsh, Sean Walsh, Dr. Allen Weinstein, Harris Wofford, Natalie Wozniak, Rose Zamaria, and Philip Zelikow.

Throughout the book I have relied heavily on George Bush's own words so that the text reflects clearly and accurately what Bush thought, what motivated him, and how he viewed the events of his life and career. His own words thus provide a more complete picture and understanding of the man and his times. I especially appreciate the time George Bush took to discuss his years in office with me. His views and recollections were most helpful. The conclusions, views, and episodes recounted in these pages, however, are in no way an endorsement by him. Furthermore, Bush has a visceral aversion to being put "on the couch"; he does not like to engage in "psychobabble," as he refers to it, nor is this work an attempt to do so. It is meant to give an overview of the man and his politics. The book presents the positive and the negative. This is in keeping with Bush's own approach. Throughout his public life Bush openly and readily admitted to his shortcomings and mistakes.

I am also grateful to Barbara Bush for her time and insights. She was most helpful, but her assistance also should not be read as an endorsement of any of the contents of the book.

A number of books were particularly helpful. *A World Transformed,* by George Bush and Brent Scowcroft; Bush's book of letters, diary entries, and memos, *All the Best, George Bush;* and his campaign biography from 1988, *Looking Forward;* Dan Quayle's memoir, *Standing Firm;* Barbara Bush's *Barbara Bush: A Memoir;* and Jim McGrath's *Heartbeat,* a compendium of Bush's speeches, diary notations, and statements, were invaluable in helping to point me in certain directions. *All the Best, George Bush* was particularly helpful for the diary notations.

George Bush's public speeches and interviews were also a rich source of information, presenting views on various events in his administration and his personal style. The Public Papers of George Bush, issued by the National Archives and Records Administration, provided ready access to the speeches, statements, press releases, press conferences, and other documents of the Bush administration.

The various lectures and conferences at the George Bush Presidential Library Center at Texas A&M University were an invaluable source of information. In particular, I am grateful for the ideas and views presented by John Sununu, Brent Scowcroft, Robert Reischauer, Arnold Schwarzenegger, and Bob Gates during their appearances and have taken the liberty to draw upon and quote from their presentations. Bush's lectures and discussions during various forums held at the center also presented a ready source of information on the issues of leadership, his administration, and the personalities he dealt with as president. I have also drawn on his postpresidential speeches, which provide some insight on his role, views, and activities as president.

I appreciate the time and effort of all who assisted in this project. Their participation greatly enriched the writing of the book by reminding me of many special events and by helping to shape the overall context of the work. Without their assistance this book would not be possible. The strengths of the book are due to their diligence and cooperation. Any shortcomings, factual or otherwise, are solely my own.

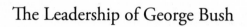

The Leadership of George Bush

One

THE MAKING OF A LEADER

I NAUGURATION DAY, January 1989, was unseasonably warm. The temperature hit a high of fifty-one degrees. It was mild, but breezy, with mostly cloudy skies. Inauguration day is a remarkable symbol of one of humanity's greatest achievements: the peaceful transfer of power based on democratic principles. The day is also fraught with emotion, touching both the outgoing and incoming presidents and the people around them. On this day, George Bush was to be sworn in as the forty-first president of the United States, succeeding Ronald Reagan, whom he had served for eight years as vice president. Bush had engineered a come-from-behind victory against the Democratic Party candidate, Michael Dukakis. Down in the polls in double digits during the summer of 1988, Bush easily swept to victory in November by an 8-point margin. He won forty states, with an Electoral College margin of 426 to 112, making him the first vice president since Martin Van Buren to succeed to the presidency.

The days leading up to the inauguration were marked by the traditional farewells and ceremonies. Nostalgia was gripping those who were moving on; they took comfort in the legacy Reagan was leaving behind—a reborn, confident nation and a strong conservative imprint on government and American society. They could point to his successor as the greatest endorsement of Reagan's tenure. Those around Bush were filled with hope and enthusiasm, eager to take the reins of power.

On January 11, Reagan's chief of staff, Ken Duberstein, hosted a party for the senior White House staff in the Roosevelt Room in the West Wing. Duberstein is an ebullient, sharp-minded Brooklynite who had come on board when Howard Baker became chief of staff. He served as Baker's deputy and then filled the position when Baker left. The staff mingled, recalling past moments and waiting to view Reagan's farewell address at 9:00 P.M. on one of the two televisions that were in the room. After his address, President Reagan came in and was met with sustained applause. He gently waved off the applause and looked around the room. His remarks were brief, focusing on his gratitude to the staff.

"I could not have gotten through the years without good staff like you," he stated. It was vintage Reagan, unassuming and with a kind word for everyone.

A week later, on January 18, the staff hosted a farewell for the Reagans in the ornate East Room. The staff presented Reagan with a horse bridle and riding gloves. The First Lady received a small decorative box. Reagan eyed his gifts with delight. An avid horseman, Reagan showed a certain joy and expectation; one could sense him looking beyond the room and envisioning the joy of being at his California ranch. With a quick shake of the head he brought himself back to the moment at hand, glancing around the room with that warm smile and head slightly tilted. He thanked everyone for the gifts and for their service over the years. Nancy Reagan, however, lost her composure, broke into tears, and could manage only a simple "thank you." The staff then joined in singing "Auld Lang Syne," adding to the emotion of the moment.

On the afternoon of January 19, President Reagan and President-elect Bush jointly met with the staff. This meeting presented Bush with the opportunity to thank the president's staff for their support over the years. He then directed his comments to the president.

"Mr. President, you have been my teacher and a friend," Bush concluded, succinctly noting the two ways that he had viewed Reagan. Years later, at Reagan's funeral, Bush emphasized this feeling during his remarks. "I learned more from Ronald Reagan than from anyone I encountered in all my years of public life," stated Bush at the memorial service.

That January day in 1989, however, Reagan gave Bush a warm smile and, with a twinkle in his eyes, Reagan moved forward.

"You have been a part of everything in my administration," Reagan stated, "and you have never taken my pulse." It was a good way to end the moment; it lightened the mood as the moment for the change of command approached and emotions were welling in all. And the change was accelerating each minute.

By 6:30 P.M. that evening all of Reagan's beloved statues of saddles and western horsemen had been removed from the Oval Office and the desk was cleared. On inauguration day, by 7:30 A.M. the photos of President Reagan had already been removed from the West Wing corridors. The West Wing is the president's world. It houses the Oval Office, the president's meeting rooms, and the offices of the senior staff. Everyone wants an office in the West Wing; it is a sign of power. It puts you on the A-list for social invitations, your words are listened to, and everyone believes you have the ear of the president. People will take an office that is a small cubbyhole with no windows in the West Wing over a spacious office with windows across West Executive Avenue in the Old Executive Office Building.[1] The building is on the White House grounds, but because of its distance from the West Wing it does not carry the same cachet. Throughout the corridors of the lower level of the West Wing, the walls are decorated with large photos of the president, rotated on a regular basis to depict the president's latest travels, speeches, or other activities. It is a vivid reminder of who is in charge.

President-elect Bush, joined by family and two hundred invited guests, attended a 9:00 A.M. service at St. John's Church in Lafayette Square. The readings were from Isaiah, chapter 26, verses 1–8, and Romans, chapter 13, verses 1–10. They reflected the self-effacement and the dedication to public service that are a bedrock of Bush's belief system. They also served to remind him of the responsibilities of his forthcoming role and the need to remain cognizant of a higher authority. Isaiah instructs, "Trust in the Lord forever! For the Lord is an eternal Rock. He humbles those in high places, and the lofty city he brings down." In his letter to the Romans, Paul reminds us, "Let every person be subordinate to the higher authorities, for there is no authority except from God, and those that exist have been established by God."

Over in the White House, meanwhile, the press was clamoring for the opportunity to record the passing of command. In particular, they wanted photos immediately after the noon swearing-in ceremony, when the photos on the walls of the West Wing were changed. Marlin Fitzwater, who had served as Reagan's press secretary and would also be President Bush's, was torn. Feeling his allegiance to both men, he refused the photographers' requests, not wanting to emphasize the abrupt change that was taking place behind the scenes.

A little before 10:00 A.M. maintenance personnel started rearranging the hooks on the walls and aligning them. Furniture was being moved around in the Old Executive Office Building. By 11:00 A.M. even the photos of Vice President Bush were down. At 12:30 P.M., after the swearing-in ceremony at the Capitol, the West Wing was decorated only with photos of Bush. A little before 2:30 P.M. the Oval Office was almost completely set up to accommodate President Bush, with family photos and favorite statues. By 4:00 P.M. the chief of staff's office was being painted.

The West Wing was quiet; the only staff members present in the late afternoon were the Press Office personnel. The focus shifted to the celebration of a new president, with special events and balls throughout the city. The new chief of staff, John Sununu, came by the West Wing at 5:00 P.M. He stopped to chat with two reporters who had run across him when they were on their way out of the White House grounds. It was an ironic moment. Sununu was gracious and accommodating to the press members, so unlike the pattern that eventually characterized the mutual relationship. That night, however, the spirit of goodwill and friendship seemed to prevail throughout the city. Beyond the White House gates Washington was awash with celebrations.

Bush was now in charge. On that day, Bush exhibited the characteristics that have come to define him as a person and as a politician and that have influenced his leadership style. He was gracious, understanding, and deferential yet confident in his actions and words and friendly toward all. In his nominating convention speech Bush had started to chart his own course when he spoke of a kinder, gentler nation, words that reflected his own personality and bearing toward those around him. Yet beneath the surface lies a sturdiness of character that manifests itself in his interactions.

When George Bush enters a room he exudes the first visible criterion of leadership: presence. Tall, standing at six feet two, with a full head of hair and a broad grin twisted to one side of his face, Bush radiates self-confidence, poise, and amiability. Now in his eighties, his full head of hair is streaked with gray. Bush has been hobbled with two hip replacements and a back operation that have given his gait a slight waddle, but there is no visible decline in the force of his personality. His broad hand gives a firm handshake and a pat on the back. Hands stuffed in his pants pockets, rocking on his heels, he engages everyone in conversation. Ever polite, he plays the gracious host, introducing, moving about the room, able to engage in snippets of conversation in a seamless movement of energy in the crowd. He carries out these activities in an unpretentious manner, showing no signs of his patrician background.

Bush has neither the demeanor nor the overt aggressiveness that one associates with a powerful politician. In 1979, when he first decided to run for president, Bush visited New Hampshire in preparation for the primary. His escort, Hugh Gregg, the former governor of New Hampshire, introduced him to Jane "Bonnie" Newman, who went on to become assistant to the president for management and administration in Bush's administration. But at that time Newman was a potential campaign supporter and worker. The two strolled the boardwalk at Hampton Beach, engaging in campaign talk as Bush casually munched on popcorn from a box. Newman immediately liked Bush. She found him to be genuine and fundamentally good and likeable. "Nice people like this just don't become president," she found herself thinking.

She signed on and, like so many others, found that Bush did not change even after he became president.

Bush does not come off as an egocentric sort of person. "I may not be the most eloquent," he stated in his acceptance speech at the Republican convention in 1988, "but I learned early that eloquence won't draw oil from the ground. I may sometimes be a little awkward, but there's nothing self-conscious in my love of country. I am a quiet man, but I hear the quiet people others don't."

Even his clothes match his subdued demeanor. They are more than likely to be off the rack rather than tailor made, and they sometimes hug the shoulders in a rumpled flow, matching the ever-askew tie that has come to be identified as the Bush style. Bush was never very conscious about his clothes. Sig Rogich, who served as an assistant to the president for public events and initiatives and is an impeccable dresser, became an unofficial clothing consultant to the president, and the two sparred humorously in conversation and in writing over Bush's dress habits. Once, as Bush was on his way to the Hill to deliver an address before a joint session of Congress on the Persian Gulf and the federal budget deficit in September 1990, Rogich rode with Bush. Bush glanced over at Rogich.

"Are we OK?" Bush inquired, referring to the preparations on the Hill.

"Everything is good except for the tie," replied Rogich, partly truthful and partly mischievous.

"What do you mean?" Bush asked, somewhat puzzled, glancing down at his tie and then over to Rogich.

"It's terrible," stated Rogich raising his voice in wonderment that Bush didn't realize the wardrobe mismatch.

"Well, what do I do?" Bush asked, puzzled about what the next step should be.

"Take my tie," Rogich stated.

They exchanged ties. Bush was wearing his standard tie—blue with red stripes. On this particular night it was a quarter-inch red stripe. Bush's idea of dramatic when it came to dress was to move from the quarter-inch to the three-quarters-inch stripe. He had numerous variations of red- and blue-striped ties in his closet. Rogich handed him his tie—a blue geometric design with a very light yellow dotted pattern. A few days later Rogich got the tie back along with a signed photo of Bush delivering the address wearing Rogich's tie. The photo was inscribed, "When it was all said and done all in that magnificent House Chamber said as one, 'Would you look at that tie.' It sent just the right message to Saddam Hussein."

George Bush has not based his own life or that of his family on recognizing individual achievement or bringing attention to oneself, one's mode of dress or one's actions. For Bush, working hard and being successful have always been the only yardsticks by which to measure one's life. By the same token he believes one should not revel in one's own success but measure what the common good is and recognize everyone's role. From this, recognition of one's own role will eventually surface. These lessons were ingrained early in life through Bush's family upbringing.

The Early Years

Bush was born in Milton, Massachusetts, in 1924, the second of five children born to Prescott and Dorothy Bush: Prescott Jr., Nancy, Jonathan, and William (Bucky). His early years were spent in Greenwich, Connecticut, where the family led a comfortable and protected life during the social and economic turmoil of the 1920s and 1930s. Early on, Bush picked up a nickname, Poppy or Pop, that family members continue to use to this day. It was the nickname of his namesake, his maternal grandfather, George Herbert Walker. At Phillips Academy in Andover, Massachusetts, Bush enjoyed studying American history, which probably helped stoke the coals of his interest in public service. One of his favorite books was Tolstoy's *War and Peace,* a vivid portrayal of Russia during the Napoleonic war. The book made such an impression on him that he read it twice, absorbing its lessons of war and the trials of life.

His teen idols were Yankee first baseman Lou Gehrig, who died in 1941 of amyotrophic lateral sclerosis, a debilitating disease of the nervous system, and tennis star Don Budge. Gehrig was a fitting role model. Quiet, productive on the field, and modest, Gehrig exemplified the characteristics that were inculcated into Bush during his youth of hard work and humility. The fact that Gehrig and Bush were left-handed first basemen helped reinforce the identity. Bush played first base at Andover and during his college days at Yale, where he was captain of the baseball team. Bush recalls those days with a mixture of nostalgia and humor.

"There was a brief time in my young life when I was absolutely convinced that I would be the next Lou Gehrig," Bush recalls. "Yes, those childhood dreams die hard and I used to keep my baseball glove from my baseball days at Yale in my desk in the Oval Office thinking that a call might come in from Yankee owner George Steinbrenner or something like that. Never happened."

As a schoolboy and a college man, Bush was well regarded and highly respected. Coupled with his upbringing, in which service was emphasized, he developed a penchant for friendliness, orderliness, and hospitality that could border on doting and worrying. "He has a concern and interest in people around him that is unmatched by any other president or high official I have ever seen," says David Beckwith, who was a *Time* magazine reporter covering the White House before becoming Vice President Quayle's press spokesman.

Indeed, Bush's desire to please and to be liked led his family to call him "Have Half" in his youth, in recognition of his willingness to share with others. One day in June 1986, Vice President Bush bounded into the Roosevelt Room, where White House staffer and avid Detroit Tigers fan Dale Petroskey was hosting a luncheon for a number of visiting Tigers ballplayers. Bush met and greeted each player and was eager to welcome his new friends to the White House. In his enthusiasm, Bush had Petroskey follow him to his office down the hall. On hands and knees Bush fumbled through some drawers.

"Ballplayers love golf balls," Bush said. "Take some of these back to them," he continued, pitching golf balls, cuff links, and other souvenirs for the players until the startled Petroskey's arms were overburdened with a barely controllable load.

This characteristic to reach out and include everyone, Bush claims, was instilled in him by his family and their strong sense of Christian ethics. Bush regards both his parents as his most important role models. "They taught me that if you have something for yourself, you should give half to your friend," Bush told a Knights of Columbus convention in 1992. "They taught me to take the blame when things go wrong and share the credit when things go right." One of Bush's fondest recollections of his youth—and one that made an indelible mark on him—was a conversation he had with his mother. As a youth, George Bush was an above average athlete. Having scored several goals in a soccer game at boarding school, he boastfully called home to report what was, in his own eyes, an exceptional achievement. After laying out his accomplishments, the silence at the other end of the line was followed by a question: "How did the team do, George?" For a youth, such a retort could be deflating. For young George it undoubtedly was, but at the same time it helped him realize the importance of teamwork and self-effacement. Indeed, to this day, Bush seeks to toe that line. In his public remarks regarding his own career successes, he states that while he feels that he and Barbara have been blessed, "no one likes a braggadocio."

The family also passed on a certain sense of social obligation. The Bushes and the Walkers on his mother's side were socially and financially prominent families who embraced the concept of noblesse oblige and who therefore imbued Bush with a spirit of service both to country and to those in need. Furthermore, his father's years of civic and political service inculcated in Bush a belief in "giving back," something that came to mark his whole life. Bush himself recognizes the privilege and successes of his life. On the outside base of the living room chimney of his summer home on Walker's Point in Kennebunkport, Maine, hangs a simple plaque with the inscription "CAVU." The letters stand for "Ceiling and Visibility Unlimited," an old aviation term that indicated the need for pilots to rely on their line of sight and clear weather to guide their planes. Simply put, it means that all's well. The sign, therefore, stands as a humble reminder to Bush that all's been well in his life and career.

While his parents were instrumental in shaping Bush's development, his mother's role is what appears to have sculpted the type of person who emerged. Bush readily admitted to the press in 1991 that his mother was "an enormous influence in my life." She was always there to provide encouragement as well as to instruct in the fine points of gentlemanly conduct. "Shortly after I was sworn into office, I received a call at the White House from my mother," recalled Bush during an address he gave at the Ronald Reagan Presidential

Library in 2007. "During our conversation, she casually said, 'And another thing, George, I always thought it was just glorious the way Ronald Reagan waited for Nancy as he exited the helicopter on the South Lawn. He's such a gentleman.'" Bush took the hint. "Fine, Mother, I promise to wait for Barbara and not walk ahead of her." His mother was the first visitor to the Oval Office after he became president. Bush gave her a tour, then seated her for a photo in the seat of honor—the armchair beside the president's in front of the fireplace. It is here that presidents sit and meet with visiting dignitaries.

In a diary notation in 1990, Bush reminisced about his mother when she visited him at the White House in her frail condition, underscoring the close relationship between the two. He wrote, "Tomorrow she leaves, and maybe I'll never see her again, but I love her very much and that's what counts. All the criticism . . . the press, and controversy—they all mean nothing. It's Mum's words: do your best; try your hardest; be kind; share; go to Church— and I think that's what really matters on this evening." The influence has not diminished with the passage of time. "I can still see her telling us to listen more than we talk, to share with others," Bush recalls, "and to find ways to be a friend."

The values of service and modesty that his family instilled in Bush in his early years were further reinforced in his school environment at Andover, where the Phillips Academy mottoes are "Finis Origine Pendet" and "Non Sibi." The former translates as "the end depends on the beginning" and the latter, "not for self." Those mottoes reinforced the family's call to live a life of service, modesty, and patience. Bush took the call seriously, becoming involved in all types of school activities, including serving as president of the senior class and captain of the baseball and soccer teams.

After graduation from Andover in 1942 Bush, buoyed by a sense of patriotism, postponed going to Yale and, on his eighteenth birthday on June 12, enlisted in the U.S. Navy. The Andover commencement speaker, Secretary of War Henry Stimson, urged the graduates to go on to college, but Bush decided to join the war effort. He became the youngest Navy pilot just a few days short of his nineteenth birthday. He was eventually stationed on the aircraft carrier USS *San Jacinto,* which was deployed to the Pacific in early 1944. That year, in September, as a twenty-year-old Navy pilot, he was shot down over the Pacific while making a bombing run in his TBM Avenger. His two crew members, Jack Delaney and Ted White, were killed, but Bush managed to eject safely. Bush faced possible capture by the Japanese before he was rescued by the submarine USS *Finback*. By his own admission, Bush faced the fear of death, yet his physical and inner strength helped him survive. Those qualities also pushed him through the defeats and victories of his future business and political careers. His military experiences were recognized by the decorations he received: the Distinguished Flying Cross and three Air Medals.

The Move to Texas

After the war, Bush was determined, despite the privilege from which he came, to build his own life and to shape his own future. A longtime friend notes that Bush was driven by a "dedicated determination" to succeed. This drive to achieve is what led Bush to leave his roots in the Northeast and move to West Texas with his young wife, Barbara, and son, George W., to build a career. George and Barbara had met at a Greenwich Country Club dance in December 1941, when they were still high school students, he a seventeen-year-old senior and she a sixteen-year-old attending Ashley Hall, a boarding school in South Carolina.

For George and Barbara it was love at first sight, and eighteen months later they were engaged. Barbara hailed from Rye, New York, and both she and Bush were the offspring of upper-class families well positioned socially and financially. Among Barbara Pierce's distant relatives was President Franklin Pierce. Her parents, Pauline and Marvin Pierce, provided the same confident and happy home life for Barbara and her three siblings that George experienced with his parents. On January 6, 1945, George and Barbara were married. Barbara left Smith College early in order to get married. With his new wife, Bush was off to Yale, from which he graduated Phi Beta Kappa with a degree in economics in 1948. After graduation, the young couple wrestled with the decision about what career to pursue.

Initially, they had toyed with the idea of pursuing a future in farming. This idea was quickly dismissed after they realized that neither one knew anything about animals or crops. The lure of farming was more of a knee-jerk reaction than a serious consideration. Louis Bromfield's popular book at the time, *The Farm,* portrayed an idyllic rural life that appealed to its readers, including the Bushes. "This is for me," Barbara Bush recalls thinking when Bromfield inspired her initial enthusiasm for the pastoral lifestyle. The reality of farm life and the associated expenses quickly dispelled any notions of a future in farming. "We couldn't afford it," she now recounts matter-of-factly.

Bush also examined corporate opportunities, but they did not come through. A family friend, Neil Mallon, persuaded Bush to try his luck out west in Texas. Mallon's advice, coupled with George and Barbara's desire "to get out and make it on our own," as Bush stated in his acceptance speech at the Republican National Convention in 1988, sealed the decision. Texas offered the lure of opportunity and distance; they would not be under the shadow of their respective families. In 1948 the Bushes packed up and headed west, where he took a position Mallon helped him secure at Ideco, an oil equipment company that was part of Dresser Industries. Bush already had some familiarity with Texas, having received military training in Corpus Christi during his stint in the Navy.

The decision to move to Texas was easy. "It was an adventure," Barbara Bush recalls. More importantly, it was what George Bush wanted, and Barbara Bush was supportive. "I was madly in love with him and still am," she explains. In Texas, George and Barbara raised their family: four sons—George W., John (Jeb), Neil, and Marvin—and one daughter, Dorothy (Doro), all born in Texas except for George W. Another daughter, Robin, was born in California when Bush was based there by Ideco, but she died of leukemia in 1953 just short of the age of four.

Bush has described the family home in Texas as follows: "We had an apartment in a tiny, ramshackle shotgun house in the oil town of Odessa, Texas. It had a makeshift partition down the middle that cut the house into two apartments, leaving Barbara and me with a small kitchen and a shared bathroom." Texas was a cultural shock to the Bushes, but they embraced it with enthusiasm. "I loved it from the minute we got there," Bush insists proudly in a video at his presidential library, "and we have been Texans ever since."

They bought their first house when Ideco transferred Bush from California to the West Texas town of Midland. It was a modest home. Their neighbor at the time and continued good friend, Gary Laughlin, describes it as being on "Easter Egg Row" because of the various colors of the houses. The house cost $11,200, which was $400 more than the other houses on the street; for the extra money, they got a carport.

The Bush family led a full, middle-class life. He coached Little League, Barbara kept score, and all four Bush boys played. Carpools, neighborhood barbecues, softball and touch football games, and church activities gave Bush an insight into the daily regimen and challenges of the typical American family, including its social disappointments and miscalculations. One backyard barbecue the Bushes planned drew no guests due to a miscommunication. Bush's casual, open invitations to stop by the house "if you have a chance" on one occasion produced not one guest. The family had loaded up on cases of soft drinks, hamburgers, hot dogs, and buns and thus had to eat their picnic food for the next few days.

Bush's drive for personal achievement led to his departure from Ideco in order to form his own oil company in 1951. He joined forces with Midland neighbor John Overbey to form the Bush-Overbey Oil Development Company. This venture eventually linked with Bill and Hugh Liedtke to form Zapata Petroleum in 1953 and the following year a spin-off, Zapata Off-Shore, of which he became president. By 1959 Bush was again willing to strike out in a different direction—offshore drilling. In that year Zapata was split, with Bush taking over an independent Zapata Off-Shore. This step necessitated the family's move to Houston to be close to the Gulf of Mexico and offshore drilling operations.

The family quickly adapted to Houston. The Bush boys continued to be normal, rambunctious lads, prone to mischief, some even bordering on the dangerous. Due to the age difference, Marvin and Neil never got much attention from the oldest, George, when he was home from boarding school. On one such occasion, George offered to play a new game that involved challenging Marvin and Neil to run down the upstairs hallway of their Houston home by the count of ten or risk being shot at with a BB gun. George pulled out his BB gun and took aim. Neil was the first up.

"Go!" shouted George.

Neil ran as fast as he could, hearing George counting slowly at first and then "six, seven, eight, nine, ten" in rapid succession. When Neil was about halfway down the hallway, George fired the BB gun, pinging Neil in the buttocks. Neil recalls this incident with some humor.

"If Saddam Hussein had known this about my brother," Neil muses, "he might have taken the president's warnings more seriously."

In West Texas, Bush had been involved in politics as a precinct chairman in Midland. In 1952 and 1956 he was involved in the Eisenhower presidential campaigns. In 1956 he served as the campaign's county chairman. In Houston, Bush's political career started a rapid rise when he became the Harris County

Republican Party chairman in 1963 and then served two terms in Congress from 1966 to 1970. After his congressional stint, Bush moved on to various appointive positions—ambassador to the United Nations, chairman of the Republican National Committee, chief of the U.S. Liaison Office to China, and director of the Central Intelligence Agency (CIA). By the time they moved into the White House, the Bushes had lived in twenty-eight places in forty-five years. The glue holding the family through all the moves and the various positions that Bush held was Barbara Bush. "I give Barbara enormous credit," Bush says regarding her ability to keep the family together. According to Bush, she was "the enforcer," the "anchor to windward," and the dedicated mother and spouse who supported the family activities. "She was always there," sums up Bush. "She represents the best of what is family."

Although Bush distanced himself from his New England family circle in order to create his own identity in the business world, he did inherit a tradition that helped him develop his political career. In observing his father, Bush appears to have learned the valuable lesson of mobility, of not being too tied to one task. Prescott Bush held many positions in various places ranging from Missouri to Ohio to Massachusetts before settling in the New York area and becoming a founding partner of the Brown Brothers Harriman investment firm. From there he went on to various community positions and served as a U.S. senator from Connecticut in the 1950s and 1960s. Bush undoubtedly observed the experiences and contacts such a path establishes, and it probably eased his own decisions in moving from position to position throughout his own career.

In that career there were some disappointments, such as the losses in Senate bids to Ralph Yarborough in 1964 and to Lloyd Bentsen in 1970 and the derailment of his presidential campaign in 1980. From that campaign, however, Bush joined Ronald Reagan on the ticket and went on to serve two terms as vice president under President Reagan.

The Impact of Bush's Business Experience

Unlike most of his predecessors as president, George Bush had an extensive business background. By the time he had become president, Bush had spent half his adult life in business and the other half in government. "I built a business from the ground up," he told a crowd in September 1992 at a national salute to the president and his black appointees. "I met a payroll, created jobs, and worked for a living." Bush went on to describe how he had studied survey and geological maps, negotiated drilling rights, and run his own company. From the latter experience, he knew the demands of meeting a payroll and the pressure of rising to challenges, particularly setbacks such as damage to an offshore drilling rig.

Barbara Bush views Bush's business experience as having had an enormous impact on his role as president. "Being in business," she claims, "you know what it means to meet a payroll and for people to depend on you." She also believes that business taught Bush how to prioritize and how to make ends meet. "He did not spend money he did not have," she notes.

In a meeting with American and Chinese students in October 2007 in Washington, D.C., Bush pointed to his business background as an important component of his presidential leadership. "I believe that my business experience might have made me a better president," he stated. "Having been in business, I took risks, and taking risks helped me to deal with situations as they arose. I found that it was a good experience." He also said that "there are some similarities to running a business and running a great big country," and both of those leadership roles required integrity and confidence. From his business experience, Bush appears to have developed a number of characteristics that were later apparent in his style of governing. One was his tendency to deal with issues as soon as they arose. In the business world, long-range planning is always ideal, but many decisions need to be made on a case by case basis. This is even truer in the oil business, where a dry well, a lost rig, or some other setback can change one's financial and long-range plans dramatically. Such situations made it impossible to rely on or even to construct a long-range plan, and they reinforced Bush's pragmatic approach to problem solving, which he carried into his presidency. Bush's oil-business experience also helped to reinforce his belief in the importance of personal relations. Business success, particularly when it comes to partnerships, such as Bush had with Overbey and the Liedtkes, is dependent to a large extent on the chemistry among the partners.

Running a business allowed Bush to cultivate both his adventurous side and his practical nature. He had to be willing to take risks, and starting his own oil business was obviously a risk in itself. He pushed to be on the cutting edge in that industry, investing in new technology, particularly in the area of offshore drilling. However, he also displayed an ability to measure situations and to decide when to take risks and when not to. Bush is, to use his own term, prudent; he knows when to move forcefully and when to move slowly. That prudence also helped him develop a "live and let live" attitude, which was valuable in his early line of work. Oil exploration is a tough business, and it was particularly so in West Texas in the mid-twentieth century. In this environment, it was important that Bush get along with competitors and associates alike in order for his business to succeed. As an up and coming business owner, Bush could not afford a head-on collision with larger competitors nor was cutthroat competition part of his nature. This attitude easily carried over into the political world, where compromise and good personal relations became the essence of his political character.

As a business owner, Bush had no time to philosophize on the nature of commerce; he had a bottom line to address and a payroll to meet. The regular need to meet the payroll probably reinforced his tendency to be mindful of others because he knew that each paycheck was important not only to the worker but also to that employee's family. Many people were dependent on Bush meeting his goals, and he took those responsibilities very seriously.

This sense of personal responsibility was evident in his approach to debt, including future campaign debts. "He paid for everything," Mrs. Bush stated. "He owed nothing." Avoiding debt or paying it off promptly reinforces strong personal relations and is evident of honesty, and Bush would have seen that in the oil fields, where a handshake and one's word were all the commitment an agreement needed. "I learned early on in West Texas that a man's handshake is his bond," says Bush. "I learned the work ethic in the oil industry where I found the people to be hardworking and honorable." Bush's oil field experience left him with a strong code of business ethics, which reinforced his own set of personal ethics. He carries the standards of honesty and fairness to this day. "It kills me to see someone breaking ethical rules," he says in regards to business practices. "It does damage to all business."

It was in the business world that Bush first experienced a taste for international affairs. Although he mostly roamed the western parts of the United States in search of oil, his business interests also took him abroad to various parts of the world. Such travels gave him an understanding of those regions and helped to hone his skills of personal diplomacy. The global nature of the oil business also required him to be knowledgeable about political situations that could affect the oil industry. It was thus in the Texas oil fields that Bush, then an employee of Ideco, got his first experience in diplomacy when he entertained a Yugoslav visitor who had come to learn about oil drilling operations. World War II, however, had left an indelible imprint on his sense of diplomacy's limits. He, like many of his generation, had witnessed the horrors of war, the need for a strong defense, and the clash of national interests and perspectives. These early encounters on the international front were sharpened by his stints at the United Nations, at the CIA, and in China. His experience as ambassador to the UN was particularly influential. "At the United Nations, I got a real feel for the importance of international relations," Bush says of his role in the world body.

Bush's Guiding Values

His early life experiences reveal four values that shaped Bush's character: faith, family, friends, and future, that is, a commitment to service that can help build a better tomorrow. Taken together, they provide the strength, patience, and foresight that helped guide him and shaped his leadership. Individually, each provides a certain reassurance and inner confidence and a sense of respect among those with whom he deals, thus strengthening his own hand as a leader.

Faith

Students of leadership often speak of moral leadership, and indeed, some presidential surveys seek to gauge a president's moral authority. For Bush, a sound moral grounding was important not only for defining one's character but also for the functioning of his presidency. Bush's character is rooted in deep convictions, as can be seen in his dedication to family values and public service. He is not, however, given to public displays of personal religious beliefs, even though he regards his faith as a source of strength and guidance. "I was never very good at discussing religion or real personal matters, such as family matters," Bush confides.

For Bush, as for Abraham Lincoln, prayer was a source of comfort and inspiration during his presidency, and he was moved by a sense of conscience and moral obligation. "Prayer is very important to George and me," reflects

Barbara Bush. "We pray every single night. He prays for people who may have hurt him."

An Episcopalian, Bush has been a regular church attendee from his youth, when going to church and praying at home were regular Bush family activities. He carried on that tradition in his own family. "Our family has always felt that church is the place to seek guidance and seek strength and peace," Bush stated in a prayer service during a visit to China in 1989. In his younger days, he taught Sunday school in West Texas, and in Kennebunkport, at St. Anne's Church, he served as a vestryman. At the beginning of his presidency, Bush told David Bates, head of the Office of Cabinet Affairs, that he would follow President Dwight Eisenhower's tradition of starting each Cabinet meeting with a prayer. Bush had Secretary of State Jim Baker lead the group at the first Cabinet session. Afterward, Bates's role, in addition to his official duties, included notifying the relevant Cabinet secretary that he or she would lead the next Cabinet meeting in prayer.

A great deal of Bush's inner strength came from praying with the Reverend Billy Graham. In 2006 Bush honored Graham with the George Bush Award for Excellence in Public Service, recognizing Graham's moral leadership not only in the United States but also in the world.[2] "No matter how deep one's faith is, sometimes you need the guidance and comfort of a living, breathing human being," Bush stated at the award ceremony. "For me, and for so many occupants of the Oval Office, that person was Billy Graham. When my soul was troubled, it was Billy that I reached out to for advice, for comfort, for prayer." The challenges of the presidency would trouble anyone's soul, so Bush's strong moral grounding was critical to his forbearance. "I believe with all my heart that one cannot be America's President without a belief in God, without the strength that your faith gives to you," he acknowledged in an address to the National Religious Broadcasters on January 29, 1990.

While he cannot point to a "born again" moment, Bush had two experiences that deeply influenced his faith. When he was shot down over the Pacific, prayer gave him the strength and inner peace that helped him survive the ordeal. "There are times in every young person's life when God introduces you to yourself," he vividly recalled during his acceptance speech at the Republican National Convention in 1992. "I remember such a time. It was back many years ago, when I stood watch at 4:00 A.M. up on the bridge of a submarine, the United States *Finback*. . . . And I would stand there and look out on the blackness of the sky, broken only by the sparkling stars above. And I would think about friends I lost, a country loved, and about a girl named Barbara. I remember those nights clearly as any in my life." When their second child, Robin, was dying of leukemia at the age of three, Bush prayed fervently, wondering why such a young, innocent life could be touched with such tragedy. The experience reaffirmed for Bush the importance of faith and the need to trust in God.

In his address to the annual National Prayer Breakfast on February 2, 1989, Bush offered some insight on his views of prayer: "There is no greater peace than that which comes from prayer and no greater fellowship than to join in prayer with others," Bush proclaimed. Equally important, he stated, was the importance of prayer in his own life. "But I can also tell you from my heart that I freely acknowledge my need to hear and to heed the voice of Almighty God." This spiritual grounding provided Bush with a moral compass that has guided him throughout his life and affected various decisions, such as his concern about limiting civilian deaths and damage to residential areas and religious sites during the Gulf War. He specifically discussed those issues with General Merrill (Tony) McPeak, the U.S. Air Force chief of staff at the time, and the general assured him that targeting had taken these issues into consideration.

During the Gulf War, the conflict between personal religious beliefs and governmental duties could be felt on the Washington scene. There was talk of what constitutes a "just war." Bush discussed these moral issues with members of the clergy. Early in 1991, shortly before the congressional resolution regarding the possibility of war, Bush met in the Roosevelt Room with his staff and addressed the issue. Bush made it clear that he had agonized over it. He reflected on his willingness to be a one-term president over the issue of a possible war. Then he stated firmly, "I have prayed. I have prayed with Billy Graham and have considered the military, tactical, and moral issues involved and even if there is not one vote in favor in Congress, I am still going. I am convinced that it is right."

Bush took his argument to the public in an address to the annual convention of the National Religious Broadcasters in Washington, D.C., on January 28, shortly after the war to expel the invading Iraqi forces from Kuwait began. The speech sought to lay out the moral justification for war and at the same time to engage critics in a dialogue by addressing the concept of "just war."

The speech reflected certain leadership characteristics of Bush. It underscored his determination and resolve in the face of adversity, an important characteristic for any leader. It also presented the rationale for his actions and rebutted the criticism that was being leveled at him. These steps underscored other aspects of Bush's leadership style: that he did not act in an arbitrary or ideological fashion; that his actions were well thought out; and that he acted in a transparent fashion, willing to expose at appropriate times his thought processes in order for the public to better understand his actions and motives. Bush clearly had this in mind when he recounted the numerous miles traveled by Secretary of State Jim Baker, the two hundred meetings with foreign officials, and ten diplomatic missions undertaken to peacefully resolve the inevitable conflict with Saddam Hussein. As he said, "Extraordinary diplomatic efforts having been exhausted to resolve the matter peacefully, then the use of force is moral." He particularly emphasized concern for the innocent victims of conflict, saying that the United States would make "every effort possible to keep casualties to a minimum."

Recalling the unrest that had swept the United States during the Vietnam War, Bush reached out to young people with an explanation of his intended actions. On January 9, the White House forwarded a letter to 460 college newspapers. In it, Bush emphasized the brutality of Iraq's leader and his own efforts to settle the issue without resorting to force, calling the choice "unambiguous—right vs. wrong."

Family

Family has always been the center of Bush's personal life. He considers his greatest success the fact that his children still come home to visit. During the dedication ceremony of his presidential library in 1997, Bush listed his three most important positions: husband, father, and granddad. These three roles are enduring both in terms of individual responsibilities and the influences they exert. In short, Bush places greater value on family and personal relations and contacts than on specific events in his life or career. Above all, he cares and reminisces about his family, his parents, and those close to him. It is those people who have touched his life and given comfort and encouragement when needed. Events and political offices come and go; they are snapshots in time, and Bush prefers not to dwell on them. He is forward looking and not obsessed with legacy. This characteristic has been useful in overcoming setbacks.

For Bush, family is a source of both personal strength and the values one needs to face life. It is in the family circle where encouragement is received, defeats soothed, and motivation provided to move forward in the face of obstacles. Bush does remember one particular personal shortcoming of his in this regard: the time his son Neil was embroiled in the savings and loan crisis, which involved the failure of hundreds of these financial institutions due to loan and investment overextensions. "I still regret not having done enough for Neil against Congress during the savings and loan situation," he says. "The highly partisan Democratic congressman Henry B. González called Neil to testify and tried to make him the poster boy for all the evils of the savings and loan situation. It was grossly unfair. If Neil's name had not been Bush, he would never have been called."

However, Bush's parental instinct to protect was evident in his jovial sparring with Democratic senator Ted Kennedy of Massachusetts. After presenting Kennedy with the George Bush Award for Public Service in 2003, Bush hosted a formal dinner for the senator in his library's rotunda. Following Kennedy's remarks to the guests, Bush, with a wide smile on his face, said in an aside to his guest, "Lay off my kid," a reference to Kennedy's sharp attacks on President George W. Bush over the war in Iraq.

Bush regards family as the source of four special values: fairness, compassion, honesty, and hard work. All are important to successful leadership. For Bush compassion is more than his public commitment to a kinder, gentler nation that he announced in his acceptance speech in 1988; it is a true commitment to helping others in need.

During a visit to Japan in February 1989, Bush learned that former ambassador to NATO David Abshire, a longtime friend who was in Tokyo on business, had fallen ill and been rushed to a hospital. Bush immediately dispatched his doctor and nurse to the hospital. In addition, he had the Japanese medical team that was assigned to him as a visiting head of state released and authorized to attend to his friend. Abshire underwent emergency surgery that saved his life.

Bush considers honesty a mark of not only trustworthiness but also dependability, and throughout his life he has been scrupulous in maintaining fair and honest relationships in his political and business dealings. With that sense of fairness, he attempts to treat people on their merits and not prejudge them. And hard work is something he has never shunned. From painting pumpjacks in West Texas to volunteering his time for various church and community organizations, Bush has tackled each challenge with enthusiasm and an eagerness to succeed.

Friends

From his early experiences and family upbringing Bush learned to reach out and maintain personal contacts. His friendliness, cordiality, and hospitality have left favorable impressions and became the hallmarks of his leadership style. He has viewed friends and others as an extended family, treating them with respect and sharing in their joys and trials. Joseph Verner Reed, a long-time family friend and chief of protocol during Bush's presidential term, best sums up the view of those whom Bush has befriended. "Unlike for most politicians," Reed states, "Bush's friendships are for real." Bush readily acknowledged to the Disabled American Veterans national convention in August 1992 that "friends have been a part of every good fortune in my life."

"George's theory is that it is better to have a friend than an enemy," explains Barbara Bush. Bush, she claims, never held grudges or let the moment of a political conflict interfere with the greater relationship. In this regard, she points to Sen. Lloyd Bentsen and Bill Clinton as examples of political adversaries who became good friends of her husband.

Bush loves to be surrounded by people and greatly enjoys entertaining. From his days at Yale to the White House, Bush has surrounded himself with friends, guests, and first-time acquaintances. Indeed, one seldom remains an acquaintance; after meeting George Bush one often becomes part of his circle. An example is Gene Van Dyke, a Houston oil man who first met Bush on a flight from Texas to New York in 1962. Bush was then head of his own oil company, Zapata Off-Shore, and was en route to meet with financial backers of Zapata. Van Dyke found himself sitting next to Bush, a stranger at the time, as they buckled into their seats for take-off, and they struck up a conversation. Van Dyke was impressed by Bush's personality, his open and honest nature, and his knowledge of world events. He took an instant liking to Bush. "This is the type of guy we need to have as president of our country," Van Dyke concluded to himself, without having any idea that Bush would eventually end up in politics and become president. From that chance encounter a life-long friendship developed, and Van Dyke became a steady supporter of Bush's political career. He entered Bush's orbit.

This veritable sea of people gives Bush energy. The more the better. At Yale, he once invited twelve guests for Thanksgiving dinner—but he only had four forks. Many of his events are usually better planned than that one, and Bush puts a great deal of personal attention into them. When he became president he had the White House staff research the types of entertaining newly inaugurated presidents undertook in their first days in order to get some idea of what he should do.

As president, Bush entertained extensively, and many times it was spontaneous. In the morning, going over his schedule, if he noticed that the evening was free, he would call the social secretary, Laurie Firestone, and ask that the showing of a movie or some other event be arranged. He would pay great attention to the arrangements, particularly the guest list, suggesting names of people who should be invited. The Bushes also entertained in the residence, inviting people for dinners and receptions. During one dinner, Bush gave his guests a tour of the Lincoln Bedroom, all the while taking photos with his Polaroid camera.

Firestone had been with the Bushes since his vice-presidential days and was attuned to their entertaining style. Bush took a keen interest in the table seating at dinners—something he still does—and preferred no green vegetables, particularly no broccoli, which he did not like. Other vegetables in disfavor were brussels sprouts and turnips; corn was a favorite. Firestone prevailed, to an extent. There must be some green vegetables—but no broccoli—at least to lend some color to the array of food on the plates. Bush's dislike of broccoli became a big story when the press broke it in 1990. It was all taken in good humor; California broccoli growers delivered a truckload of their produce to the White House and it was then donated to a homeless shelter.

Entertaining was more than just a social or personal enjoyment in the Bush White House. He and Barbara regarded it as their responsibility to open "everyone's house," as Bush referred to it, to as many people as possible, for everything from formal dinners to impromptu tours for guests and friends. At the conclusion of many of these various events, Firestone would see the guests off and be struck by their comments. Guests often expressed surprise at the graciousness and consideration of the Bushes both as a couple and as hosts.

Bush's enthusiasm for entertaining was evident when Britain's Queen Elizabeth visited in May 1991. During an Oval Office session months earlier, Joseph Verner Reed had suggested to Bush that the queen would be amenable to making a state visit. Bush eagerly leapt at the idea.

"Absolutely," beamed Bush. "Make her the star for May."

Arrival ceremonies for state visits take place on the South Lawn, with the White House serving as the backdrop. White House staff, guests, and staffers from various agencies crowd the South Lawn, waving the American flag and the flag of the guest country, and provide an enthusiastic audience for the honor guard, the twenty-one gun salute, and the speeches. For Queen Elizabeth's visit, Sig Rogich tried something different in an effort to make the occasion more memorable. He decided to reverse positions, placing the podium so that it would face the White House, thus leaving the Mall and the Washington Monument as a picturesque background for the news photographers. Rogich believed that the traditional shot, with the White House as the background, was too mundane and did not allow for a broad photograph. He discussed the possible new setup with Bush, who quickly decided to allow Rogich to proceed with the innovation.

The queen arrived to the appropriate fanfare, and Bush escorted her to the podium. Bush gave his welcoming remarks and then stepped back to allow the queen to present her remarks. Bush towered above the petite monarch, and he was supposed to pull out the riser so that she could stand above the podium. Reed caught his breath as he saw Bush step back and no one moving to pull out the step. In the instant while he debated whether to shout to Bush to pull out the riser or go do it himself, the queen took her place. All that could be seen of the queen by the audience and the photographers was her hat, thus giving rise to the "talking hat" humor surrounding the visit. Bush, however, was not amused. After the ceremony he cornered Reed by the Rose Garden.

"How could you have done this?" asked Bush. As the consummate host, he was mortified at the breakdown of protocol.

Reed mumbled incomprehensibly, fully realizing the president's embarrassment, yet cautious enough to know that nothing at the moment could be said to assuage Bush's anger. In his own defense, however, Reed finally countered with the admonishment that Bush was supposed to pull out the step. It was the wrong thing to have said.

Bush was not pleased. "I am president of the United States," stated Bush, "you are the chief of protocol. That is your job."

Then Bush gave Reed the ultimate warning.

"Barbara is angry with you," Bush told him.

As chief of protocol, Reed was indeed responsible for making the ceremony move forward flawlessly. It was now his responsibility to right the situation, and Bush wanted it done immediately. "You better go and explain to Her Majesty that it was your fault," he instructed Reed.

Reed hurried over to Blair House, the official guest residence across the street from the White House, where the queen went following the ceremony. She was very understanding, dismissing the incident and deeming it all quite funny. Her husband, the Duke of Edinburgh, however, was more taciturn and proper and was not amused. The next day, in her address to Congress, Queen Elizabeth showed her humor by starting her presentation by remarking that she hoped everyone could see her.

To this day Bush's social spontaneity is still part of his character. A close friend relates how Barbara remembers when she was a new bride and trying to blend in with the Bush family in Kennebunkport. During those days there was a tradition for families to gather along the waterfront of the River Club, down the road from Walker's Point. Each family brought its own hamburgers, and mealtimes were an opportunity to make acquaintances, especially for any newcomers to the community. Barbara recalls those early sojourns as awkward for her since no one spoke with her. With this in mind, George and Barbara Bush have always been sensitive to welcoming newcomers who have taken up residence around their home in Kennebunkport. In August 2005, the Bushes hosted such a gathering, entertaining about one hundred guests. Bush had already invited a famous country western music group for the same day, so instead of postponing either event, they blended the two into a diverse mix of friends, strangers, and staff.

Service: Building the Future

The relish with which Bush tackled his entertaining activities was mirrored in his career activities. In taking on various government positions, Bush was living the philosophy of service that had guided him since his youth. "I was taught to do what the president wants you to do," he explains, "if you feel you can do it." Of all his positions, the Republican National Committee post was the most difficult. "Worst job I ever had in my life," he explains, referring to the Watergate scandal and President Richard Nixon's resignation, both of which occurred during his chairmanship. "It was terrible," he says, in his simple summation of the post and the events surrounding it. His Democratic National Committee counterpart, Robert Strauss, whom Bush later appointed as ambassador to the Soviet Union, commiserated with Bush over his predicament. Bush's job reminded Strauss of "making love to a gorilla"— you cannot stop until the gorilla wants to.

It was part of Bush's character to undertake any task assigned to him, tackle it with enthusiasm, and do the best he could. In hindsight, it was the variety of positions he held that became one of his strengths as president. The diverse jobs had given him a wide array of leadership experience that was a great source of strength during his presidency.

This history of service underscores a core belief. To Bush, leadership means more than just leading and being in a position of authority; leadership also requires a willingness to undertake and fulfill tasks at the behest of others. Such service creates bonds of loyalty, embeds great experience, and thus provides an opportunity for advancement. In short, to lead, one must first be willing to serve. Overall, Bush was guided by a sense of noblesse oblige, a drive to better the conditions of those around him. It could be detected in the prayer that he offered at the beginning of his inaugural address. "Make us strong to do Your work, willing to heed and hear Your will, and write on our hearts these words 'Use power to help people,'" Bush prayed. "For we are given power not to advance our own purposes, nor to make a great show in the world, nor a name. There is but one just use of power, and it is to serve people. Help us remember, Lord. Amen."

Bush regards public service as a noble calling, and in his address to Congress on February 9, 1989, he stated that "any definition of a successful life must include service to others." He is troubled by the negative connotations that public service seems to raise, particularly with regard to politicians. Bush believes that the public tendency to view politics cynically because of individual transgressions by particular politicians is unwarranted. "What gets me is when people say all politicians are crooks," he says. "Well, it is not true."

Bush's own public service did not end when he left the government arena. He remains actively engaged in various endeavors, the three most important being cancer research, volunteerism, and education, represented, respectively, by the University of Texas M. D. Anderson Cancer Center, where he served as past chairman of the University Cancer Foundation Board of Visitors; the Points of Light Foundation; and the Bush Presidential Library Center. Until 2004 Bush served as honorary chairman of M. D. Anderson, and he continues in the same role at what has become the Points of Light Institute.[3] At the Bush Presidential Library Center, comprising the Bush Presidential Library and Museum, the George Bush School of Government and Public Service, and the George Bush Presidential Library Foundation, he remains a frequent lecturer and discussant, appearing with various public and private sector leaders, including such world leaders as former German chancellor Helmut Kohl and former Soviet leader Mikhail Gorbachev. Such activities are part of his effort to instill a sense of public service in the younger generations.

For Bush, the library is not an icon of personal success. Indeed, he never asks about attendance at the library—a measure by which "success" of presidential libraries is viewed. For him, the library center is seen as a place to meet old friends and to establish new friendships. He is enamored by the traditions of Texas A&M, especially the Corps of Cadets, the Singing Cadets, the football games, the Aggie Wranglers country western dance troupe, and the exceptional hospitality and friendliness that has come to be known as the "Aggie Spirit." While Bush has deep respect for his alma mater, Yale, it did not instill the same sense of values that he has come to admire at Texas A&M. Indeed, Bush humorously notes that he has been hung in effigy at Yale.

The George Bush School of Government and Public Service is a particular focus of his attention. The school's mission of preparing students for careers in public service dovetails with Bush's own high regard for public service, and he is delighted to see the nation's youth show an interest in serving their country. He takes every opportunity he can to meet with the students both inside and outside the classroom. For George Bush, there is a special interest in helping to guide the nation's youth. As president, he pointedly stated in a talk to the Youth Leadership Forum in 1990 "that America can be really transformed by youth engaged in service. There's no problem in America that young people cannot solve or certainly help solve."

Starting in 2005, Bush became actively involved with former president Bill Clinton in humanitarian relief efforts. He was, however, careful to stay away from policy issues that could impact the presidential administration of his son. "Because of my son, George, I stayed out of causes," Bush says. "I have my own niche worked out. Family and friends is what it is all about at this stage of my life. I put my energies into raising money for charitable donations, such as working with Clinton on relief efforts for the tsunami and Katrina victims and helping UN Secretary General Kofi Annan with relief for Pakistan."[4]

Two

BUSH'S PRINCIPLES OF LEADERSHIP

D R. ALLEN Weinstein, who founded and headed the Center for Democracy, and one of its board members, Senator Richard Lugar (R-Indiana), came to visit President Bush in the Oval Office in December 1989. The center was preparing to monitor the Nicaraguan elections to be held in February 1990, and Weinstein, who had just returned from a visit to that country, came to brief Bush on the progress of the election process. It was the first time that Weinstein had met Bush. He did his briefing and presented the president with a T-shirt emblazoned with a slogan in Spanish that translated as "Your vote is secret—use it." Soon afterward, back at his office, Weinstein received a handwritten thank-you note from Bush and an autographed photo of their meeting. Years later, in March 2005, Weinstein, then the archivist of the United States, met with Bush at his presidential library. One of the first things that Weinstein recounted was that first meeting and Bush's courtesy with the note and the photograph. This episode underscores Bush's reliance on personal contacts as a mechanism for placing his stamp of professionalism and courtesy on the political world.

Positive personal relations may be an inexhaustible commodity. You may not be able to repay a favor, you may not be able to support someone, you may not be able to lend money, but you can always empathize with a person's situation, treat them in a decent manner, or give them a friendly hearing, all of which create a certain bond and respect that both friend and adversary will remember and appreciate. Such behavior is not only a courtesy but also a link that reaffirms a friendship or relationship. It gives the recipient a feeling of inclusion in an inner circle, reaffirming a sense of obligation and friendship toward Bush. This sort of professional courtesy was the currency that Bush utilized, not in a Machiavellian mode but as an extension of his personality and upbringing. His notes and contacts were a way of reinforcing friendship and expressing gratitude. He appreciated what people did for him and wanted to make sure that they realized it. Such manners helped create a vast network of contacts and, equally important, the image of a likeable and decent individual, which, in itself, became a source of power and influence.

Personal correspondence is a practice that Bush holds dearly. Pecking away at his typewriter—now computer—Bush is notorious for misspellings and grammatical errors made in his haste to get the note out. He often added "self-typed" to the note or one of his staffers would add the notation. By doing so, he protected the credibility of his secretary as a professional typist but, more importantly, confirmed for the recipient that they were in possession of a unique document, one that had been personally attended to by Bush. Many of his notes were written at the end of his working day in the residence of the White House, and he would bring them into the office early the next morning. And although he sometimes typed them, most of his notes were handwritten, thus adding an extra personal touch. As president, his note writing practice came up against a formidable increase in the volume of mail that he received. In 1989 alone, he received more than 5 million pieces of mail, the vast majority of which he never saw. In his postpresidential years, Bush has become an avid e-mailer. His frenetic pace of letter writing and phone calling has not abated; he has simply worked e-mail into his daily routine.

Bush puts such a great emphasis on the practice of personal contact that he regards it as something that should be passed on in the family. Indeed, he follows in the footsteps of his father, who was an avid note writer. Once, on a return trip to the White House on Marine One from Camp David with his young grandson, George P. Bush, son of former Florida governor Jeb Bush and his wife, Columba, he took the occasion to instruct the youngster on the need for thank-you notes. George P. had received a number of gifts for his birthday and, like any youngster, was more impressed with the gifts than with where they came from.

"George, you need to write thank-you notes to the people who gave you gifts," Bush instructed. Then he reaffirmed the admonition by adding, "It is really important that you write thank-you notes when someone gives you something or does something for you."

Bush's Rules of Behavior

Bush has always operated on this basis of personal ties and connections. On two occasions when Bush was writing down his thoughts on leadership and success he underscored the personal characteristics necessary for each. In an alcove at the Bush Presidential Library and Museum that contains exhibits detailing Bush's congressional days is a list of Bush's four rules for congressional excellence and leadership, drawn from his 1988 campaign autobiography, *Looking Forward*. They revolve mainly around individual strengths and character, underlining Bush's view that leadership starts with the makeup of the individual; they are more a prescription of individual behavior rather than a template for management.

Bush believes that, foremost, one must never be personal when it comes to policy debates or struggles. Isolating an individual on an issue can come back to haunt you when you need support on another issue. Therefore, it is incumbent upon a person not to hold grudges or demean anyone. Next, it is important to know the subject matter at hand; knowledge is an important leadership tool. If you know what you are talking about, people will listen and you can lead them. This helps enhance a staff's and the public's respect and support, thus reinforcing one's stature as a leader. Bush was often able to mention bits of information he had retained on occasions when others around him had perhaps forgotten. "President Bush was perhaps the most seasoned public official ever to have been elected to the presidency," notes Joseph Verner Reed.

At times, his breadth of knowledge made up for errant staff work. During a visit to China in 1985 as vice president, Bush prevented an embarrassing situation. Speech cards prepared for his use by his staff referred to Li Peng as a vice minister, not vice premier. Bush caught the mistake and delivered the speech without incident. The wrong identification would have been not only a personal affront to the Chinese leader but also an embarrassment for the United States. The incident prompted a momentary burst of vice-presidential anger at the responsible party. He warned the staffer to be more careful and, true to form, explained how embarrassing the mistake would have been.

Bush also believes that persuasiveness is more effective than intimidation.

"The emphasis is on cooperation, not confrontation, as the surest route to progress," he said at an Associated Press (AP) business luncheon in 1989. He also stressed the importance of being considerate to those around you no matter how high or low their position. A practical reason for such consideration is that at some point in the future you might be dealing with that individual again, and the quality of the early relationship will color all future interactions. His theory is, in short, that if you treat everyone well, you are likely to have more allies as time goes on. Bush treated everyone the same, whether they were a head of state, a Secret Service agent, or domestic staff at the White House. He was able to empathize with their situations and reinforce their own confidence by sharing his own shortcomings.

Bush credits various congressional leaders on both sides of the aisle as being the inspiration for his own rules of how to succeed in Congress. This point could be considered Bush's fifth principle for congressional excellence: he sought to learn from those around him. He absorbed knowledge, analyzed it, and figured out what worked and what did not.

In a 2003 handwritten note to Henry Dormann, editor of *Leaders* magazine, Bush presented ten rules of behavior that young people might use as a guide when facing challenges. "I cannot single out the one greatest challenge in my life," Bush wrote. "I have had a lot of challenges and my advice to young people might be as follows:

1. Don't get down when your life takes a bad turn. Out of adversity comes challenge and often success.
2. Don't blame others for your setbacks.
3. When things go well, always give credit to others.
4. Don't talk all the time. Listen to your friends and mentors and learn from them.
5. Don't brag about yourself. Let others point out your virtues, your strong points.
6. Give someone else a hand. When a friend is hurting, show that you care.
7. Nobody likes an overbearing big shot.
8. As you succeed, be kind to people.
9. Don't be afraid to shed a tear when your heart is broken because a friend is hurting.
10. Say your prayers!!

Bush's Rules of Management

All of the numbered points above reflect in some fashion Bush's own leadership style. Beyond these points and his congressional rules of behavior, there are nine elements (with some overlap with the noted points and rules) that guide Bush's leadership and management style: standing up for your beliefs; telling the unvarnished truth; loyalty; expecting mistakes and admitting your own; communication; giving credit to others, as stated in his note to Dormann; showing your human side; realizing that all actions have consequences; and ensuring that everyone has and knows his or her role.

Standing Up for Your Beliefs

As a public office holder, Bush was not politically rigid. Although he has a set of political beliefs, such as limited government, he, like any politician, wrestled with the lure of compromise and the drive to succeed politically. In such cases, he faced the dilemma that every leader confronts: making the best choice. Sometimes this involved compromise while at other times, such as in his exercise of the veto, it involved eschewing any compromise. In the end, however, his decisions were colored mostly by his sense of stewardship or doing what he believed would benefit the greater good. Thus, although Bush might be accused of exercising the political opportunism that comes with the territory, one might also have a hard time making this accusation stick because many of his decisions did not yield political success; he paid a price for doing what he saw as the right thing.

"So often politicians do the easy things, the popular things," Bush told an audience in South Carolina in 1992. "But it's the tough things that tell you about character and honor and leadership. Anyone can demagogue, but presidents must make decisions. . . . I think you elect a president to say what America needs to hear, even when it's not what people want to hear." He was not swayed by polls or political fads; he had a clear vision of and dedication to individual policies that he pursued irrespective of political costs or benefits. In the early part of 1990, Bush's approval ratings were 80 percent or higher. He ignored this type of public opinion, stating matter-of-factly that he did not believe in polls. "That's not the way I try to call the shots on the policy," he told the press in March of that year.

As a member of Congress, Bush came out in favor of the Fair Housing Act of 1968 that forbade any form of discrimination, including racial, in housing. It was a very progressive position given the fact that in the 1960s the South was only in the preliminary stages of the racial transformation of American society. Furthermore, Bush represented a heavily conservative Houston district, from which he received much criticism for his vote. As president, Bush broke his "no new taxes" pledge in order to get a pathbreaking budget agreement. Although he was accused of having used the pledge to boost his chances in the presidential election of 1988, the budget agreement ultimately laid a foundation for economic growth in the 1990s.

In an effort to move the Middle East peace process forward, Bush, in 1992, forbade U.S. loan guarantees that would have helped fund the expansion of Israeli settlements in the occupied territories. The move, taken to signify U.S. evenhandedness in the Arab-Israeli dispute, undermined Bush's political support in the American Jewish community. There was intense pressure from the American Jewish community over the issue. Bush, however, was firm in his position. "I believed there was no room for compromise," he says. He has no second thoughts about that decision, although he believes that it did have a negative affect on his reelection campaign in 1992. He felt comfortable that he had taken a stand that was evenhanded. "Our position told the people of the Middle East and Europe that the United States was not going to be opting always for one side and be a part of financing settlements that the United States and the rest of the world felt violated key United Nations resolutions and that totally went against the legitimate concerns of the Palestinian people," Bush has said in retrospect. Likewise, even though some veterans groups were critical, Bush attended the funeral of Japanese emperor Hirohito in 1989. He believed it was the right thing to do for a country that had become a strong U.S. ally.

Since his days in Congress Bush has considered ethical behavior in government and the private sector to be critically important. As a freshman House member Bush introduced an ethics and disclosure resolution aimed at having members disclose their financial holdings. The effort did not succeed, but when Bush became president in 1989 he pledged to have the most ethical administration on record. He introduced a set of guidelines, but while he personally sought to maintain a high ethical standard, some members of his staff ran into problems. The most glaring was John Sununu, whose personal use of government transportation led to his resignation as chief of staff. But there were others. In the first days of the administration Dr. Louis Sullivan, who served as Bush's secretary of health and human services, faced questions of whether he would receive salary payments during his leave from the Morehouse School of Medicine. In February 1989 Sullivan issued a statement through the White House saying that, in order to avoid any appearance of a conflict of interest in his position as secretary, he was taking an unpaid leave of absence from the school.

More recently, in 2003, Bush received considerable criticism for giving the George Bush Award for Excellence in Public Service to Senator Ted Kennedy. Many supporters of the Bush Library across the country contacted the George Bush Presidential Library Foundation to complain, and some canceled their memberships. Irrespective of Kennedy's personal background, Bush believed that Kennedy's record of public service was admirable and needed to be recognized despite the obvious political differences between the two men. Bush wanted to convey, moreover, that, as Americans, individuals may have political disagreements but that such disagreements are part of our political process and are what give the nation its strength.

The Unvarnished Truth

From his staff and himself, Bush expected two things: loyalty and what he calls the "unvarnished truth." Bush is well aware of what might be termed the "Oval Office syndrome," in which people withhold their opinions and criticisms when faced with the power and trappings of the presidency. "When you are president," says Bush, "people are reluctant to tell you what they think you may not want to hear." As a result, Bush made it clear that he always expected everyone's full and honest expression of views. In this regard, Bush was prone to place himself in a listening mode in order not to inhibit visitors from expressing their true feelings and views. Bush's social manners helped set visitors at ease, giving them a more open environment in which to express their views. Bush expected the staff to be truthful in their views and opinions on the issues. Once he made a decision, Bush then expected the full loyalty and support of the staff in carrying out the decision.

Loyalty

Bush is a firm believer in the adage that you do not neglect friends on the way up or on the way down. The nomination of Clarence Thomas to the Supreme

Court became such a test of loyalty. In the face of various accusations leveled against Thomas, including allegations of sexual misconduct, Bush stuck by his nominee and successfully saw him through the Senate confirmation process. In the days after the storm of allegations broke, Bush invited Thomas to the White House. He made a point of walking with Thomas along the driveway of the South Lawn in full view of the press, in a clear signal to Thomas and the public that he was standing by his nominee.

Such a move is indicative of Bush's understanding of the importance of symbolism and loyalty and the signals that they send to others. Much of what he believed regarding loyalty he most likely learned from his own experience. As vice president, Bush had experienced the awkwardness of standing in the shadows of President Ronald Reagan, how that could constrain his own style, and the image it could project to the public and the media. As vice president, George Bush kept his advice to Reagan private. He was not inclined to speak out during Cabinet sessions or share his views with the press. He maintained this routine out of loyalty to the president, probably realizing that in the politically charged White House he was not fully accepted by those in Reagan's inner circle. After all, during the presidential primary season and before he was selected by Reagan as his running mate, Bush had accused Reagan of positing "voodoo economics" as the prescription for the country's economic ills. George Bush's conservative credentials were suspect in their eyes.

Bush knew that his low-key approach would reinforce Reagan's trust in him and allow him to be an effective confidant and adviser. It would also serve as an example to his own staff, thus strengthening their loyalty. A freewheeling staff devoid of any loyalty can quickly become a burden in the internecine squabbles and competition of the White House and Washington. A staff lacking loyalty could also undermine his effectiveness with Reagan and the latter's confidence in him. Bush firmly realized the limits of the vice presidency; it was not a leadership position. "You have no power as vice president," Bush states. "Your power is to preside over the Senate and to vote when there is a tie. Power is given to you by the president." Then, for emphasis, he adds, "You have no powers other than those assigned to you by the president." Therefore, loyalty is important in the relationship in order to maintain the trust of the president and to carve out a role for oneself.

His loyalty, therefore, was meant to cement his relationship with the inner circle and make himself a more effective vice president, but it was also genuine. There is only one president, and both the officeholder and the president's agenda should be served. Bush's commitment to the president was dramatically underscored when he rejected his staff's proposal that, in the wake of the assassination attempt on Reagan in March 1981, he should arrive quickly at the White House by helicopter. In rejecting their advice, Bush noted that only the president lands on the White House grounds.

Bush's sense of loyalty throughout his public career remained strong, even in the face of events that undermined his own standing and credibility. As ambassador to the United Nations, Bush privately and publicly argued for the continued membership of Taiwan in the world body at a time when the UN was debating whether to include China and expel Taiwan. The Nixon administration, despite its stated dual representation policy, had apparently already moved to a position of accepting the expulsion of Taiwan yet did not forewarn Bush. Secretary of State Henry Kissinger's visit to China at the time of the United Nations debate sent that body a signal indicating in which direction U.S. policy was headed. Even earlier in the year the administration had been discussing with China the possibility of Nixon making a state visit. As envoy to China, Bush was not made privy to all of the plans Kissinger's State Department office was making, yet he never publicly complained. He maintained his composure and remained a team player. Bush undoubtedly was well aware of the workings of Washington power politics; complaining could result is ostracism by the powerful inner circle. It could also further undermine one's credibility and emphasize one's being out of the loop. Bush surely learned from these experiences, and they helped reinforce his tendency toward secrecy and compartmentalization of information and decision making that marked his own management style.

The Watergate scandal challenged Bush's sense of loyalty and compelled him to preserve his own credibility and that of the Republican Party. Bush, as chairman of the Republican National Committee, refused to let the besieged White House draw him into any hardnosed political measures to defend Nixon at the expense of truth and the good of the country. In a letter written on August 7, 1974, Bush urged Nixon to resign. In doing so he joined a growing chorus of calls for Nixon's resignation. The distinguishing characteristic was that Bush, as chairman of the party, signaled the party's formal rejection of its president's stand, thus breaking its links to Nixon. Faced with his party's rejection and growing political and legal problems, Nixon resigned on August 8.

Based on the ways his own sense of loyalty had been challenged, Bush was sensitive to the difficulties and extra burdens borne by his own vice president, Dan Quayle. The selection of Quayle as his running mate was a bold move, an attempt to show that the future was in the hands of the post–World War II generation. Quayle was to represent this passing of the torch and to symbolize Bush's empathy with the new generation. Bush viewed the young senator from Indiana as an effective and knowledgeable politician with good political instincts and connections to conservative forces. Quayle's selection was a political calculation that was expected to reap benefits in the campaign. Furthermore, Quayle did not have the high profile or personal ego that many other potential vice-presidential candidates had, such as Senator Bob Dole of Kansas. Dole, with a national reputation and a political record of his own, could prove to be a strong personality who might raise friction with Bush over policy issues. Bush was not comfortable with confrontation; it was not his nature. Quayle, with his lower political profile and being much younger than Bush, would not pose this threat; he fit Bush's political and personal needs. Prior to his selection, Quayle had known Bush for about ten years, going back to when Bush campaigned in Indiana on behalf of Quayle's first Senate victory in 1980. Prior to that Quayle had served two terms in the House of Representatives. Quayle, like Bush, viewed his selection as an outreach to the new generation of Americans. Specifically, he regarded his relationship with Bush along the lines of the Eisenhower-Nixon model. Eisenhower was seen as an elder statesman with expertise in foreign policy who reached out to a younger Nixon with similar credentials. At the time of Nixon's selection as the vice-presidential candidate he was younger than Quayle was when Bush tapped him. Nixon was thirty-nine; Quayle was forty-one. Like Quayle, Nixon had a connection to the conservatives and an expertise in foreign affairs. Unfortunately, Quayle's initial exposure to the national scene was not flattering, and it set a negative tone that persisted in the media.

Quayle's reaction to his announcement as the vice-presidential choice and the controversy regarding his National Guard duty quickly painted the eventual vice president as an unsophisticated and naïve son of privilege. At the time of the public announcement, Quayle demonstrated a gleeful enthusiasm in his outdoor appearance with Bush, playfully punching him in the arm and bobbing excitedly. His National Guard service was portrayed mostly as an effort to escape service in Vietnam through arrangements made by his influential and wealthy family. The press went into a feeding frenzy, painting Quayle with negatives that were to dog him during his tenure. To offset this negative image and to neutralize any jockeying that traditionally takes place between the presidential and vice-presidential staffs, Bush constantly highlighted his support of and confidence in Quayle. He determined to define Quayle's role in the administration, appointing Quayle to head the administration's Council on Competitiveness, which helped trim government regulations that hampered business. In addition, Quayle represented the president in numerous overseas trips and was the administration's point man on values issues.

Despite these efforts, when the 1992 campaign was shaping up there was speculation about replacing Quayle. This speculation was nothing new in the drama that has become presidential elections. Every vice president suffers this ignominy. The press, pundits, and various campaign officials engage in the ritual of dissecting a president's strengths and weaknesses in the reelection bid, and one of the inevitable questions that arises is what benefits the vice president brings to the ticket and who might be a suitable replacement.

Bush and Quayle had established the same type of working code as had existed between Reagan and Bush. Quayle gave advice and kept the confidences. They got together for a weekly lunch, and Bush included Quayle in all major meetings and issues. Quayle is proud that there were no leaks of their interactions. The relationship, therefore, was close and personal. More so than the Reagans and the Bushes, the Quayles and the Bushes socialized. The Quayles had the Bushes over to the vice president's residence for dinner a couple of times, and Quayle pointed to the president as a role model for his own three children, telling them that they should grow up to be like George Bush, "an honest, decent, caring individual."

Dealing with Mistakes

During one of the presidential debates in 1992 Bush stated, "I've admitted it when I make a mistake, but then I go on and help try to solve the problems." For Bush, knowing and admitting one's shortcomings is a sign not of weakness but of strength. You can learn from your mistakes and provide a more relaxed work environment if people realize that you are reasonable and are part of the process of seeking a solution rather than of affixing blame.

For Bush, that sort of work environment also meant sometimes overlooking mistakes and offering words of encouragement during difficult as well as good times. This approach, he believes, brings out the best in people. Jim Baker, who as secretary of state helped manage the diplomatic response to the dissolution of the Soviet Union, ascribes any success he had to Bush. Baker says it was the special relationship he had with the president that allowed him to be a good secretary of state. "Even when I would screw up," Baker recalls, "he would support and defend me."

As press secretary, Marlin Fitzwater was always on the firing line. The intense verbal parrying with journalists inevitably led to some mistakes. At one press briefing, Fitzwater referred to Gorbachev as a "drugstore cowboy" in reference to the Soviet leader's seemingly endless release of arms proposals. After the briefing, Fitzwater was seized with concern that the remark could cause a diplomatic flap with the Soviet Union. He went to see the president. Bush, however, was understanding and forgiving. No incident developed.

Early in his administration, Bush attended a Marine drill team performance at the Marine Barracks in southeastern Washington, D.C. It was a foggy night, with a blanket of moisture on everything. The crisp drill proceeded with a precision that made the viewers admire the skills of the young Marines. All was going well until the drillmaster, in the exchange of rifles, dropped the weapon. In a slow, graceful motion, the drillmaster knelt, retrieved the rifle, and continued with the drill. Two minutes later, in front of his commander in chief, the drillmaster once again dropped the rifle. The crowd could feel the tension of the assembled Marines. No one spoke.

The next morning, one of the first things out of the Oval Office was a note from Bush to that drillmaster admonishing him not to worry and pointing out that he—Bush—messes up things all the time. Most importantly, Bush noted that, as commander in chief, he was proud of what the Marines do.

Communication

Proper communication is important to the functioning of any organization. It underscores your interest in those around you, picks up on brewing concerns, and facilitates the work of an organization. In this regard, it is important that leaders not be isolated and that they maintain an open line of communication. The leader's goals must be clearly known, and a feedback mechanism must be in place so that the effectiveness of policies and the organization as a whole can be judged. Bush made it a habit to learn what others were thinking, and he was willing to be a sounding board. On occasion, Bush, after finishing up in the Oval Office for the day, would pop into the press office on his way over to the residence. The early edition of the network news would be coming on, and the drop-in visit gave him an opportunity to get a read from Fitzwater of how the coverage was going. Equally important, it gave him an opportunity to interact with the press office staff. Those few moments of unexpected contact and conversation helped bring a personable end to a twelve-hour day that was spent fielding incessant queries from the press and constantly guarding against a slip of the tongue that could shape the coverage of the White House. It also gave the staff an opportunity to discuss issues with the president in an informal and relaxed manner outside the constraints of formal settings and oversight by other staffers.

Sharing the Credit

Bush is a strong believer in the adage that everyone likes to be associated with success. A strong leader, Bush believes, puts ego aside and distributes accolades to the staff. True to his belief, Bush readily gives credit to others, providing them with a sense of accomplishment and inclusion, thereby maintaining staff morale and offering an incentive for success. After his trip to Europe in 1989, during which he announced his plan for conventional force reductions in Europe, Bush dispatched a series of notes to the staff. Typical was one sent to an aide in the press office: "I am very pleased with the way the press coverage turned out—foreign and domestic = positive. Thanks for a job well done. George Bush."

Bush's role as vice president provides a classic example of how his strong sense of getting the job done overcame any prodding for him to grandstand or arrogate credit. While Bush publicly took a backseat role, his participation in policy and the policy process were very influential on a wide range of issues, including defense, trade, and drug interdiction. Much of the success in persuading America's European partners to accept the deployment of Pershing missiles in the early 1980s was due to Bush's role. In particular, his trips to Europe in 1983 were key in persuading the Europeans. The deployment was important, for it underscored the Reagan administration's determination to expand the U.S. defense posture and thus challenge Moscow in defense spending. Moscow could not face this spending challenge, and it was one of the elements that helped bring an eventual end to the Soviet Union.

Showing Your Human Side

Socializing with and entertaining all levels of employees helps ensure greater empathy. Everyone seeks some exposure with the boss and a window on his or her personal life. It gives one a sense of belonging and a greater comfort level as well as a greater identity with the organization, its goals, and its leader. Typical of this social rapport with the staff were Bush's horseshoe tournaments at the White House. In addition, Bush is not shy about baring his emotions. During his last stay at Camp David, Bush was given a surprise greeting with thunderous applause by the staff and their family members in the Marine One hangar. Bush spoke of how special Camp David was to him and thanked all the military staff for their service to the country and to him at the camp. He told them how he appreciated the honor and dignity they brought to the country and how special the men and women of the armed forces are. The emotion of the moment overwhelmed the staff and Bush. The event turned teary, an exhibition of emotions that George Bush is never wont to conceal but that reinforces the human, down-to-earth side of his character and that endears him to those around him.

Realizing That Actions Have Consequences

Bush was very aware that each action has consequences. To Bush, therefore, leadership means that one has the responsibility to address the long-range view. Decisions need to be well thought out so that a hasty decision does not lead to unwanted consequences. This principle was evident in his reaction to the Tiananmen Square massacre in China in June 1989. Starting in April of that year, pro-reform demonstrations rocked Beijing. The demonstrations were sparked by students in response to the death of Hu Yaobang in mid-April. Hu, who had served as a general secretary of the Communist Party, was an early reformer who was removed from office in 1987 because of his efforts.[1] In response to the demonstrations, the government declared martial law in May. The show of force eventually led many of the demonstrators to disperse. However, in an effort to clear the square on June 2, unarmed government forces were stymied by the remaining demonstrators, prompting the regime to dispatch tanks and troops the next night to retake the square by force, killing a number of demonstrators and creating a world outcry. Bush imposed sanctions on military sales to China in order to underscore the United States' disapproval. "You just couldn't stand there and see the violations of human rights," he explains. However, Bush kept options and relations open through a secret visit to Beijing by National Security Adviser Brent Scowcroft in July and a public visit by Scowcroft in December of that year.

In addition, Bush opposed efforts by Congress to extend Chinese student visas after they expired, thereby providing them safe haven. Bush favored providing an extension via a presidential order. He feared that the congressional action would offend China and would prompt it to close down the exchange program, undermining what Bush saw as one of the key factors that was helping to liberalize Chinese society. It was a close fight. Baker and Scowcroft were concerned that the president's position would not hold on the Hill, but Bush dismissed the political concerns and the possibility of defeat. "I want to see us fight and win," Bush declared to them. The bill, sponsored by Rep. Nancy Pelosi (D-California), passed with what appeared to be veto-proof margins in both houses. Bush, however, was successfully able to veto the congressional action. "I was determined to keep the relationship going even though what they had done was horrible," Bush recalls, referring to the Chinese government actions.

Bush has a special affinity for China. "The U.S.-China relationship," Bush states, "is the most important relationship." Not only had he lived there and become acquainted with its people and leaders but through that experience he had witnessed the birth of modern China—the budding international giant that is now increasing its economic and political position in the world. He witnessed and followed these changes from their early stages, which gave him a special appreciation for the political role of China in the international community and the particular challenges that it would pose to the United States, ranging from the differences over Taiwan to economic competition and possible hegemony in Asia. Bush is optimistic about China's future. He does not worry about China seeking hegemony and does not foresee Beijing taking over its neighbors.

Bush notes that the Chinese never forgot his veto of the student visa legislation and appreciated his support, and he feels vindicated in his early belief that China would evolve toward a better future. "I was right," he stated in retrospect in February 2004 in a discussion with Bush School students. "There are more human liberties today in China." In addition, the ideological nature of the Chinese government and society is changing. "In the days when

I was president they would stick to Marxist ideology," Bush stated in 2003 to a gathering of Bush School students, "but that's not where they are today. I don't think they are rigidly communist at all." Capitalism, he believes, is bringing Chinese society forward.

China's special place in Bush's orbit even affected seemingly unrelated issues. There was a clamor among some staff for Bush to take public credit for the fall of the Berlin Wall and the liberation of Eastern Europe. Jim Cicconi, head of the White House Staff Secretariat, the office that oversees the paper flow to and from the president, was one of the White House staff who urged Bush to declare "the cold war is over." Cicconi believed that the fall of communism and the events in Eastern Europe were not only a historic achievement but that there were political benefits Bush could reap from being visibly identified with the ending of the cold war. Bush, as usual, resisted any chest thumping.

During one Oval Office session in mid-1990, however, Cicconi appeared to have prevailed in his entreaties. With Scowcroft listening, Cicconi made his case to Bush, who finally succumbed to Cicconi's persistence and agreed to what could be considered a speech declaring the cold war over.

"Well, Brent," stated Bush, "I think Jim has a good argument here. Maybe we should go ahead and do this."

"Well, okay, Mr. President," stated Scowcroft in a slow, even voice. Scowcroft had preferred to maintain the low profile that Bush had been following and, thus, had been at odds with Cicconi.

Cicconi was elated, amazed by the prospect that he had won a foreign policy argument over Scowcroft. Cicconi, still reveling in his perceived victory, and Scowcroft then moved to exit the Oval Office. Scowcroft, however, was not to be outdone.

"I just worry what the Chinese will say," Scowcroft stated slowly and dryly, casting a furtive side glance at Bush.

"The Chinese?" exclaimed Bush, jumping to a new level of attention. "What do you mean?"

"The Chinese might be suspicious that we had done some secret deal with the Russians if we declared the cold war over," Scowcroft continued, with the confidence of one who knew he had just won the argument.

Scowcroft was well aware that he had hit a sensitive spot with Bush. Although the cold war was over, China's government was still a communist regime. With the Chinese cultural tradition of "saving face," any claims of victory over communism could hit a raw nerve with Beijing and complicate relations for Washington, particularly in the wake of the Tiananmen Square incident. In addition, any appearance of a back-door agreement between the United States and Russia could unsettle the Chinese, who might see it as being made at their expense. Bush was very familiar with these Chinese sensitivities and concerns. He also put a great emphasis on the U.S. relationship with China and did not want to do anything unnecessary that could complicate that relationship. As soon as Scowcroft spoke, Cicconi realized that his victory had been premature. No speech was to be given.

As they exited the Oval Office, Cicconi admired the handicraft of Scowcroft and laughed at how he had been outfoxed by the latter's deft tapping into Bush's sensitivity over China.

"You know, Brent," said Cicconi in good humor, "that was dirty pool."

Scowcroft, slightly hunched and with head tilted to the side, looked up at Cicconi with a wide smile.

"All's fair . . . ," he said, and before he could finish they both broke into laughter.

Ensuring That Everyone Has a Role and Knows What It Is

Bush was keenly interested in the process of decision making. Based on his Washington experience, Bush was aware of the need to delegate and to establish clear lines of authority in order to have a smooth decision-making process. In this regard he built a hierarchical management structure through which advice and decision making were funneled and in which responsibility was delegated with the expectation that individuals would know and carry out their responsibilities. Thus, staffers knew and operated within clear lines of authority. This arrangement reflected Bush's personal temperament: he is organized and seeks order.

Bush trusted staff to the extent that he did not believe his physical presence was needed at all times. On the evening of Iraq's Scud missile attack on Israel during the Gulf War, Bush stayed in the residence and remained in touch with his key advisers by telephone. Secretary of Defense Dick Cheney was at his office while Vice President Quayle, National Security Adviser Brent Scowcroft, Secretary of State Jim Baker, Deputy Secretary of State

Larry Eagleburger, Deputy National Security Adviser Bob Gates, National Security Council staffer Richard Haass, and Fitzwater and his deputy set up command in Scowcroft's West Wing office and stayed in touch with Bush by telephone.

Overall, Barbara Bush sees her husband's leadership strengths as his ability to delegate authority and loyalty. "Delegating is important in leadership," she observes. "George always delegated authority and had loyalty to his people." She is emphatic on the latter point. "Loyalty," she states, "is not only up but down."

These characteristics embody the spirit of George Bush's leadership style. There is nothing extraordinary or special about any one of these points. Many are simple rules of human relations. Any management book would present more detailed and even complicated criteria for measuring success and leadership. But for Bush, leadership is not complicated: it is an ability to accomplish ends. That all starts with people skills.

March 20, 1989. Bush meets with Mexico's foreign secretary, Fernando Solana, seated in the armchair next to the president. This is how it looks from the president's side when he meets with the press.

April 14, 1989. President and Mrs. Bush host staff and guests at a movie party in the Family Theater in the East Wing. Special guests for the evening were the British ambassador Sir Antony Acland and his wife.

June 2, 1990. President Bush and Mikhail Gorbachev pitch horseshoes at Camp David. Bush often took advantage of the informal atmosphere of Camp David to pursue negotiations.

August 16, 1990. Bush fishes off the coast of his home, Walker's Point, in Kennebunkport, Maine, and reads at the same time.

January 2, 1991. President Bush drops in at Press Secretary Marlin Fitzwater's office to review the press stories of the day with Fitzwater and the author. Fitzwater had Bush's complete trust and great credibility and relations with the press.

January 29, 1991. President Bush starts a Cabinet meeting with a prayer. Prayer was important to Bush in dealing with the challenges of the presidency.

February 20, 1991. Briefing the president in the Oval Office. Seated in front of the president's desk (*left to right*): National Security Adviser Brent Scowcroft, Deputy National Security Adviser Bob Gates, Chief of Staff John Sununu, and the author.

February 25, 1991. President Bush, playing host, lights a fire in the fireplace in the Oval Office as Vice President Quayle watches. Secretary of State Jim Baker is seated in the background. Standing is the president's Air Force military aide, Major Bruce Caughman.

August 19, 1991. President Bush heads from the main house at Walker's Point to address the press regarding the coup against Soviet leader Gorbachev. *Left to right:* National Security Adviser Brent Scowcroft; President Bush; Linda Casey, assistant to Andy Card; the author; and the president's personal aide, Michael Dannenhauer, followed by Secret Service agents.

August 19, 1991. President Bush, National Security Adviser Brent Scowcroft, and the author leave Marine One after arriving on the South Lawn of the White House. Bush was returning from his vacation in Kennebunkport to deal with the coup against Gorbachev.

September 2, 1991. A meeting on the patio deck at Walker's Point in Kennebunkport. *Left to right:* National Security Adviser Brent Scowcroft, Deputy Chief of Staff Andy Card, President Bush, Press Secretary Marlin Fitzwater, and the author.

September 3, 1991. The author briefs President Bush and Secretary of State Jim Baker in the Oval Office. Baker's close relationship with Bush made him a central figure in the administration's handling of foreign policy.

April 1, 1992. Chief of Staff Sam Skinner and the author consult as President Bush announces to the press in the White House Briefing Room that the United States will provide an assistance package to the former Soviet Union.

May 26, 1992. The author and his wife, Judith, with their children Catherine, Gregory, Matthew, and Mary, with President Bush, on the occasion of author's swearing-in ceremony as the first U.S. ambassador to Ukraine, 1992.

Three

~~~

THE VISION THING

THE PRESIDENT'S ability to convey a message to the public is an important element of official leadership and can determine the overall success of the administration. FDR's New Deal and Kennedy's New Frontier rhetoric and philosophy, for example, instilled hope, optimism, and a sense of exhilaration in the American electorate, thus strengthening their respective hands as leaders. Bush was unable to demonstrate a similar skill. During his term in office, Bush received much scrutiny and criticism for his apparent lack of "vision," that is, his definition of how and where he wanted to lead the country. However, many of Bush's problems in this regard stemmed not from the lack of any guiding philosophy but rather in the nature of his own management philosophy and in the failure to present his vision to the public in an effective way.

Bush was not comfortable with high rhetoric and the need to sell oneself. His emphasis on teamwork and self-effacement undercut opportunities to seize the rhetorical high ground. He disliked dealing with oratory for the sake of exhortation. In his inaugural address he stated, "Some see leadership as high drama, and the sound of trumpets calling, and sometimes it is that. But I see history as a book with many pages, and each day we fill a page with acts of hopefulness and meaning." For Bush, the essence of the presidency was to provide moral leadership. The president was to set a tone of dignity and tolerance and provide an environment for individual opportunity and national growth and harmony. Rhetoric for the sake of rhetoric did not fit this vision of the office.

Bush's reluctance to engage in the marketing of his policies was also partially linked to his view of the media. He believed that there was a liberal bias in the media and that the media were therefore unfair in the way they portrayed his policies and intentions to the American public. He was thus reluctant to respond to press criticism or to see the press as an instrument to be cultivated for leadership purposes. "I do not feel compelled or pressed because of a column here or a column there to reach out for something dramatic," he explained to the press in 1989.

The main impediment to Bush's presentation of a clear vision for his administration, however, was his own view of government and management. Despite his brief stint on the faculty at Rice University in Houston in the late 1970s, Bush does not have the patience for the intellectual conceptualization or discussion of an issue; his impatience is noted by his reference to academic exercises as "yellow pad sessions." "I'm no student of history," he said at a White House luncheon for journalists in 1989, summing up his personal aversion to such intellectual pursuits. From the oil fields in West Texas, where he built a successful business, through his series of government positions, Bush has relished solving the challenges at hand. He dealt with the realities that confronted him, whether it was the challenge of a dry well or rebuilding morale at the CIA; his was not a world of abstract ideas. These experiences also colored his view of governing, which he saw as a process of problem solving. Bush, simply stated, was a man of action. If there is an issue, it should be solved, not talked about interminably. He believed it was his record that mattered in the end and by which he should be judged; invariably, he pointed to his résumé and record of accomplishment. Coupled with this habit, Bush also has a very nuanced view of issues. He seldom sees events and issues as simply black or white. This view comes, partially, from his foreign policy experiences, where cultural and historical influences can affect perceptions and interpretations and where patience and negotiation—and not the bravado of rhetoric—are important for finding solutions.

Bush's many years of private sector and government positions helped him develop management skills that included the ability to deal with people one on one, to understand the complexity of an issue, and to zero in on what would benefit the organization and the greater good. Bush worked largely through compartmentalizing problems and tackling them one by one, rather than blending them into a single overarching framework or vision. He believed this approach made it easier to plan and to marshal the proper forces to accomplish a specific objective. He saw no reason that issues should be placed in the context of a bigger movement and believed that the public would not be swayed by gimmicks but would rally around successes on a case-by-case basis. This pragmatic approach is seen in his analysis of the budget negotiations of 1990, in which he sacrificed the "no new taxes" pledge he had made at the nominating convention. He saw the budget deal as a simple process of outlining the benefits to be realized and believed that the public would then support him. In a news conference, Bush outlined for the press how he foresaw himself explaining an eventual agreement: "This agreement is going to be good for future generations. It's going to be good for the economy. It's going to be good for jobs. Then people will say: Look, we support the president." It was a very practical and pragmatic statement, but it was not a politically astute one. In line with his budget comment, Bush pointedly stated in his State of the Union address in 1992, "And the test of a plan isn't whether it's called new or dazzling. . . . The only test of a plan is: Is it sound, and will it work?"

Bush viewed issues individually, with each issue having a different set of circumstances. Improving the protection of civil rights in the United States, for example, would involve circumstances different from those that would promote action to address environmental issues. Achieving success in various categories would add up to a positive cumulative effect for society as a whole. Bush's vision worked from the bottom up; it was not a rhetorical umbrella under which various goals could fit but was instead the sum total of the individual goals.

Bush's piecemeal approach to policy and his fondness for challenging issues as they arose was underscored in his convention acceptance speech in 1988, when he described himself as "a man who sees life in terms of missions— missions defined and missions completed."

"I have always operated on the basis of defining a mission and setting out to attain it," Bush now explains. "I did not view myself as developing some sort of grand design by which to plan my life. I have always believed in meeting the challenges at hand and doing your best at whatever task you face."

Andy Card, who served as Bush's deputy chief of staff, explains that "Bush's vision was based on the reality of the world." This pragmatism stemmed partially from the many different positions Bush had held, which gave him a vision of the future based on experience and on the personalities he had encountered rather than on abstract idealism. Bush's vision was tempered by the question, "Where can we go given the state of reality?" This perspective was evident when the Soviet Union was breaking up and new states appeared to be emerging. "Bush shared the vision of democracy in the Soviet space," explains Card, "but his vision was shaped by the reality of the cold war. He did not allow an idealistic vision of the future to interrupt the important steps that needed to be taken to achieve that end."

Furthermore, while Bush has often received high marks for his affability and social skills, he is not necessarily a natural politician. His success appears to be more the result of his energy and determination rather than of any natural political instincts. This undoubtedly prevented him from judging the political winds of the presidential campaign of 1992 and from realizing the importance of political rhetoric. Bush himself recognizes this shortcoming. "I was not able to counter the cries for change and make the case for our agenda," he explained in his 1997 Gauer lecture. Closely allied to this political shortcoming was the fact that Bush was, in many ways, the quintessential Washington insider. The various positions that he had held gave him an understanding of the personalities and institutions in Washington. In this world that his experiences had created, personal contacts and bonds were more important in shaping deals and solutions than ideological or rhetorical confrontations. The bonds that tied Bush to Washington seemed to limit his maneuverability; he knew the system and many of the players and was willing to work with both. His political and insider shortcomings were evident the one time Bush took a stab at defining his "vision"; he wound up with a listing of various generalities, many of which first appeared in his State of the Union address in 1992. Sequestered one March day in 1992 at Camp David he wrote a note to the speechwriters in which he offered as examples of his vision the need for the American family to be strengthened, the need for community action programs, the need for health care, and the need for educational excellence, among other points. Most important was the need for world peace, with a strong United States to help maintain the peace. The exercise did not prove to be helpful; there were few specific programs to attach to the effort. It did underscore, however, the fact that, while Bush sought to dismiss criticism regarding his purported lack of vision, the issue did concern him somewhat, particularly in the election year.

Bush felt misunderstood and somewhat defensive about the criticism. "I didn't like it all the time," he admits. "No one likes to be hectored and criticized, but sometimes it takes time for that record to be appreciated. In terms of foreign affairs, it will be a pretty good record. If the historians look at the changes that occurred while I was in office, they may say that maybe I was not the best rhetoric man but look at all the changes that occurred under him. As to press criticism about my vision, I do not worry about journalists."

Bush believed he had a clear concept of his goals and how to lead the United States. "It depends on how you define it," says Bush. "I believe I had a vision. I am content to leave it to historians to decide. Look what happened when I was president—and it happened peacefully—such as the implosion of the Soviet Union without a shot being fired and the Berlin Wall came down. I think, eventually, they will say this guy had vision—they'll realize the vision of a unified Germany, the ending of the cold war, democracy in Panama, and other successes."

"Contrary to perception in this country," claims John Sununu, "he had a very clear idea of what he wanted to do internationally and an exceptionally clear idea of what he wanted his domestic agenda to be." Ron Kaufman, who served as Bush's political director, summarizes Bush's dilemma: "It was not a matter of no vision but a matter of not articulating the vision he had."

If there was one guiding theme for Bush's domestic policies, it was the "Good Society," a term that he used on a number of occasions to describe his domestic goals. In describing the Good Society, Bush stated in June 1991 to the National Federation of Independent Business, "We want to build a society of shared hopes and helping hands, a society in which all benefit from growth and prosperity. We want to make this kind of society—a good society—the hallmark of our administration." A month earlier, in a commencement address at the University of Michigan, Bush drew a distinction between past efforts linked to heavy government spending and what he envisioned in his Good Society. While he praised the ideals of President Lyndon Johnson's Great Society, Bush believed that "the programs weren't always up to task. We need to rethink our approach." Bush stated that the United States did not need "huge and ambitious programs" run by the government. "We need a Good Society," Bush stated, "built upon the deeds of the many, a society that promotes service, selflessness, action." Thus, the Good Society was a combination of economic opportunity and individual action aimed at advancing society. Bush wove these ideas throughout his policies, reflecting his conservative belief system and his philosophy of government. Bush viewed social and economic change as being the result principally of personal and market forces. For Bush, the philosophical foundation of domestic policy was empowerment, the idea of giving people a stake in their futures and a greater say in the activities that affect their lives. The role of government was to be minimal; indeed, it was up to the president to make sure the role of government did not expand to undermine natural market forces and individual initiative.

Bush's philosophy, outlined in his acceptance speech in 1988, can be pictured as a set of concentric circles. At the core stands the individual, who, through his or her initiative and drive, shapes society. To do this, the individual must remain unfettered and free to pursue his or her goals. In the next circle is the family, an extension of individuals and the source of strength and stability that gives the individual members the platform on which to pursue their goals and dreams. The next circle is the community, an amalgam of individuals and families associated with each other voluntarily to pursue various interests. This is the web that binds the nation together and that generates its strength and values. Finally, there is the government. As Bush sees it, "Government is part of the nation of communities—not the whole, just a part."

What is more important, he believes, is that government should not be intrusive; it must set the parameters within which individuals and communities operate, but it must not dominate. The role of government, Bush explained in a salute to the black appointees in his administration in September 1992, is "to create opportunity . . . and not stifle it, and to clear the path for individual accomplishment, not to block it; to facilitate, not to dictate." It is a true conservative image of limited government, with the role of government focused on providing individual opportunities via such policies as free and fair trade, lower taxes, and limited government.

Bush summarized his vision on February 12, 1992, when he announced his candidacy for reelection. At that time he stated, "I believe government is too big, and it costs too much. I believe in a strong defense for this country and good schools, safe streets, a government really worthy of the people. I believe that parents, not government, should make the important decisions about health, child care, and education. I believe in personal responsibility. I believe in opportunity for all. We should throw open wide the doors of possibility to anyone who has been locked out."

In addition to his overall philosophy, Bush was guided by a set of principles for shaping his policies and garnering public support, and he detailed them in April 1989, in an address at an Associated Press business luncheon in Chicago. True to form, Bush did not view these principles as a vision peculiar to his administration. Rather, he regarded them as enduring American principles that have guided national behavior throughout the decades. These principles are: freedom for individuals and nations; fairness, or equal opportunity and standards; strength at home; self-confidence on the world stage; gaining the respect of adversaries; and excellence in all we do, both in the public and private sectors, marked by accountability for what we do.

An important component of his philosophy of limited government is Bush's strong belief in volunteerism, the organizing principle of the Points of Light Foundation. The president coined the phrase in his acceptance speech at the Republican National Convention in 1988, when he spoke of a "thousand points of light," referring to the cumulative effect of volunteer efforts throughout the nation. He established the Office of National Service at the White House, headed by Gregg Petersmeyer, which provided public recognition for the volunteer service of individuals or groups throughout the country. The concept was institutionalized in the Points of Light Foundation and supported through congressional funding. In Bush's view, volunteerism cannot replace government efforts, but as he stated to the Points of Light Foundation in 1991, it is "a critical answer to America's social problems." The "points of light" concept ran through the course of his administration and came close to being a theme by which to identify his leadership.

Scowcroft attributes much of Bush's vision problem to the press. In particular, Scowcroft points to columnist George Wills's characterization of Bush in 1986 as Reagan's "lap dog." Saddled with this label and with a *Newsweek* cover portraying Bush as a "wimp" in 1987, Bush found it difficult to buck these negative designations. The *Newsweek* piece particularly upset Bush, since it questioned whether or not he had the toughness to be president. Much as Quayle had been portrayed as clueless, Ford as bumbling, and Carter as the victim of a "killer rabbit," Bush was characterized as divorced from the realities of everyday life and devoid of both a political philosophy and a vision for the future. The first impressions that the press paints are sometimes difficult to overcome. Fitzwater was aware of the perception issue and sought to have Bush hit the ground running when he took office, but with Bush's aversion to rhetoric and self-promotion Fitzwater faced a difficult task.

Fitzwater was someone the president admired and trusted implicitly, so his comments had a chance of swaying Bush. Fitzwater hailed from Kansas, where he came from a farm family; however, he had decided to seek his fortune in the big city. He attended Kansas State University, held a number of newspaper positions in Kansas, and eventually found his way to Washington, where he began a career in the federal government, first with the Appalachian Regional Commission and eventually with the Treasury Department. His work ethic and professionalism led him to be recruited as a deputy to President Reagan's press secretary, Larry Speakes. From there, Fitzwater wound up as Vice President Bush's press secretary, and he developed a close personal bond and trust with Bush. Fitzwater left Bush for a two-year stint as Reagan's press secretary, replacing Speakes, who had gone to the private sector, before rejoining Bush during his presidential term, thus becoming the only press secretary to serve two presidents.

Fitzwater's even, avuncular demeanor could have a calming effect on an otherwise high-strung press corps. Fitzwater would often meander down to the press working area in the West Wing of the White House, take a seat, and lean back, puffing on his cigar as he ruminated on the day's events with the assembled press, helping to ease any tensions and guard the president against major flare-ups. The press gave him high marks for honesty, accessibility, and his overall professionalism. Bush confided in Fitzwater, giving him a heads-up on many events that were tightly held secrets. The press's knowledge that Fitzwater had Bush's confidence and spoke with authority added to his effectiveness as the president's spokesman.

On January 10, 1989, in his West Wing office, Fitzwater discussed setting up "getting to know the president" sessions with the press and holding a press conference during the first week of the administration. These plans addressed the mechanics of leadership, but they did not tackle the message the new president wanted to convey—or should be conveying. One press staffer, Alixe Glen, noted that no long-term planning had been done regarding the themes that should be pushed by the administration during its first one hundred days. But such planning was not the domain of the White House Press Office. Fitzwater shared Glen's concern. He noted that Bob Teeter, who had been the campaign's pollster, had declined to take a position in the White House, and, as a result, there would be no long-term strategy formulation or conceptualizing taking place. It was a prescient statement of a problem that continued to plague the administration.[1]

In keeping with Fitzwater's plan, Bush started his administration with numerous media events, including an interview and a full press conference during his first week in office. In an Oval Office interview on January 25, a pair of print reporters charged that Bush had no active agenda. Instead of confronting the question and listing his goals, Bush waxed philosophical, basing his response on the realities of the first week. "Well, I've been a president since January 20," he stated, "and I think it's a little early to make conclusions one way or another on all that."

Two days later at a news conference Bush once again was confronted regarding his agenda. Journalists pointedly asked if he was concerned that there might not be any meat to back up his words. Once again, Bush sidestepped the issue by stating that it was his first week on the job. He also explained that, as in the case of foreign policy, it was important to conduct a policy review. Such explanations did little to mollify a press corps trained to search insatiably for news.

Equally important to Bush's press image was that serving as Reagan's vice president for eight years had not only given Bush a wealth of experience but also affected the way the press viewed him. Critics maintained his presidency was nothing more than a continuation of the Reagan agenda. Moreover, the press viewed him as "out of the loop" during those years, partly because he would not reveal what advice he provided Reagan and partly because he claimed he was unaware of the Iran-Contra scandal.[2]

Bush knew full well that his administration was intertwined with the Reagan legacy. In some ways this link was a political necessity. Given the popularity of President Reagan, it was wise politics to recognize his impact on America and to stay at least within the shadow of his political mantle at the beginning of his own administration. In this regard, Bush stated in his inaugural address, "There is a man here who has earned a lasting place in our hearts and in our history. President Reagan, on behalf of our nation, I thank you for the wonderful things that you have done for America." While this can be viewed as a standard acknowledgment of a popular predecessor, for Bush it was something more. Bush realized that he owed his political success on the national level to Reagan and that his ability to govern would be influenced to some degree by placating the electoral forces that Reagan had been able to put together.

As Bush entered office, therefore, the press and part of the public held expectations of him as being a nice fellow whose strength would be in serving as a caretaker of the Reagan legacy. Much of the criticism of Bush related to the yardstick by which presidential leadership has come to be viewed. In the press and even in academic circles, there is a tendency to equate leadership with action; the more dynamic a person and the more innovative in terms of policies and initiatives, the more the person is viewed as a leader. Thus, a president like FDR is regarded as a dynamic, visionary leader based on his use of the instruments of government to create new initiatives and to pursue goals. Much of the press criticism also stemmed from Bush's inaugural address, which some in the press viewed as devoid of substantive initiatives.

The White House added fuel to the fire of expectations when staffers spoke in the first days of the administration of the need to get a fast start. Buoyed by their new sense of power, exhilarated by their new positions, and being naïvely optimistic that they could somehow scale the walls of policy quicker than their predecessors had, they soon encountered the realities of governing. No amount of optimism could dislodge initiatives from the bureaucratic turf battles that inevitably arise within the White House and between the White House and various Cabinet departments and government agencies.

Four

ORGANIZING THE LEADERSHIP STRUCTURE

A s AIR Force One started its descent, Souda Bay stretched out below, the blue color of this inlet of the Mediterranean shimmering under the sun. Two ships, the USS *De Wert* and the Greek naval vessel *Limnos,* proudly sat stern to stern, reaffirming the cooperation of the two countries in the recent Gulf War. Bush was coming to the island of Crete in July 1991 to thank Greece for its support of the war. In the spirit of diplomacy, Bush next planned to visit Turkey, also an ally in the Gulf War. He was well aware of the historic sensitivities of each country and the need to treat both sides equally. The president scanned the horizon and the ships.

On the ground, the president and his staff motorcaded to the event site. At the end of the motorcade Phil Brady and David Demarest were twisted with anxiety. Brady had replaced Jim Cicconi as staff secretary when Cicconi had gone back into the private sector. Previously Brady had been general counsel at the Department of Transportation. Demarest was a longtime Republican political operative who had served in positions at the Republican National Committee, in the Reagan administration, and on Bush's presidential campaign. He joined the Bush administration as director of communications, a position responsible for supervising the speechwriting staff and maintaining contacts with the public.

Brady and Demarest had prepared the president's remarks; they were good remarks except that their notes stated that the ships were moored bow to bow, something that they had realized, too late, was inaccurate. They envisioned the embarrassment that would ensue for a president who had had a distinguished naval career. Unfortunately, circumstances prevented them from unobtrusively alerting the President, since their part of the motorcade was separated from Bush's.

Bush and Greek prime minister Constantine Mitsotakis toured the ships and then moved to the podium to deliver their remarks. Brady and Demarest felt helpless and unsure of how to get the President's attention and help him avoid the blunder they had unwittingly built into his speech.

Bush was animated, his spirits lifted by the warm welcome and the pomp of the military surroundings. The warmth of the sun led him to shed his Air Force jacket and Navy tie, drawing laughter when he stated that now he could "go to work." Bush then started his prepared remarks. He thanked the U.S. and Greek service members for their work in the Gulf War and then turned his attention to the ships. "And today, just as these two ships are moored stern to stern, . . ." he intoned, and the life came back to Brady and Demarest.

Back on Air Force One, Bush passed to the two men in the staff seating area a note that ran along the following lines: Phil and David: My resident geniuses. The bow is the pointy end of a ship. The stern is the squared off part. Your humble servant. George Bush.

This was not the only time that day that Bush had to improvise on the remarks his staff had provided him. Later that day, Bush was scheduled to make another address to guests assembled for his visit to the bay. Demarest and the speechwriting staff had expected a large audience and had provided a text prepared for such an event. Instead, Bush's talk was scheduled to take place before a much smaller group. The more intimate setting for the occasion meant that it would be awkward to have Bush pull out the cards on which the speech was prepared and deliver the remarks to the assembled few. Bush again rose to the occasion. To the great entertainment of the guests, Bush recounted his staff's gaffe regarding the different ends of a ship. Then with a flourish he waved his speech cards above his head for everyone to see and plopped them onto the small podium, stating, "So I think that I will speak off the cuff rather than use the text prepared by my crack speechwriting team."

This was neither the first nor the last time that Bush would carry his staff. With his discipline and drive to take in details, Bush assimilates information from disparate sources and retains it, without appearing to pay attention to his surroundings. These skills informed the way he structured his White House and managed his team.

Organizing the White House

Bush places his management style somewhere between that of Jimmy Carter and that of Ronald Reagan, who were at opposite ends of the management spectrum. Carter was interested in even small details, while Reagan tended to voice a grand view of policy and delegate everything else.

"I did not want to be a micromanager," states Bush emphatically. "I did, however, want to be involved, more than Ronald Reagan, in the final formulation of policy. I had a broad management view and so I guess you can say I was in between Carter and Reagan."

Much of Bush's leadership style reflected his view of the presidency as embodied in his two favorite presidents: Theodore Roosevelt and Dwight Eisenhower. Bush admires Roosevelt for his activism as an environmentalist, hunter, and public servant and for his limitless personal energy. Roosevelt's public service at all levels—local, state, and national—in particular wins his admiration.

"And there's Ike, Dwight Eisenhower, hero to a generation, a man who, once he became president, didn't appear to seek the spotlight," Bush recounted for the press in 1989. "He understood the value of quiet, steady leadership and led this nation through a decade of growth and progress and prosperity." Bush especially admires the role model Eisenhower presented as a military hero and the stability and respect that he brought to the office of the presidency. Bush is an amalgam of the two: a lifelong public servant in the vein of Teddy Roosevelt and a quiet, effective chief of state in the tradition of Eisenhower, with great respect for the office and an emphasis on stability.

One advantage that Bush had coming into office was that he already fully understood how the decision process should work, thanks to his experience as vice president and in his various other roles in government. Organizing the White House, therefore, was one of the first things he tackled after his election. In late 1988, he appointed Jim Cicconi as staff secretary. Cicconi had worked in Ronald Reagan's administration and had gotten to know Bush through that connection.

In their initial meeting, Bush made it clear that although Cicconi reported to the chief of staff, he in fact worked for him and that he expected a high degree of trust. Bush put a great emphasis on confidentiality; he wanted to make sure that no one felt that advice to him would be compromised by leaks or sharing with others. Equally important, he wanted classified materials to be handled properly and in a close-hold fashion.

Bush emphasized that he wanted to be exposed to all information and all views. He also expected feedback regarding tasks he assigned and the status of decisions. As Cicconi soon found out, Bush has a knack for keeping a mental checklist. To stay abreast of the tasks, Cicconi kept a written checklist and kept Bush informed regarding the status of various issues. Cicconi would type status notes to Bush and detail what he had done to follow up on the president's behalf. In addition, he spoke with Bush at least once a day and summarized long, complex memos for him on key issues. Cicconi also kept the chief of staff informed.

There were two types of correspondence, not including family correspondence, in which Bush exhibited particular interest and gave special instructions for handling. The first type was letters from his friends. He insisted on setting up a system to ensure that he personally saw all such letters. For the most part, the system worked efficiently. The second type of special correspondence was from former presidents. Bush instructed that such letters not be staffed out and that no copies be made. The letters were to be forwarded directly to him without anyone else, including the chief of staff, seeing them. President Carter was the most consistent correspondent, sending about two or three letters per year. Addressed "To President Bush," the letters usually concerned reports on his trips overseas.

Cicconi oversaw three parallel tracks of paper flow to the president through his office: from the Staff Secretariat, from the Office of Cabinet Affairs, and from the National Security Council (NSC). White House staff would send memos for the president to the Staff Secretariat, which, if necessary, would "staff" the paper out to other offices for comments and input. The final product, once fully vetted, would go to the president.

Cabinet secretaries would use David Bates, head of Cabinet Affairs, as the conduit. Bates would assemble reports from individual departments and then forward them to the Staff Secretariat. Bush made every effort to keep in contact with the Cabinet. He saw the Cabinet secretaries as the daily supervisors and implementers of the respective policies affecting their departments. The president set the policy and the general parameters of operation. The secretaries were expected to funnel their recommendations and advice to the president. To facilitate the communication process, the president adopted a reporting system that Don Regan had used when he was secretary of treasury and that was tailored to White House needs by David Bates, who had been at the Treasury Department under President Reagan.

Each Cabinet department reported to the White House on a weekly basis regarding the issues they were confronting and the matters they expected to be dealing with in the upcoming week. This practice not only kept the White House updated on the work of the various departments but also permitted the White House to prevent duplication of efforts or straying from administration policy. The reports were then condensed into a double-spaced document outlining the issues in each department in bullet form. The reports were due at the White House by Thursday night; the White House document was prepared on Friday and was ready to be delivered to Bush on Saturday morning, usually at Camp David, where Bush spent many of his weekends.

Bush was a dedicated reader of the Cabinet report; he relied on it for much of his information. If it did not arrive on time, he would call Bates to inquire about the delay. After he was finished reading it, Bush sent it back to Bates with various notes and questions scribbled across the pages asking for more information or reaffirming the need to push on a certain issue.

While the reports were helpful, Bush fully understood that the Cabinet secretaries needed to have a direct channel to him. Direct access would strengthen the standing of the secretaries in their own departments and also make them feel that they were part of the president's management team. To facilitate direct access, the president indicated that any Cabinet secretary could send a personal note to him using the vehicle of the Cabinet report. The note was to be at the White House by Friday so that it could be forwarded to the president along with the report. The secretaries were careful not to abuse the system. On average, Bates forwarded about one note per week.

To strengthen the secretaries in their own departments and give them an opportunity to discuss issues with the president, Bush made it a practice to lunch with individual secretaries every month. He would also gather the whole Cabinet for informal discussions, sometimes on a relaxed Saturday at Camp David or during a dinner at the White House. In addition, Bush made sure that he met with the heads of the sub-Cabinet agencies, such as the Office of Personnel Management, the Export-Import Bank, and the Overseas Private Investment Corporation. These gatherings took place every three or four months over lunch in the Roosevelt Room.

On the National Security Council side, there was a similar paper flow process, centered on the executive secretary, Bill Sittmann, who held a ground floor office in the West Wing. The structure was Scowcroft's design. The key component was the Deputies Committee, which was composed of the deputies of the major foreign policy agencies and handled the analyses and recommendations that were presented to the Principals Committee. The latter consisted of the National Security Council minus the president and the vice president. It was an innovation that Scowcroft formulated, an important intermediary step, as he envisioned it, where recommendations could be vigorously vetted before being presented to the president. This structure proved effective during the course of the administration. It was overshadowed early on, however, by an informal gathering of a core group of advisers plus the president and the vice president. Included in this group were Baker, Scowcroft, Gates, Cheney, Sununu, and, at times, Eagleburger. Also, during the Gulf War period, Fitzwater and General Colin Powell, chairman of the Joint Chiefs of Staff, were added. While formal NSC meetings continued to be held, the informal structure proved the norm for decision making. It was most evident during the policy process related to the Gulf War.

Action items on major issues were usually first tackled by the Deputies Committee, chaired by Scowcroft or his deputy, Gates. Each of the departments of that committee would provide their input, which was forwarded to the NSC Executive Secretariat. Sittmann would have the papers logged in and then forward them to the proper NSC staff director. The director's task was to put the views and recommendations into a manageable format. If necessary, the director could send parts or all of the work back to the relevant Cabinet departments for more input. The final document would be forwarded to Sittmann, who would do a check of all the principals to make sure they were comfortable with their department's input. The product would then go to Scowcroft, who would have his own opportunity to present the president with options and give his recommendations.

It was Cicconi's task to digest all the paper flow and ensure that it reached the president in a timely and efficient manner. Cicconi soon found out that Bush was in a more thoughtful mood on the weekends. During the week, the president is inundated with so many memos, telephone calls, meetings, and other events that there may not be much time to reflect on issues. As a result, Cicconi started sending many of the papers up to the president at

Camp David. Over coffee and with no distractions, he liked to sit back and do his reading then. Cicconi soon found that many of the papers he would give the president for weekend reading would come back with comments and thoughtful responses. The pieces that needed careful attention were often foreign-policy related. With Scowcroft's concurrence, Cicconi had the discretion of holding an NSC paper for weekend reading, even if it arrived in his office early in the week. However, given the close working relationship between Bush and Scowcroft, Cicconi could not keep tabs on everything. Scowcroft would visit with the president in the Oval Office, at which time he could hand him papers and reports that fell outside the staffing process.

The natural conflict that could develop between the NSC and the rest of the White House did not embroil the Bush administration. "I think during the Bush administration there was an unprecedented level of cooperation between the domestic side of the White House or the chief of staff's operation and the national security side, particularly under John Sununu and Brent Scowcroft," observes Gates, who worked on the NSC for a number of presidents. "I don't think that the system ever worked better than it did under these two and the sharing of information," he says. Some of this cooperation can be attributed to Sununu's acceptance of Scowcroft's dominance in foreign policy. Sununu was involved in all issues; foreign policy, however, was one area in which he would tread cautiously, deferring to Scowcroft. The personal relationship between the two was excellent, with Sununu often popping into Scowcroft's office to touch base on evolving issues or just to chat. The latter, although quiet and unassuming, refused to cede his area of expertise to Sununu. Furthermore, much of Scowcroft's influence stemmed from his close relationship with Bush, which precluded Sununu from becoming a major player in foreign policy. Scowcroft, however, was attuned to the need to keep Sununu informed so that greater personality or policy conflicts did not arise between the two or their staffs.

Shirley Green supervised most aspects of the tightly controlled system for dealing with correspondence for the president's attention as well as outgoing correspondence. She is a longtime Texas associate of Bush and served as deputy assistant to the president for presidential messages and correspondence, which meant that she had a finger on the pulse of the American public. Nearly every day Green sent Bush a folder through the Staff Secretariat containing correspondence divided into three categories: letters from friends, letters from

VIPs, and samplings of correspondence on significant issues penned mostly by representatives from organizations associated with a particular issue.

In addition, every Friday Green forwarded a report to the president and Cicconi on the mood of the country. The report had two elements: incoming mail that reflected the pros and cons of issues dominating the public's attention and telephone messages, also broken down into pro and con positions, regarding the top issues of the week. Attached to the report was a sampling of pro and con letters from the public regarding the issues reflected in the letters and calls, with prepared responses, already vetted by the staff, for Bush's signature. Green also included a sampling of responses that she sent out under her own signature. The purpose of this practice was to expose the president to an unvarnished sampling of the opinions, recommendations, and requests from the public.

This weekly report was provided only to Bush and Cicconi, who was the conduit for delivering it to Bush. The chief of staff, while not on the distribution list for the report, was not excluded if he wanted to see it. Fitzwater, on the other hand, was someone who did not want to see the report since he believed that it would put him in a difficult position with the press. Credibility is the most important asset of any press secretary, and Fitzwater did not want to jeopardize his standing with the press. The press was always asking about the public's reaction to or views on the president's actions and policies. Fitzwater believed that if he had access to the report he would have had knowledge of the public mood and would have been in the awkward position of having to admit his knowledge and, thus, might inadvertently create a story by speaking about it or risk undermining his own credibility by avoiding the question. With no knowledge, he could simply state, "I don't know." Furthermore, Fitzwater did not believe that letters and calls to the president were an accurate reading of public opinion since they tended to reflect the views of people whose opinions were strong enough to motivate them to write or call.

In the first two months of his administration Bush faced a particular dilemma regarding correspondence. In late December 1988 Pan Am flight 103 was blown up over Lockerbie, Scotland, in a terrorist act that killed 270 people, including 11 on the ground. The terrorist act eventually was tied to Libya. Family members of the victims sent letters to President Reagan, but the letters never received his attention. The coming end of the Reagan administration limited the staff's time and attention as they packed up and prepared to turn the reins over to Bush. In addition, the NSC staff, knowing that Reagan could become very emotional over the letters, sought to protect him from dealing with the issue as he was leaving office and recommended that the letters be sent to the Transportation Department for handling. As a result, by the time Bush came into office there was some disgruntlement among those family members because President Reagan had not acknowledged their losses. Cicconi seized the issue, and, after a discussion with Sununu, the latter agreed to have Bush deal with the correspondence. Bush responded to every letter.

The lesson was not lost on Bush. Later on in his administration, Bush personally signed the letters addressed to family members who had lost relatives in the Gulf War.

Cicconi was in an unenviable position. He had to not only keep tabs on all the papers coming through his office but also ensure that no one was circumventing the system. The procedures he put in place worked well, with some notorious exceptions. The biggest culprit was the Press Office. Oftentimes, in order to meet press deadlines or to get a statement out quickly, the Press Office bypassed the Staff Secretariat. It would take valuable time to follow established procedures, and doing so would thus undermine the rationale of press relations, which is to make sure that the administration's views are part of the news cycle. An established pattern soon emerged. A perturbed Cicconi would accost Fitzwater or one of his deputies, complain about the lapse in following procedure, and note the importance of working with the Staff Secretariat. Cicconi's victim would nod sympathetically, apologize for the lapse, and assure him that it would not happen again. While frustrated, Cicconi's good nature and sense of humor made these routine encounters enjoyable banter.

Outside this paper flow mechanism, Bush set up a three-tier advisory system early in his administration. The National Security Council was charged with foreign policy. The Domestic Policy Council was charged with developing, coordinating, and implementing domestic and social policy. The Economic Policy Council was to advise the president and deal with both domestic and international economic policy, since the domestic and international economies are closely interrelated. It was believed that this structure would provide close coordination and a comprehensive treatment of economic issues. Each of these councils was tasked with coordinating the relevant information, advice, and recommendations from the Cabinet departments. The NSC soon developed into a formidable and effective instrument of administration policy. The other two councils, however, performed erratically.

The Economic Policy Council was chaired by Secretary of the Treasury Nick Brady, while the Domestic Policy Council was headed by Attorney General Dick Thornburgh. Both councils operated more on the basis of personal contacts among various staffers rather than by a bureaucratic structure. On the Economic Policy Council, staff of various agencies and departments worked out among themselves what issues were assigned to what offices. The two councils fell under the purview of Cabinet Affairs, but their work was facilitated by Roger Porter, assistant to the president for domestic policy, and the White House staff functioned as staff members for both councils. Porter also spearheaded the president's domestic policy agenda, conducting many of the negotiations with Congress over various pieces of legislation.

The Economic Policy Council met a couple of times a week, while the Domestic Policy Council's sessions were less frequent, running about two or three meetings per month. Whenever an issue needed attention, a sub-Cabinet working group representing the agencies relevant to the issue was set up to examine options and to forward them to the respective full council.

This system existed until 1992, when the two councils were merged into the Policy Coordinating Group and put under the supervision of Clayton Yeutter. Yeutter had been brought over to the White House from the Republican National Committee to serve as counselor to the President for domestic policy. There was some political motivation for the reshuffling. With the president under increasing political attack for the stagnant economy during that election year, the White House sought to portray Bush as being engaged in the development of economic policy. Centralizing the process presented a picture of presidential involvement.

The success of any process depends on the quality of the individuals filling the various roles. The linchpin for making Bush's hierarchical process work efficiently and for maintaining the loyalty of the staff was the chief of staff.

John Sununu was an early backer of Bush's bid for the presidency and had first met Bush in the early 1980s. In 1982, Sununu won the gubernatorial primary in New Hampshire. His war chest depleted, Sununu approached Vice President Bush about attending a fundraiser on his behalf. Bush quickly obliged, and the successful event raised almost all the funds Sununu required to win the general election. From then on, a personal relationship developed, including social visits to Bush's summer home in Kennebunkport and the vice president's mansion.

Sununu's efforts on behalf of Bush in New Hampshire helped deliver that state to Bush in the 1988 primary and set the course for Bush's nomination. Besides being grateful for this political support, Bush was impressed with Sununu's intellect and the prospects for his ability to deal with Congress. As a former elected official, Sununu had political skills and had been exposed to public pressure, something with which Washington fairly vibrates; he also had experience making decisions in the context of legislative pressures and bargaining. He was decisive and confident; he could be expected to help push the president's agenda through the morass of Washington politics. This combination of factors led Bush to appoint Sununu as his chief of staff.

The strength of any presidency is dependent to some extent on the effectiveness of the White House chief of staff. The purpose of the position is not only to be a gatekeeper for the president but also, more importantly, to shepherd the White House staff and external constituencies in support of the president's agenda. A good chief needs management skills, communication skills, good political antennae, and great interpersonal skills. Sununu possessed excellent skills in all areas save one: interpersonal relations. His sharp intellect, witty mind, and bombastic personality made him an intimidating force. Many a time he cowed his own staff and outsiders, including members of Congress and the media.

Sununu started the White House working day with a half-hour senior staff meeting at 7:30 A.M. in the Roosevelt Room, across the hall from the Oval Office. At the meeting, the possible press interests of the day were raised, and each office head reported on expected activities and potential problems. Sununu gave direction on how to proceed.

Sununu laid down the law with an iron hand his first full day on the job, foreshadowing the problems he would eventually have with the staff and the press. On Monday, January 23, Bush held a Cabinet meeting after which Sununu warned against anyone discussing with the press what went on in the meeting. Fitzwater, nonetheless, put out a written statement summarizing the key points of the meeting. He was fully aware, based on experience, that if such a step were not taken, each participant would be spinning a version to the press. "Sununu," Fitzwater said, "will have to learn how this town works."

The natural consequence of Sununu's style was an alienation of much of the staff and a tendency not to delegate responsibilities fully, both of which eventually hampered the smooth functioning of the White House. Sununu, understandably, had to play the hard-nosed administrator in order to protect access to the president and to drive his agenda through the government bureaucracy and Congress. His approach, however, was far too rough and dismissive of others, as seen in his disdain of the press. Sununu did not view the press as an important player in the Washington scene, and he never established a cordial working relationship with the media. The press is, however, an important component of the policy process in Washington; how it portrays an issue, an event, or a government proposal can have a major impact on how the public and Congress receive it. Thus, any astute policy maker cultivates the press. Sununu's dismissive treatment of the press probably added to the critical reviews of the administration and eventually led to his own downfall when the press hounded him over the use of government transportation for private travel. "John is very bright and he was very loyal to me," recalls Bush. "I trusted him. I hated to see him go down the tubes. The press far outweighed the few minuses that he had."

Andy Card, Sununu's deputy, enjoyed a close, longtime relationship with Bush, and over time, Bush relied on him for more and more assignments even before Sununu encountered his travel scandal. Card first met Bush in 1974 when the latter came to Boston as chairman of the Republican National Committee to give a speech during the Watergate crisis. Card got a free ticket—a sure sign that the organizers feared a low turnout. Indeed, it turned out to be an almost empty room. Bush, however, while not dynamic, gave a strong defense of the Republican Party. The qualities that many have come to admire in Bush—his patriotism, kindness, and commitment to service— attracted Card. The two struck up a correspondence in 1978, and at the beginning of 1979 Card signed on to Bush's presidential bid, driving him to sites in Massachusetts and New Hampshire; he has been a close family friend since. Over the years Card gained a reputation as a selfless public servant, always fair in his dealings and not harboring a personal agenda. Card had done a stint in the Massachusetts legislature, and with a background in engineering he has the attention to detail that comes with that profession. Bush eventually appointed Card as secretary of transportation in 1992, a move Bush was happy to make. However, in hindsight, Bush regrets that he had not kept Card closer to him by making him chief of staff after Sununu resigned. Card went on to serve as George W. Bush's convention organizer in 2000 and eventually became his first chief of staff.

Card first met Sununu in 1971, when both were involved in local politics in their respective states. Card had a very candid, relatively close relationship with Sununu and never felt isolated from him. Much of that relationship was shaped by Card's view of his job. Card recognized and appreciated the pressures that Sununu felt in his position. Therefore, Card regarded himself not only as a sounding board but also as the one on whom Sununu could vent his frustrations. By playing the latter role, Card believed he could spare other staff members from being berated or being the objects of Sununu's frustrations. In this way, Card served as the loyal deputy and at the same time protected the staff.

Beneath Sununu's outbursts, however, lay his compassionate side and an eagerness to assist people. The period leading up to the Gulf War was a hectic time at the White House, with long hours and high tensions. Many of the meetings were held in Sununu's office and were facilitated by Katie Maness, his executive assistant. Maness started working with Sununu during the 1988 transition, and in addition to working the grueling White House schedule she was attending law school at night. Following one particularly late meeting in December 1990, Sununu continued with his work and Maness decided to assist him rather than attend her classes that evening. Sununu, aware that her exams were nearing, insisted that Maness attend her classes, but she demurred, showing the loyalty that White House staffers often exhibit, choosing to remain until the task was done. Raising his voice and demanding that Maness leave for the evening did nothing to persuade her. Finally, pacing his office in exasperation, his shirt rumpled and beginning to hang out over his belt from the long day of work, Sununu announced that he was leaving for the night.

"I can get these things done in the morning," said Sununu. "I'm going to go home now. Katie, please call for my car."

Maness made the call, Sununu left, and Maness followed close behind. Sununu entered his car and had the driver circle twice around the White House. Then, with Maness off the White House grounds, Sununu quietly slipped back to work.

One of Bush's strengths—one that gave those around him extra incentive and confidence—was the way he treated the staff. George Bush believed in the abilities and loyalties of the individuals with whom he surrounded himself. He assumed and expected competence and loyalty from everyone and judged them on their actions and performances and not the innuendo or self-serving criticism and whispering that can permeate any staff. This sense of loyalty, while a definite strength, also exposed a certain weakness. Bush was reluctant at times to face the reality that a staffer had become a detriment to the administration.

Bush was not enthusiastic about dealing with personal confrontation or thorny personnel issues that would inevitably arise. Bush is considerate of everyone; like most politicians he enjoys making people feel at ease and does not enjoy conflict. He expected issues and disputes to be settled in a gentlemanly manner. Even more importantly, he expected individuals to acknowledge their own shortcomings or any action that might be detrimental to the administration. If such a problem were to arise, the staffer should show their loyalty by leaving. As a result, Bush was expert in using the wordless gesture to send signals of pleasure or displeasure. In most cases it was enough to avoid a direct personal confrontation, which might exacerbate the situation or put the individual in an embarrassing position.

When senior staffers got crosswise with the highly demanding Sununu, Bush, to calm the waters and to restore peace on the staff, would offer a gesture of confidence, such as having the staffer walk out to Marine One on the South Lawn, sometimes with Bush's arm draped over the staffer's shoulder, in plain sight of Sununu. Bush, therefore, was torn in his loyalties to Sununu when he got embroiled in his travel problems.

In April 1991 the media broke the story that Sununu had been using government aircraft and autos for private purposes. The uses were not illegal. A directive issued by President Reagan in 1987 had authorized the use of government transportation for the chief of staff and the national security adviser in order to keep the officials readily available for the president and to protect them from any possible hijacking to which the use of commercial transport might expose them. However, it was the appearance of impropriety and the purposes to which Sununu was putting the perks that rankled the press. Sununu used the transportation to visit his dentist and his home in New Hampshire, among other reasons. Sununu thus appeared to be using the government trough to support a convenient lifestyle for himself. The press hounded him; it was their

chance to undermine a man who had over the years mistreated them, sometimes even threatening to destroy them. Eventually, the opposition spread to
the White House staff and members of Congress whom Sununu had treated
dismissively over the years. While at first Sununu believed that he could not be
toppled, by the time he was forced to resign he was pleading for his job. It was
left to Andy Card to approach Sununu with the word that his continuation as
chief of staff was hindering the administration and that it would be best that
he resign, something that Sununu did in December 1991.

Bush was not completely divorced from the process. He carefully worked
behind the scenes with telephone calls to various staffers, including to their
homes on weekends. In the calls, Bush solicited the staffers' views on the level
of support that Sununu enjoyed among the staff. He took every measure possible to be fair in gleaning information and in making his judgment.

Sununu did have his supporters.

"I love John Sununu," Barbara Bush states exuberantly. "I enjoyed John
Sununu a lot."

Barbara Bush has a particular memory of Sununu's help in the presidential campaign of 1988. "He was a great comfort and joy, particularly in New
Hampshire, after George lost the Iowa caucus," she recalls.

"When we got off the plane in New Hampshire, John greeted us," she
further recalls.

"'Don't worry, we are going to win New Hampshire,'" she says Sununu
stated emphatically to her.

Barbara Bush believed him. About a year later she got the truth from him.

"'I lied,'" she recalls Sununu confessing with a mischievous smile. "'I didn't
think we would win.'"

Once Sununu left, Bush settled on Sam Skinner, his secretary of transportation, to run the White House apparatus. After the chief of staff, the
next line of support for the president is his staff. Under Bush, the senior staff
was smaller than in the Reagan administration, but more importantly, it was
set up as a low-profile staff. This mirrored Bush's and Sununu's views that
the White House staff was not to be a buffer between the president and the
outside world with its own dynamics, but rather a facilitator. Bush relied on
personal contacts developed over years of service to be able to get in touch
with anyone at anytime. Sununu, with his supreme self-confidence, believed
he needed no intermediaries. Overall, Bush had great confidence in his staff

and was very supportive. "I had a great staff," recalls Bush. "They were loyal and imaginative people. Unfortunately, the staff was evaluated because of Sununu's image."

In addition to the paper flow mechanism, a careful process was put in place for dealing with the president's schedule. Control of the president's schedule is an important function, impacting whom the president will see and for how long, travel destinations, and every action taken. A careful mechanism was established to maximize the use of the president's time and to ensure that Bush's goals would be met. Joe Hagin headed the scheduling office during the first two years of the administration. In 1990 he was replaced by his deputy, Kathy Super, who had been in charge of appointments under Hagin. About once a week the heads of the various White House offices would meet in Super's ground floor office in the West Wing to review scheduling issues. The session was chaired by Card. Before each meeting, Super had already vetted numerous requests, denying obvious ones, getting surrogates for some, or staffing out others for recommendations. The staff had five days in which to get their scheduling recommendations to Super's office.

Once all the recommendations were in, a folder was prepared for each participant in the meeting. The pros and cons of each of the requests were discussed, with Card serving as the final arbiter. The process did not end there. A memo, based on the discussion of the meeting, was then prepared for the president, who had the final say regarding what went on the schedule.

Bush was very disciplined when it came to his schedule, as was everyone else around him. Sununu and Scowcroft needed much flexibility regarding scheduling, given the pressures of their positions and the need for Bush's time or involvement as issues arose. Despite these pressures, neither of the two men put anything on the schedule without first checking with Super. Bush was conscientious regarding the process. He would himself call Super to check if something could be added to his schedule. Ironically, while Bush himself was part of the scheduling process, it was one of the few things that he complained about, particularly if he felt overscheduled. "Why am I doing this?" would be his frustrated plea. He would, however, plow through the events. Sometimes the schedule was adjusted, but oftentimes it was not and the staff learned to live with these intermittent complaints.

Despite the attention to detail, there was the occasional glitch. The underwater explorer Jacques Cousteau was persistent in his requests to meet with Bush. Sununu, however, opposed such a meeting, fearing that Cousteau might use the meeting and the White House as a platform to push his views regarding the environment. Super, therefore, dutifully kept rejecting the requests. However, at one point Super and Green consulted and decided to let one such letter go through to the president. When Bush received the letter, he gladly wrote across it that he would not be averse to a meeting.

Super staffed Cousteau's request, and it was favorably reviewed, eventually finding its way as a recommendation for the president, who then formally agreed to add the meeting to his schedule. On the day of the meeting in the fall of 1990, Sununu became concerned, fearing the worst scenario, one in which Cousteau would trot out to the lawn to criticize the president in front of the press. Bush became concerned over Sununu's dire warnings. He summoned Super into the Oval Office. Super reassured the president, explaining that it was a courtesy meeting. Cousteau patiently sat in the West Wing Lobby as the frenzy unfolded.

With no alternative, Bush gladly greeted Cousteau. They walked the grounds of the South Lawn, engaged in enjoyable conversation. There was no pressure, no criticism. Bush reflected on the meeting afterward, viewing it as nice and delightful.

The scheduling process seemed to work efficiently for the most part, but staffers noted some breakdown when Skinner replaced Sununu. Overall, Skinner was everything that Sununu was not: more personable, easygoing, and able to work with various constituencies, particularly Congress. Skinner came in pledging to maintain the integrity of the scheduling process, realizing the importance of not abusing the president's time. The stated intentions, however, were not realized as Skinner apparently fell victim to his own background. Some staffers felt that Skinner, as a former secretary of transportation, was not able to make the transition from executive to staffer. He was more comfortable giving directions than carrying them out. Whether he was managing the daily staff needs or trying to be collegial, Skinner did not exhibit the decisiveness of Sununu, which further loosened the staff structure. Skinner, however, was in an untenable position. He had come into his post at a time of turmoil; Sununu had left under a cloud, the primaries were about to begin, and the campaign was still seeking to find its footing. After almost twelve years of Republican rule, the party's energy and initiative seemed to have slipped, and the problem was reflected in the inability of Bush's campaign to get on track. A number of Bush's associates, such as Roger Ailes, the media consultant, opted out of campaign politics to pursue private sector opportunities; Lee Atwater, the engine behind the campaign in 1988, had died. Beyond the campaign, the established procedures of the White House veterans were not malleable in the hands of an outsider coming in toward the end of an administration.

Bush's Personal Style

An organizational structure outlines the flow of authority and responsibilities. Making it work smoothly, however, depends on the people who fill the slots. In the case of the White House organization, the president is key to the personal dynamics. How presidents view the office and the enthusiasm they bring to it can shape the overall functioning of the staff.

Besides his family, the one thing that George Bush enjoyed most was being president. He enjoyed the challenges, the responsibilities, and the trust of governing. He enjoyed the daily interaction and activities, the telephone calls, and the give and take of negotiations. In short, he loved the job and misses it to this day. However, although he liked the work of the presidency, he was not enamored by the trappings. He shunned any attempts to project power or to be ostentatious in its use. He approached the office as a sacred trust, to be used for the common good, to advance the needs of the nation and not as a tool for furthering a personal legacy. There was a sense of stewardship in his view, that it was incumbent upon a person to leave the world a better place and that the common good overrode all other considerations. Bush's enthusiasm for the presidency was an added strength in his leadership arsenal. The energy and positive attitude he brought to the position helped invigorate the staff, but, more importantly, they gave Bush a sense of confidence and enjoyment, two aspects of psychic strength that helped him tackle his challenges with relish and with the attitude that he could succeed.

Bush believes that his view of and approach to the office of the presidency were as much a part of the job as the daily activities. He holds a deep respect for the office, viewing it as the symbol of the nation, a beacon of its hopes and its future. The presidency is entrusted to an individual for a certain period. For Bush, any individual who holds it should be cognizant of two things: the power of the office to move the country forward through policies and, equally as important, the president's responsibility to leave the office in the dignified and respected state that it warrants. It was for the latter reason that Bush viewed the Nixon resignation and the Clinton scandals as so tragic. If the office is tarnished, then much of its strength is undermined, both in terms of the federal policy process and, politically, in the eyes of the public. For Bush, "duty, honor, country" was more than a motto; it was a way of life and a code to which one should be held accountable. Above all, Bush wanted to be remembered as having served in the presidency with honor and integrity.

In both his personal and his professional life, Bush has always been well organized. He is an early riser and was usually in the Oval Office a little past 6:30 A.M. He found that the early morning offered a certain solitude, without the small distractions and noise of human traffic through the West Wing that the rest of the day brings. That quiet time gave him a jump on his work, a sense of accomplishment before most of the offices had tackled their in-boxes. When Bush reached the office, his aide, Tim McBride, was awaiting him and the two would go through the day's schedule.

Bush would usually head to his study off the Oval Office, where he would start the day with paperwork over coffee and a grapefruit or some other light breakfast. Barbara Bush would usually poke her head in at the Oval Office around 7:00 A.M., en route to the heated outdoor pool. The study was Bush's favorite place for lunches, meetings, and the work of the day. He found it a relaxing haven in the midst of the whirlwind of activity that marks the West Wing. When he heard an aide playing background music to soften the pressures of the job, he quickly picked up on the practice, bringing in a stereo from the residence, sometimes playing soft music and other times something from his collection of country and western music.

Before his first daily meeting, Bush had already been through the press, tackled some paperwork, or penned a few notes to friends, supporters, or members of Congress. At 8:00 A.M. he was ready for his national intelligence briefing in the Oval Office. Scowcroft and Gates did the briefing, but the meeting also included Sununu and Quayle. After the briefing, Scowcroft and Gates left and Bush reviewed various domestic issues with Sununu and Quayle. After that, Bush was at the mercy of the daily schedule of meetings, briefings, and trips mostly arranged weeks ahead of time. He tackled each part of the day with enthusiasm.

Sometimes before the morning intelligence briefing, he would take a few minutes to meet with visiting friends—perhaps a fishing or golfing buddy or some other acquaintance. Barbara Bush would often join him on these occasions. These events were not on the official schedule, and they let the Bushes have some contact with their private world to counterbalance the fishbowl exposure of their daily routines. When Bush was occasionally able to escape for dinner, he liked to go to the Peking Gourmet, a favorite Chinese restaurant in northern Virginia, on the outskirts of Washington. Contact with his extended family, spread all over the United States, was rather sporadic and consisted mostly of stop-by visits. Christmas was the one occasion when most of the family sought to gather at Camp David.

Bush would end each day making sure that the in-box was cleared, that telephone calls had been returned, and that all was ready for him to tackle the tasks the next day was to bring. Being an early riser, he also liked to be early to bed. Whenever possible, Bush would get a massage before bedtime. After a massage, he would typically head to bed around 10:00 P.M.

It is said that Abraham Lincoln was driven by an engine of ambition that knew no rest. George Bush too is driven. He seemed to evaluate his day in the Oval Office by the number of things he had accomplished during his waking hours. Bush spent (and still spends) his waking hours on the telephone, giving speeches, "recreating" (as Bush referred to sports activities), and writing letters and notes. His energy is complemented by and feeds his competitive nature. Bush thrives on competition, whether in the political or sports world. There is no such thing as a simple game of tennis or golf. Bush strives for— and expects—victory in every such endeavor. He had the stamina and drive to move quickly from one thing to another, but this activity level also came with a bit of impatience. There is the famous moment during one of his debates with Clinton when Bush glanced at his watch, a sign of impatience and readiness to move on. Bush's energy is an important part of his leadership skill set; staffers marveled at the stamina he had despite being in his mid- to late sixties during his term. There was no slowdown after he left office. He parachuted from an airplane to mark his seventy-fifth birthday. And, to mark his eightieth birthday in 2004, Bush did a tandem parachute jump at his presidential library. The only thing that held him back from a solo jump was the wind and the recommendation of the Golden Knights, the army's elite parachute jump team that helped orchestrate the event. In November 2007, to mark the tenth anniversary of his library, Bush did a surprise tandem jump, assisted once again by the Golden Knights.

Bush was not the only one who kept such a frenetic pace. Barbara was his equal. From the first days in the White House she made it clear that she wanted to play a role beyond the traditional social scene. She had always had causes that she espoused or supported. During the vice-presidential days she seized on the problem of adult literacy needs, and her involvement helped bring the issue to the fore in American society. Thus, her desire to stay active and involved came as no surprise to her staff when they met in the East Wing during the first week of Bush's presidency. After stating her desire to be active in her new role, she turned immediately to her director of projects, Julie Cooke. "What am I doing tomorrow?" she demanded.

Cooke, a diminutive, energetic woman, had worked for the Bushes during the Reagan administration and the presidential campaign. She knew Barbara's energy, and within a few days she, with the creative guidance of Barbara's chief of staff, Susan Porter Rose, had filled the First Lady's calendar with various events; the calendar remained full for the next four years. In addition to accompanying the president on various domestic and foreign trips, Barbara expanded her role in literacy to include family literacy and broadened her interests to include libraries, schools, AIDS, organ donation, and volunteerism. Besides her public functions, she filled every minute of private time with such activities as keeping her scrapbooks up to date, keeping the family connected, and maintaining her swimming regimen.

Ann Brock recognized Barbara's drive from the moment they met. Brock became the First Lady's director of scheduling in March 1989 and remained in the position through January 1993. Brock had started her political journey in 1979 with Rep. G. V. "Sonny" Montgomery (D-Mississippi), first as a receptionist and then as the scheduler in Montgomery's office. Montgomery entered Congress in 1966, the same year that Bush won election from his Houston district. Montgomery was considered a Republican in Democratic clothing, and the two quickly struck up a close and lasting friendship that continued until Montgomery's death in 2006. The two played paddleball in the Capitol gym, a "recreation" that Bush took up again when he became vice president and then president. Montgomery had foreseen Bush's presidential success. He shared his feelings with Brock in 1980.

"My friend is going to be president some day," he told Brock. Then he gave her some advice. "You need to get on board."

Brock took the advice and signed up at the Bush for President campaign headquarters in Alexandria, Virginia. That year, though, Bush became Reagan's vice-presidential running mate. Brock continued to work for Montgomery and then went on to work as an assistant scheduler for President Reagan. After a stint in the private sector, she found herself being interviewed by Barbara Bush in February 1989. During the interview, Barbara confided that Montgomery had called her on Brock's behalf, and that endorsement was good enough for her. Her next statement gave Brock the first glimpse of the drive and energy that was to characterize the next four years.

"I want to do something every day that makes a difference," she instructed Brock.

Despite their similar frenetic routines, the Bushes are complementary of each other in social and public settings, each playing off and supporting the other. Barbara Bush is very natural, with a sense of humor and a manner that makes anyone in her company feel relaxed. This bearing has been a boon to Bush throughout his career, presenting to the public a couple that are at ease with themselves and with those around them. Barbara, however, can be critical, often masking her criticism in humorous tones that provide Bush with a perfect foil. Too much a gentleman himself, Bush would often parry off to Barbara to provide the critical observation or curt dismissal in their own version of "good cop–bad cop."

Her critical observation was evident when eldest son George W. announced his presidential ambitions. She was skeptical of his chances. Years later, recalling that moment, she muses that her first thought was: "He doesn't have a chance." Then again, she recalls that she had given him the wrong counsel when it came to the Texas gubernatorial race. "I told him not to run for governor," she now laughs. "I didn't think he had a prayer." Six months after that March date in 1999 when George W. announced his exploratory committee, however, she admits that she felt much better about his presidential chances.

From the elder Bush's own bearing and self-confidence flows a natural empathy toward the people around him. As Bush interacts with friends, staff, and even first-time acquaintances, he quickly makes them feel at ease. In a one-on-one setting, Bush lets his guest hold the floor, which not only shows respect for the guest but also offers him the opportunity to glean information and learn the views of his guests. Bush holds to the old adage that you learn more by listening than by speaking. In group gatherings, Bush gave his attention to those in the room, making everyone feel part of the gathering.

Some of this ease dissipated when Bush was dealing with staff outside the established chain of command. As a result, the ease and familiarity that Bush enjoyed with many of his senior advisers did not extend to their staffs. Bush could noticeably be seen fidgeting and looking past any such staffer, awaiting the arrival of their superior. This characteristic underscored the emphasis he put on maintaining a hierarchical chain of command and handling issues on a personal basis with those whom he knew best. While always courteous, Bush had a clear signal for when he was finished with business and it was time for a staffer to leave: he simply stopped looking at the person and returned to his work.

Bush's aversion to the trappings of the office and anything that smacked of an imperial presidency occasionally led him to micromanage and fret over minor logistical matters, such as the size of motorcades and the number of staffers on Air Force One. In these instances, Bush had a distorted view. As vice president, his logistical support tail had been short. A president, however, has an extended support tail ranging from military to medical personnel and various advance personnel and policy staffers. Still, there were caps on the number of staff who could accompany the president on trips, but senior staffers often tried to bypass such caps. Bush's attention to the size of the traveling staff diminished, however, as the administration wore on.

It was because of the large entourage and complicated logistics that Bush hated visiting New York City. His distaste for such travel was actually considerate; motorcades disrupt traffic, set back schedules for the public, and are a strain on local law enforcement officials and municipal budgets. Such trips are not much easier on staff. Once the president is seated the motorcade moves, leaving behind any dawdling staffer. Therefore, as the president departs an event, there is a mad scramble down stairwells, through hotel kitchens or backstage corridors, to get to the motorcade on time. During Bush's trip to China in 1989, one reporter was left behind when he did not get to the tarmac in time to board the press plane. To this day, Fitzwater says he still has nightmares about missing motorcades.

Patience has its limits, and Bush is no exception to this rule. Saddled with an overstaying conversationalist, Bush will listen politely, his jaw dropping, as he ponders a way to extricate himself. When he feels uncomfortable or does not want to do something, he tends to fidget. His eyes will not focus on the individual confronting him and his lower jaw moves back and forth, his lips and teeth partially open, and in a chair he will tend to slouch. His eyes will move, set with a noticeable twinkle and a pleading stare at an aide or anyone who can help him escape an overly long social obligation. Barring such a rescue, he will, finally, try to change the subject and, politely once again, suggest that time has gone by so quickly. In such circumstances, however, Bush remains diplomatic and gracious. When pop star Michael Jackson came to the Oval Office, Bush found himself having to play host when he needed to turn his attention to other matters. Grabbing the telephone, he called Barbara and boomed how Jackson would really like to see the residence area of the White House. She understood this as a code meaning that she was needed to rescue the president. She quickly whisked Jackson away for the tour. She soon found her famous guest to be quiet and self-effacing. When Mrs. Bush urged him to join her at the window and wave to tourists exiting by the North Portico, Jackson did so, but rather reluctantly. His appearance created a stir, but then he moved back from the windows to stay out of sight.

Bush's interpersonal skills, while a great asset, also had some drawbacks. In addition to not liking confrontation, Bush hates to be openly critical of people. Either situation, Bush fears, can break the bonds that tie an individual to Bush and break the gentlemanly decorum in which Bush prefers to operate. He thus tended to keep his feelings and frustrations to himself rather than sharing them with the objects of his emotional stress. When he vented his frustrations, he did so in front of a neutral observer. Oftentimes he would use Scowcroft as his sounding board.

Bush made sure that he was knowledgeable on policy, but for the execution of policy and its detailed specifics he relied on subordinates, particularly the Cabinet secretaries. Unfortunately, this practice sometimes did not work as smoothly as it should have. Jack Kemp, secretary of housing and urban development, often spoke out against administration policy. This problem is not unusual when a manager is surrounded with strong-willed individuals. But Bush would have it no other way; he did not want weak, overly agreeable people in critical positions.

One of the challenges any staff has is providing advice to the principal. As any staffer will attest, reactions can be affected by the amount of advice being provided, the timing, and the personality of the leader. Bush is a leader who is easy to deal with and to whom to offer advice. He did not have problems with listening to advice, whether in agreement with him, contrary to his views, or mixed. Indeed, he welcomed it and was pleased that conclusions and recommendations were put forth without inhibitions.

Bush had no particular preference as to how he was briefed. He was orally briefed and was also presented briefing papers that he could read at his leisure. The key to the latter was brevity. Bush did not enjoy long reads—nor was this a practical use of a president's time. Scowcroft made a point of limiting national security memos to an average of three pages, and Bush avidly read everything sent his way. The papers came back with exclamation marks in the margin and key words underlined or circled. Seldom, however, would he write notes in the margins nor did he have to. In the case of foreign policy, he trusted Scowcroft to present an issue in a balanced manner. Bush was not a passive recipient of information, however; he brooded on it, analyzed it on his own, and sought explanation until he was comfortable with what he was told. A worrier by nature, this characteristic served as an anchor that inhibited rash actions and helped him survey the whole issue and the range of options. In the prelude to the Gulf War, Bush had been briefed by General Tony McPeak at Camp David about the devastating impact that the U.S. Air Force strikes would have on Iraq. Bush fretted over whether or not McPeak's analysis was valid. He confided his skepticism to Scowcroft, who supported McPeak's analysis. A few days later, after McPeak had returned from a visit to the Gulf region, Bush invited him over to the White House. In the quiet of the upstairs dining room in the residence, McPeak repeated his assurances, to Bush's satisfaction.

In discussing Bush's attitude toward meetings, a senior aide has described him as "distracted." His abundant nervous energy could not be contained and made to focus; his mind appeared to be fixed on his next event. The exception to this tendency was during any kind of crisis; in those circumstances Bush always rose to the challenge of dealing with issues that needed immediate attention and solution. It put into place the forces that he knew best how to handle and that he felt most comfortable with—his immense reservoir of personal contacts. Crisis meant the need for immediate consultation and decision making, and personal contact was for him the best approach, not interminable meetings or position papers. The latter was left for staff and the various Cabinet bureaucracies to supervise and send up the chain of command. Bush, therefore, operated much like any other typical CEO: he closed the deal by telephone or in person based on his force of personality and his knowledge, both of the subject at hand and in many cases of the individuals with whom he was dealing. One former staffer has characterized him as being probably the best behind-the-scenes president the nation has ever had. A prime example was his success in pulling together the grand coalition that expelled Saddam Hussein's forces from Kuwait. This effort underscored Bush's interpersonal skills and his adept use of telephone diplomacy as a tool of policy making.

Bush's meetings were marked by a relaxed, bantering style, more akin to a gathering of friends rather than a formal session examining various intellectual angles and ideas. Furthermore, meetings were not a decision-making mechanism for Bush. They served to provide information that he then digested along with any briefing papers or conversations he had had on the issue. It was common for him to ask individuals to see him privately after a meeting so that he could pursue an issue further. In addition, he would consult with other White House staff and then telephone people throughout the government to get as broad a perspective as possible. Cabinet meetings fit this mold. Bush, along with the chief of staff, would usually set the agenda, but when it came to the actual meeting, Bush was mostly in a listening mode, punctuating his silence with a question or two. The purpose of the Cabinet sessions was to open a dialogue on an issue and for Bush to be exposed to a range of opinions.

On national security issues, the fact finding was more extensive. Bush, finding some free time in his schedule, would often telephone Scowcroft and ask him to stop by the Oval Office. The two would then examine a wide range of foreign policy issues, specific in some instances and rambling in others. It was the type of discussion Bush engaged in with relish.

While much of the foreign policy process operated on an informal basis between Bush and Scowcroft, the latter, as the national security adviser, did have a set routine for gathering information. Once a week Scowcroft tried to host a breakfast in his office for Baker and Cheney. The difficulty of meshing all three schedules precluded adhering consistently to the weekly sessions, but the gatherings did help to reinforce the personal bonds among the three. More importantly, free of staff, the three could openly discuss the issues and plan strategies without any fears that they would be leaked to the press.

In formal meetings, Bush prefers not to be the center of attention nor appear as being specifically in charge. In national security meetings, he let Scowcroft moderate the proceedings. As in Cabinet sessions, Bush rarely revealed his views during these meetings except by the nature of the questions that he posed. In this manner Bush was able to learn what his advisers believed without preempting their boldness or their recommendations with his own views. This practice also fit Bush's pattern of learning by listening. The one time that Bush sought to take the initiative, he was dissuaded by Scowcroft.

Scowcroft believed that the first meeting held on August 2, 1990, on Iraq's invasion of Kuwait had gone poorly. It had not properly dealt with the issue and the options that the United States faced nor had it underscored the president's determination to deal with the issue. Scowcroft, therefore, believed that another meeting was needed as quickly as possible, and he broached the idea to Bush.

"I would like to start out the meeting and lay out why Kuwait is important, " offered Scowcroft.

Bush reflected and quickly agreed. He realized the importance of Kuwait and the need to develop a coherent and forceful administration response. Any prolonged delays could portray the administration as indecisive and send Iraq the wrong signal.

"Why don't I do it," stated Bush with a note of determination that indicated his words were more a statement than a question.

"No," counseled Scowcroft. "The discussion would quickly be over." He realized that the participants might tailor their views to the president's and, thereby, preclude an open and fruitful examination of the issue. "If I run the meeting, then we will see how others think."

Bush readily agreed.

The next day, Bush convened the meeting, and Scowcroft opened with the terms of consideration. While the previous meeting had been a rambling, inconclusive discourse, the new meeting concluded with a strong sense of the president's clear determination to stand up to Saddam Hussein. Sandwiched between the two meetings was a quick trip to Aspen, Colorado, where the president met with Prime Minister Margaret Thatcher of Britain. Iraq dominated the discussion, and, in a joint news conference at the end of the meeting, Bush and Thatcher called for Iraq's withdrawal from Kuwait.

There never was any hesitation in the president's determination to oust Saddam from Kuwait. Saddam had come into full power in 1979 after forcing President Ahmed Hassan al-Bakr to retire. Saddam soon embarked on a policy of ruthless subjugation, killing his opponents and terrorizing the Iraqi population. He created the world's fourth-largest army and set his sights on neighboring states. In 1980 he turned a border dispute in the Persian Gulf into a war against Iran. The conflict ended in a stalemate in 1988, and in 1990 Saddam turned his attention to Kuwait, which he claimed was historically a part of Iraq. The invasion not only undermined international law and threatened the world oil market but also unnerved nearby states such as Saudi Arabia and Israel. Earlier that year, Saddam had spoken of destroying Israel. Bush spearheaded the international community's response to the invasion by getting the United Nations to pass various resolutions, including UN Resolution 678, which authorized the use of force against Iraq. Bush also formed a coalition of more than thirty states to join the effort against Saddam and was also able to generate international financial support to cover the costs of the U.S. military action.

Bush did not worry too much about appearances. He had no problem sitting back and listening at a meeting, even though it might appear that he was not "in charge." True to his emphasis on personal relationships, Bush was always attentive to how people behaved at meetings. His main concern was to make sure that the meetings were productive and proceeded in a harmonious fashion. When Bush sensed the tension rising, he would often make a joke or a humorous remark, thereby dissipating the tension. He was fully aware that the development of personal animosities could cloud judgments and recommendations. He saw his ultimate goal as being the facilitator of a harmonious gathering. In this way, he believed he received his advisers' best recommendations.

Hidden from public view but well known by his staff and those around him is Bush's sense of humor. Bush used it not only to reduce tension in meetings but also to build camaraderie among staffers. Bush presented an "award" to Scowcroft for his tendency to doze off in meetings yet jerk to attention and appear as if he had been listening attentively all along; soon, the "Scowcroft Award" became a tradition, granted to anyone who was caught dozing off. If the event was caught on camera, the award consisted of a photo signed by Bush; otherwise it was an award in name only. And one time Bush received the gift of an outfit and sombrero from President Carlos Salinas of Mexico. Bush gleefully donned the complete outfit and posed for a photo. He sent the autographed photo to Salinas.

Bush's jovial side was contagious. Recognizing Bush's lighter side, the staff readily reciprocated. On his birthday, the NSC staff would throw a surprise party in Scowcroft's West Wing office. Bush would be presented with birthday cards—one for each year of his age—with notes and signatures from various staffers. In addition, the names of world leaders, such as Thatcher and Gorbachev, were inscribed on the cards by the staffers. The notes and signatures were on self-adhesive paper, allowing Bush to discard them but keep the cards. The rationale was that given the nature of his job, it could not be possible for him to get out and buy cards. Bush, thus, had a reservoir of cards that he could re-use for his personal friends.

Bush is an avid storyteller with a gift for making the mundane and the serious humorous and enjoyable. He readily shares his anecdotes with family and friends. Typical was an e-mail he sent out recounting a walk he took with Sadie, the family English spaniel that was a gift from Queen Elizabeth, around the pond at his presidential library in 2002:

> On Good Friday I was quietly fishing our pond. I looked up and saw Sadie with what appeared to be a white bag. She had dragged it up on top of the hill. . . . The agents went to look. It was, yes, a white duck.
>
> But here's Sadie's side of it. I examined the duck and the blood on the duck was near the tail. There was no blood on our beloved Sadie. It is my story, and I am sticking to it, that some snake bit the duck in the ass or perhaps a beaver did the duck in.
>
> In case there is an inquiry I want you to know that Yes, the second duck has now bit the dust, but until definitely proved guilty Sadie is innocent—well reasonably innocent.
>
> The surviving duck, the littler one, the one Sadie almost did in, was quacking in sorrow and this did make me sad.
>
> I cannot bawl Sadie out for doing what she was trained to do at Her Majesty's kennel.
>
> If a funeral is required the duck was last seen in the bottom of the creek where I had thrown it to keep well trained Sadie from Re-retrieving [sic] the darn thing. End of report.

Bush's social style is not stilted, and his relaxed manner is apparent and often serves as a quick antidote in tense situations. On one occasion Bush hosted the Joint Chiefs of Staff at a White House luncheon. Seated to his left was Admiral David Jeremiah, vice chairman of the Joint Chiefs. Jeremiah served four years as vice chairman, first under General Colin Powell and later under General John Shalikashvili. He served as commander of the Pacific Fleet and was involved in various military exercises, including the Gulf War of 1991, the capture of the *Achille Lauro* hijackers, and the action against Libya in the Gulf of Sidra in 1986. A soft-spoken individual, Jeremiah had been steeled by his experiences, and one could not imagine anything unnerving him. As the wide-ranging discussion progressed, Jeremiah leaned back in his chair to allow those to his left to direct their conversation to the president. Suddenly, there was a loud snap. The admiral's balancing act had not been successful; the chair had broken. Everyone in the room knew that the chair had broken. An awkward silence grabbed everyone. A horrified Jeremiah thought, "I have just broken the president's chair," and he seemed unsure of what to do next. Before he or anyone else could say anything, Bush looked at Jeremiah and stated reassuringly, "My brother did exactly the same thing last week." Whether with a word or a gesture, Bush makes sure his guests feel comfortable and leave with a positive experience. He would have it no other way.

On policy matters, Bush's willingness to gamble occasionally put him ahead of his staff. When the issue of congressional support for the impending war against Saddam was raised, many on the White House staff were hesitant; there was a widespread belief that Congress would not support the president. Bush felt very strongly about having such a resolution. Unlike many of his advisers, Bush believed that he could obtain congressional support. In an Oval Office meeting he was adamant and confident. He told those around him, "I don't want to be an LBJ." President Johnson got Congress to pass the Gulf of Tonkin Resolution after North Vietnam attacked a U.S. ship, and he used the vote as proof of congressional support for the subsequent escalation of U.S. involvement in Vietnam. Bush wanted clear and unarguable support before any military action was taken. On January 12, 1991, Bush got the vote, days before the military campaign was launched. In a joint resolution, the Senate voted 52–47, and the House supported the president by a vote of 250–183.

Bush also took a chance when he relied on his first impression of Gorbachev at their initial meeting in 1985 at the funeral of Soviet leader Konstantin Chernenko to guide his views on the evolving situation in the Soviet Union. In a cable he wrote back to President Reagan, Bush indicated that he saw Gorbachev as a different sort of Soviet leader and as someone who could clearly do business with the West. During his visit to France in July 1989 for a G-7 meeting Bush pushed his advisers on the possibility of a meeting with Gorbachev. Both Baker and Scowcroft were skeptical, fearing that the president could be blindsided if a firm agenda were not set ahead of time. Bush, however, overruled them. On the return flight home, he penned a letter to Gorbachev proposing a meeting, which eventually became the Malta Summit in December of that year. This was the start of a close personal working relationship between the two leaders as well as the beginning of cooperation between the two countries on various issues.

Over the years, Bush came to enjoy Gorbachev's friendship and his sense of humor, particularly his willingness to tell jokes about himself. For Bush, Gorbachev's call on Christmas day in 1991 to tell of his resignation as the Soviet leader was particularly emotional.

"Felt like I lost a friend," Bush subsequently stated about the event.

Ironically, Bush, while a very social and outgoing individual, exhibits a secretive nature in terms of decision making and information. This penchant for secrecy is possibly an outgrowth of Bush's social background. Raised in a patrician world of private clubs and a member of the secret Skull and Bones society at Yale, Bush's world revolved around friendships and gentlemanly conduct, where one's word was one's bond and what was said was not for general consumption. His experiences in the worlds of diplomacy and intelligence probably served to reinforce this tendency. An experience early in his career embedded in Bush a profound distaste for press leaks and strengthened the penchant for secrecy. As CIA director, Bush participated in the famous Team A–Team B exercise that pitted a team from the CIA (Team A) with a team of outside experts (Team B) to gauge the effectiveness of CIA analyses of the Soviet Union. The exercise highlighted some of the weaknesses in CIA analyses. In and of itself, this exercise was a very useful project that helped strengthen the analytical approach of the CIA, but the results were leaked, putting the CIA in a bad light. Bush was infuriated: not only was his organization made to look bad but the guiding principle of that organization—secrecy—had been violated. Thus, Bush's personal and career experiences together underscored the importance of secret negotiations, of saving face, and of maintaining open lines of communication, but often behind the scenes.

This approach was paralleled in many instances throughout the Bush administration. Baker had established a very close-knit structure at the State

Department. His circle of advisers included a number of political appointees, to the exclusion of career officials. At the NSC, Scowcroft not only had a smaller staff than had his predecessors in the Reagan administration but also relied heavily on Gates as a sounding board.

There was also a practical side to the penchant for secrecy. On the foreign policy front, Scowcroft shared the president's concern about press leaks and the damage they did by exposing internal debates and recommendations. Scowcroft believed in two simple points: that people, for ego or policy reasons, leak to the media and that leaks cannot be prevented. To minimize leaks, Scowcroft and the president resorted to informal rather than formal meetings of the National Security Council. This tactic had the benefit of limiting the number of people in attendance. In formal meetings, each of the principals was allowed to have two aides attend, which greatly increased the risk of a leak. However, there was a drawback to the smaller, informal sessions. "This approach tended to leave out some experts that had crucial information relative to a discussion," admits Scowcroft.

As within any organization, the formal structure and various personalities were at times circumvented. Fred McClure, the president's senior staffer for congressional relations, despite his good relationship with Sununu, nonetheless utilized various means to stay abreast of things besides the formal meetings he had with the chief of staff or the president. Vice President Dan Quayle, in particular, was a valuable ally who served as a conduit to the president and to Capitol Hill. As a well-respected former member of the Senate, Quayle used his close relationship with conservatives on the Hill many times to calm down Republican Congress members' concerns about administration actions. Likewise, while members of the White House may have been reluctant to share information with each other due to bureaucratic turf battles, members of Congress were more than willing to do so. If a staffer needed to speak with the president, a few minutes of hanging out in the West Wing could lead to a chance encounter that could provide an opportunity for a discussion. In these situations time would be short and the opportunities were open to chance. The West Wing is a small enclave in the White House, and it thus seems like it would be the perfect environment for a close encounter with the president; nothing could be further from the truth. For practical purposes, the president might as well be a thousand miles away from each office. There is little opportunity for contact with the president except for those privileged to enter the Oval Office, and entry is tightly guarded by the chief of staff. When the president walks out, every movement is carefully orchestrated and monitored. A monitor in the chief of staff's office reports the president's location; a call to the Situation Room by the signal operator lets the watch team know where the president is at any particular moment. The president's path is cleared by Secret Service agents, front and rear, throughout the West Wing and the entire White House. Bush himself used such chance encounters to get up to speed on issues. He enjoyed getting firsthand accounts. In the days leading up to Operation Desert Storm, staff in the White House Situation Room, the nerve center for classified communications, were constantly badgering the Joint Staff at the Pentagon for updates and various information. The calls came each day at all hours and were fielded by an increasingly exasperated Pentagon staff that had nothing new to report. At about five o'clock one morning a marine in the Command Center was sitting at his station when a call came in from the White House.

The marine grabbed the telephone and bellowed, "What do you want now?" in an exasperated and tired voice.

At the other end came a polite voice, almost apologetic for the inconvenience at that early hour.

"I was wondering if you had any photos from the overnight take," said the voice. It was the president. The marine quickly snapped to attention, fully awake and apologetic. The president brushed aside the apologies, understanding the strains that a long duty can bring in the early morning.

The glue that held much of the decision-making structure together was Bush's personal relationship with key officials, particularly in the foreign policy area. "The people he chose to be in the system all had worked together before," explains Scowcroft. "Secretary Baker, Secretary Cheney, CIA director Bill Webster, and I had all been together under other circumstances," he adds. Bush enjoyed a close relationship with Baker, one that spanned more than twenty-five years. The ties with Scowcroft dated back to the Ford administration, when Scowcroft served as Ford's national security adviser and Bush was CIA director. At Treasury was Secretary Nick Brady, another longtime friend; at Commerce there was Secretary Bob Mosbacher, a friend from Houston; at Defense, Dick Cheney, whom Bush had known from the Ford administration, when Cheney served as chief of staff. It is quite understandable, therefore, that Bush relied on personal contact in small groups rather than on elaborate presentations of policy discussions. One of the strengths of this type of small friendship circle is that it makes decision making congenial and that the level of trust and openness is great. The individuals share similar values and goals and expect certain outcomes. The one drawback, as noted by Scowcroft, is that such a system may serve to isolate the decision makers from various sources of information and alternative views. Bush, however, was careful to avoid falling into this type of quagmire.

A hallmark of good leadership is a willingness to be exposed to differing views. It is incumbent for a leader not to be isolated, acting solely on preconceptions, whether personal or belonging to those in the inner circle. Bush, from his years of Washington experience, understood this challenge well and made sure that, while he maintained a tight-knit group of decision makers, he also went beyond them to listen to and to learn different views. Bush, therefore, sought to cast a wide net in which to gather information. Many of his meetings consisted of a host of U.S. officials from various agencies. In addition, he wanted to seek views from outside government. When it came to major issues, such as China, the Middle East, and the Soviet Union, Bush hosted sessions with scholars, which helped balance the official views of experts within the government. He usually held such sessions in a relaxed atmosphere, either at Camp David or at Kennebunkport, where all formalities were put aside. In this environment the guests could feel less inhibited by the aura of the presidency and be more relaxed and open in their comments. In addition, Bush was an avid reader of books, mostly of a historical nature. At times, his readings could be reflective of his policies. In the lead-up to the Gulf War, Bush was reading a book on World War II that probably played a part in influencing him to refer to Saddam as Hitler.

The person who spends the most time with a president and thus has the most opportunity for influence is the spouse. As a result, there is always speculation in the media regarding the impact of a presidential spouse on a policy and the president's decision making. George and Barbara Bush were like any other normal married couple: they discussed various issues, but Barbara was careful not to cross the line into the policy realm. "George knew how I felt," she now explains. "We didn't agree on everything, but I didn't offer advice." The closest that Barbara believes she may have come to having had a role in a decision was in regard to the National Literacy Act of 1991. "He heard me blowing about it," she says. "He knew I had a big interest."

Bush also drew on the advice of former high-level officials, but such situations created their own unique challenges. On January 28, 1989, Bush met with former secretary of state Henry Kissinger at the White House. The meeting lasted more than an hour, and Kissinger used it to brief Bush on his discussion with Gorbachev during a recent trip to the Soviet Union. Bush appreciated the report but was concerned about the public impression such a meeting could have. Kissinger could easily leverage such encounters to portray himself as having a larger role than was actually the case. Indeed, in a letter to Bush, Kissinger himself realized the misleading nature of appearances. In that letter, Kissinger assured the president that Scowcroft, Bush's new national security adviser and a former protégé of Kissinger both in the Ford White House and in business, was not his surrogate. The White House photographer took a picture of the January meeting, but the photo was not released; it was believed that it would give Kissinger too much publicity and could make him look like an intermediary with the Soviets. In addition, after his session, Kissinger was escorted outside the West Wing to the press area, so as to undermine any perception that he was being sneaked into and out of the White House.

After a decision, Bush, like anyone facing the pressures of uncertain developments, would seek some form of affirmation and understanding from those around him. One of the dilemmas of leadership is that it is also a lonely process. Even though one can study the impact of a decision and the possible factors that helped influence it, no one can fully fathom the personal insights, considerations, or emotions behind a decision that one person has made. It is something that only the decision maker can fully realize and appreciate. While Bush eschewed the idea of the presidency being the "loneliest job," in reality he, like other presidents, could not escape the truth of it.

The night the air war commenced against Iraq, Bush, done for the day in the West Wing, wound his way to the residence. Moving slowly and in deep thought he stopped at the Medical Unit. He went inside and plopped down on the couch. Dr. Larry Mohr, a colonel in the Army Medical Corps, was on duty that night. He sensed the president's contemplative mood and the weight of the decision to start the air war. Bush peered at him, as if signaling his intention to converse, but Mohr figured he should leave the first step to Bush. The last thing the president needed, Mohr thought, with a war weighing on him, was some forced small talk. It did not take Bush long to open the conversation.

"I had to make a really tough decision to start the bombing," Bush stated. His voice was tired and his comments seemed directed more at himself than at Mohr. Mohr gave Bush his full attention, sensing that this was going to be more a monologue than a conversation. Bush did not wait for a response. "I know that some of my friends will be upset with me for starting the bombing, but, Larry, I know it is the right thing to do."

Bush moved slightly on the couch and then continued. "We have to stop Saddam Hussein now," Bush stated firmly. "We can't let him go any further."

Then he resorted to a historical analogy. "The world would have been very different if Hitler had been stopped before he invaded Czechoslovakia and Poland," he said and then, looking directly at Mohr, he concluded, "I think the same thing applies to Saddam Hussein."

Mohr came over to Bush. "I know that this was a tough decision, Mr. President," Mohr offered. "But the American people will know it was the right thing to do and the American people will support you."

Bush nodded and got to his feet. He thanked Mohr and moved on slowly, deep in thought.

Five

BEHIND THE SCENES

W HEN HE was national security adviser to President Reagan, Frank Carlucci held the view that by 6:00 P.M. the work day should be finished and one should set off for home. It was an appealing notion, and Carlucci was often able to meet his own deadline. Unfortunately, for a White House staffer there is no magic end to the work day and the sacrifices that a staffer must make. All too often one thinks only of the financial sacrifices. Public salaries cannot compete with private salaries, and there are frequent reports of officials who leave their government positions for the private sector to be able to deal with children's college bills and even the daily costs of maintaining a home and family.

Overall, the White House is a career incubator. Its staff have moved on to successful careers in business, politics, education, the media, the nonprofit sector, and other areas of government. However, before many of these careers are embarked upon there are sacrifices other than financial that officials endure in the political world of the White House or the various departments and agencies. And their sacrifices greatly impact family life, put undue pressures and responsibilities on a spouse, and disrupt the memorable experiences of their children.

Working at the White House is a twenty-four-hour-a-day job. Much of a staffer's waking hours are physically spent in the complex, including weekends, and when not in the office a staffer is on call or mentally replaying the latest meeting, planning the next meeting or event, making telephone calls, or reviewing how a task has been carried out. Working literally from sunup to well beyond the onset of evening, many days go by without an opportunity to interact at length with children or one's spouse. Furthermore, extended domestic and foreign trips bring long separations, when a spouse is left with all the parental responsibilities. Usually these trips mean missing birthdays, First Holy Communions, and other religious and family events that are part of a child's—and family's—experiences that should produce fond memories. For the children of many White House staff members, there is a void in the photos and memories.

The Extended Staff Family

George Bush was aware of the sacrifices the staff endured and sought to soften the hardships as much as possible. He understands that all success starts with people and that how you treat them and respond to their strengths and failures will shape the outcome of any activity. Whether it was in the world of diplomacy, intelligence, or politics, Bush held to this philosophy.

It was this characteristic that shaped President Bush's relationship with the staff and helped to inspire those around him. Bush understood the need to create and maintain an environment that was friendly, helped motivate people, and provided the incentive to work hard and enjoy the challenges that they faced. "The fact is that one of the best ways to keep people focused," states Sununu, "is to let them understand that what they are dealing with is serious." However, they should not take themselves too seriously, Sununu says, and it's best to have a president "who is smart enough to be able to balance the seriousness of the issue with the opportunity to create a system and a process and a climate in which people like to work." Writing notes of appreciation to staffers and others as a means of reward and incentive was an important part of Bush's style. In addition, the White House made a point of giving out certificates suitable for framing to recognize accomplishments, ranging from a staffer's initial ride on Air Force One to helping out at a summit or other special event. According to Sununu,

> one of the hallmarks of President Bush is that he knew how critical
> it was to keep a staff inspired and to keep a cohesive agenda and
> that his role in doing that by stroking the staff was absolutely

critical. It is amazing how important . . . the most trivial of rewards in terms of their materialistic perception is in stimulating people when that reward is delivered by a president. Whether it's a cuff link or a presidential note written on a paper napkin or a handwritten note or typographically—a note written and typed by the president on his own computer with 1200 typos in it—the fact is that when you receive that and it thanks you for a job well done, it makes all the difference in the world in inspiring a staff to move forward.

One of the things George Bush is excellent at is making those around him part of a tight-knit political family. Staffers were always invited to various social events that involved the president and the First Lady. Interspersed with the staffers were press people and others. Cocktails and coffee in the residence of the White House made everyone feel they were being given a special treat because the residence is not open to the public or the staff; visits to the president's living quarters are by invitation only. Relaxed and talkative, the president would give a tour, explaining various features. During one such tour, he eagerly sat down at a new computer to demonstrate his skills.

At other times there were screenings of newly released films in the Family Theater in the East Wing. Conversation started off the evening before everyone settled in with bags of popcorn for the evening movie feature. The president and First Lady would take the first row with whomever had been invited as their special guest. The night that *Field of Dreams* was screened in 1989, the president had the British ambassador, Sir Antony Acland, and his wife as his guests. The movie deals with a father-son relationship wrapped in a baseball theme, and, as usual, Bush exhibited his emotions, welling up during various poignant scenes in the film. On another occasion, following a press conference at the American ambassador's residence in Paris in July 1989, Bush showed spontaneous hospitality by inviting the one hundred or so reporters for a tour of the ground level of the house. Following the tour, he and Mrs. Bush, joined by Scowcroft and Sununu, lingered on the grounds, casually chatting with reporters.

Bush's personality also makes him a worrier. One of the things that he often worried about early in his political career but eventually became inured to was political criticism. He came to realize that there is nothing one can do about it; someone will always be displeased with a decision and the press will always highlight the negative and controversial aspects. Bush worries whether someone is affronted, if a new staff member has settled in comfortably, or if someone might take away an inaccurate impression about something, and he worries about those around him. Since family has always been of utmost importance to Bush, he worried about and knew the importance of including staffers' families in many of his functions. He was well aware that a harmonious family life is very important to the success and motivation of any individual. Extending an invitation to whole families helped strengthen the family and helped remind everyone what the administration and staffers' individual sacrifices were all about.

When the new Camp David chapel was dedicated in April 1991, the event became a family affair. That April day children had the run of the famous presidential retreat and all of its athletic and other facilities before settling down for an interdenominational service and hymn singing. After the Saturday Camp David retreat, staffers entered the White House with a renewed vigor and inspiration, leaving at home a happy family reinvigorated to manage the long hours and separations that Monday morning was going to bring again.

Staffers, however, were not averse to reducing the stress on their own. "I think one of the deepest secrets of the White House, particularly during the time that we were all there, was how much fun it really was," says Gates. "And I suppose that the way we dealt with a lot of the pressure was through some of the fun that we had." From pizza delivery to office parties, the staff tried to make the atmosphere as relaxed as possible. Speechwriter Curt Smith, an admirer of President Nixon, would don his Nixon mask and trenchcoat and roam the Old Executive Office Building in a passable imitation of Nixon, with slumped shoulders, hands held high above his head, and fingers spread in the familiar victory sign. He would pop into offices to give the staff a pep talk. Marlin Fitzwater tended to put his feet up and smoke his cigar and distract himself with his hat collection; Sig Rogich entertained himself and colleagues as a wine connoisseur. He provided wines to the president on occasion and even made recommendations for the state dinners.

A key benefit for staffers was the opportunity to meet various celebrities either at the White House or on presidential trips. These occasions afforded opportunities for photos, autographs, and interaction with leading sports, entertainment, and business figures. So it was when Arnold Schwarzenegger came to visit Bush. Schwarzenegger always enjoyed his time with Bush, whom he regarded as a role model and mentor. He campaigned for Bush in 1988 and was affectionately referred to as "Conan the Republican," a reference to one of Schwarzenegger's films, *Conan the Barbarian*. Bush appointed Schwarzenegger to be chairman of the President's Council on Physical Fitness and Sports, a position he tackled with relish. Schwarzenegger was struck by the president's dedication and commitment to physical fitness and, with the president's support, he gave the organization a new vitality. Among the new activities Schwarzenegger organized was the annual "Great American Workout." Schwarzenegger recalls that while he was doing this, "the president had a few more important things on his mind—like the end of the Soviet Union, the war in Kuwait, the economy. But George Bush never acted like he was too busy for me or our movement." As a result of the friendship and the activities, Schwarzenegger visited with Bush many times at the White House.

On one visit early in Bush's administration Schwarzenegger began to squirm in his chair in the Oval Office, trying to shake off a growing pain in his side as the conversation continued. The president noticed his discomfort and persuaded him to go to the White House Medical Unit to get checked out. The doctor was summoned. By the time the doctor got to the Medical Unit, Schwarzenegger was lying naked, with just a towel around his waist, surrounded by female nurses. They were attentively bent over Schwarzenegger, poking his side. Dr. Mohr rushed to Schwarzenegger's side. Mohr is a low-key, personable individual and has a reassuring bedside manner, like that of a country doctor, but what he saw startled him.

"What are you doing?!" exclaimed Mohr.

"We're just doing a thorough physical examination. You didn't think that we would pass up this chance," said one of the nurses in a moment of honesty that had nothing to do with medical care. Dr. Mohr determined that Schwarzenegger had nothing more than a minor muscle strain.

Of course, White House staffers had an opportunity to be celebrities themselves, as happened with Colonel Charles "Chuck" Krulak, who served as the deputy director of the White House military office. Krulak was a tough marine who eventually went on to become commandant of the Marine Corps. Beneath the stony exterior hardened by two tours in Vietnam, Krulak possesses a great sense of humor, a soft heart, and a social gregariousness that endears him to those around him. It also helped set him up for some unexpected assignments from his commander in chief. In 1989, with the annual White House Easter egg roll approaching, Bush decided to break the tradition of the Reagan years, in which someone who was not on the White House staff would don the Easter bunny outfit. Bush wanted the role to go to someone in the White House family. Krulak's administrative assistant, Joni Stevens, quickly volunteered him to the organizers. She went a step further, building him up as the perfect Easter bunny. When the role of the bunny was finally assigned, the choice was not surprising: Chuck Krulak.

Krulak, who had thought nothing would come of the matter and was unaware that the selection was basically rigged, was aghast. The image of a tough marine hopping around as a bunny chilled him. He protested but relented when he was assured that he would not have to remove the costume's head. Skeptically, on the appointed day he stepped out on the White House lawn and was instantly mobbed, poked, and grabbed by countless children. In the finest tradition of Bush, it truly became a family affair. Krulak's partner for the day was an hour late to don her Mrs. Bunny costume, and so Krulak's wife, Zandi, filled in until she arrived. At the end of the afternoon Krulak shed the costume, comfortable that no one recognized him, and went home greatly relieved. The next morning he was in the office at 6:15 A.M. when a call came in from the Marine Command Center; the commandant, General Al Gray, wanted to speak with him.

"Krulak, what are you doing over there?" shouted Gray.

"Well, sir, I'm the deputy director of the White House Military Office," responded Krulak innocently and with a bit of confusion as to where the conversation was headed.

"No!" barked Gray. "I'm talking about today's paper."

Krulak quickly motioned to an aide for the morning's *Washington Post*. Rifling through it he came across Gray's source of consternation. The newspaper had reported Bush's new tradition: a staffer would play the Easter bunny and Colonel Krulak had won the part that year.

"Krulak, I didn't send you to the White House to be an Easter bunny!" snapped Gray. From then on, Krulak received friendly ribbing, being dubbed "General Bunny."

Viewed from the outside, the White House seems like a world of glamour, excitement, power, and other attributes too numerous to enumerate. For those on the inside, the world is one of human beings—with all the strengths and weaknesses that people in every walk of life exhibit. One is not immune to pain and hurt feelings in the White House, nor is a person spared from quirks of fate, no matter how minor. If anything, being at the White House only compounds the mishaps one must face since its busy staffers often do not have the time to deal with or correct them as other people do.

Nor are presidents immune from the daily travails of life. One winter evening, with Baker and others gathered in the Oval Office, Bush decided to play gracious host by lighting the fireplace. He forgot, however, to open the flue, and smoke soon filled the room. Nor do presidents always get their way, even in nonpolicy areas. After Hurricane Hugo in September 1989, Bush traveled to view the devastation in South Carolina. After landing in Air Force One, he was scheduled to view the affected area from Marine One. However, the pilot objected, claiming that the ceiling was too low and any flight would be dangerous. Staffer Bonnie Newman, sensitive to keeping the president on schedule and knowing that there was no backup plan to the helicopter flight, grilled the president's marine aide in an effort to have him persuade the pilot to fly, but she only wound up supporting the pilot's assessment. Bush was upset and pushed firmly for the chopper flight. He lost and wound up taking a hastily arranged motorcade. On another occasion, in January 1991, while sledding with grandchildren at Camp David, Barbara Bush sustained a minor fracture in her left leg. Bush made a judgmental error: he decided to remain with the couples' weekend guests and did not accompany Barbara to the hospital. As it would be for any married couple, the decision was controversial: he heard about it from Barbara later on.

Bush's Hospital Stay

In May 1991, Bush experienced shortness of breath while jogging at Camp David. An electrocardiogram taken at the Camp David clinic showed Bush to have an irregular heartbeat of the type known as atrial fibrillation. The decision was made to take him immediately to Bethesda Naval Hospital for evaluation, where he was eventually diagnosed with Graves' disease, a condition caused by an overactive thyroid gland, a condition that, coincidentally, also afflicts Mrs. Bush.

When the helicopter landed on the grounds of the hospital, Bush climbed out wearing sneakers, blue sweats, a polo shirt, and a blue jacket. His right arm, free of the jacket, was bent at the elbow, and his hand, tucked up against his armpit, was hooked up to an I.V. bag. The free arm of the jacket hung over his shoulder. An aide dispatched to meet him greeted the president and asked how he was feeling.

"I'm okay," said Bush, trying to make light of the whole thing.

A nurse held the IV bag while Bush walked to a waiting car. At the president's wing, Bush got out of the car and headed into the building and then the elevator. Standing in the elevator he continued to joke. He looked around him.

"I need a tall nurse," he said looking at the short nurse alongside him, "to hold the IV up high."

The event, however, was far from humorous. Only nervous laughter greeted Bush's efforts to make light of the whole matter. The president's illness not only was a personal issue but also had wide political ramifications. Issues of world reaction, particularly in the financial markets, possible presidential succession, and the impact on the president's political future were all intertwined.

That Saturday morning, May 4, Bush had flown to Ann Arbor, Michigan, to deliver the commencement address at the University of Michigan, where he talked about "political correctness." After returning to Andrews Air Force Base, Bush boarded Marine One for Camp David. Never one to rest, Bush continued his whirlwind of activity, including the late afternoon jog, during which he experienced the shortness of breath and was then whisked off to the hospital.

Sunday morning, Vice President Quayle planned on visiting the president, but it was decided that he should not come. The White House sought to maintain as much of a normal routine as possible; the vice president's visit, it was believed, could raise additional press speculation regarding the president's condition. To maintain as much normalcy as possible, Bush appeared briefly at his room window and spoke with the press pool. In addition, a photo of him being briefed by Sununu and Scowcroft and with Doro's children milling around was released.

By Sunday afternoon, the issue of invoking the Twenty-fifth Amendment arose since the doctors were considering the possibility of a cardioversion or electrical shock in order to bring Bush's heart back into normal rhythm. The

procedure was being considered for Monday morning. Bush was being treated
with medication, but it was not bringing his heart into a normal rhythm. The
cardioversion would be done under anesthesia, which meant that Bush would
be incapacitated, thereby prompting the implementation of the Twenty-fifth
Amendment. The amendment, passed in 1967, calls for the vice president
to serve as the acting president in the event the president is unable to carry
out his duties. Sununu favored having the announcement of invoking the
Twenty-fifth Amendment made Monday morning; Fitzwater favored an announcement on Sunday in order to prepare the American public and to make
the medical procedure look routine rather than appear to be a last-minute
decision. Furthermore, since the medical procedure was being scheduled for
early Monday morning, it would be less of a shock to the public to hear it and
digest the situation the night before rather than when they were waking up
and going off to work and hearing that a different person was in charge of the
country. Fitzwater's concern prevailed. Around eight o'clock Sunday evening
Sununu, Dr. Burton Lee, the chief White House physician, and a press aide
visited with the president to review Fitzwater's draft opening statement. Bush
was sitting up in bed; he was in his pajamas, his chest exposed. He carefully
read the statement. He liked it but objected to the great detail it contained
about the Twenty-fifth Amendment. Bush then spoke by telephone with Fitzwater and suggested to him that he keep that part of the statement brief.

Fitzwater did his briefing without incident. By 10:30 P.M., however, Bush's
heart had reverted to a normal rhythm on its own. It was decided, however,
not to announce the change in his condition but to see how things proceeded in the morning. During the night Bush's heartbeat became irregular
for a short period of time. By 5:00 A.M. Monday Bush's heart had returned
to normal rhythm in his sleep. At 5:30 A.M. the doctors met to review Bush's
condition.

Phil Brady had arrived with the paperwork regarding the Twenty-fifth
Amendment, but events proved that this step would not be necessary. The
heart condition was something the doctors determined could be treated with
medication. At 6:00 A.M. Sununu called Quayle to inform him that the president was scheduled to leave the hospital at 9:00 A.M.

Bush left the hospital under cloudy and rainy skies. It was a fitting threshold and metaphor. From that point on, neither the president nor his administration were the same. The battle to maintain his thyroid function sapped

much of his strength; the medication appeared to drain some of his energy and intensity, and while he would not admit it, his drive during the following months and leading into the reelection campaign was slowed. His illness also came at a high point in his popularity. The Gulf War had ended in February, and in the aftermath Bush's favorable poll ratings surged into the low 90s—historic numbers. Never again was Bush to be at such a level of popularity. As Bush rode off in the motorcade for the White House, he was a changed person facing a rapidly changing political environment.

Traveling with the President

On overseas trips, the staff often worked through the night, putting finishing touches on position papers and working to meet press deadlines several time zones away in the United States. The trips were often grueling yet exhilarating, given the excitement of the work and the very travel itself. "Tiring and exhausting but good," is Barbara Bush's view of these trips, mirroring the view of the staff.

During the president's Thanksgiving trip to Dhahran, Saudi Arabia, in 1990 to visit the troops, the White House Press Office staff worked around the clock for forty-eight hours, starting with an initial stop in Jiddah. The only time off was for a shower before boarding the flight across the Arabian desert from Jiddah to Dhahran. From Dhahran it was off to Cairo for meetings with the Egyptian government and then on to Geneva for a meeting with the Syrian president, Hafez al-Assad. The meeting with Assad fell short of the pomp and dignity that usually accompany a president upon his arrival in a foreign land. Swiss security, tense over the meeting, displayed an over-zealousness that broke the rules of diplomatic decorum. The traveling staff and press were manhandled and roughed up upon arrival and departure from the airport. A press photographer was taken into custody and then released, Joseph Verner Reed was threatened with a machine gun, and Sununu was verbally accosted at the hotel.

During presidential trips various conveniences were put in place. Those conveniences were intended to make the staff more efficient in carrying out their duties rather than to provide for their individual comfort. Air Force One provides all the comforts for the president. The current airplane, a Boeing 747, was ordered by President Reagan, but Bush was the first president to use it. It has facilities for sleeping and eating, a shower, an infirmary, and various work and conference facilities and state-of-the-art communications equipment. The White House Communications Agency equipped staff hotel rooms with telephones allowing instant communication among the traveling staff, the White House, and, indeed, the world. At each stop a room dedicated to the senior staff was stocked with food and telephones in order to ease the all too often all-night working sessions. There was also a briefing room where the press could work on their laptops and make telephone calls and where Fitzwater could hold his press briefings.

There were some travel comforts. Whether on Air Force One or the accompanying press plane, staffers' luggage was delivered to their rooms and just as conveniently picked up from the rooms at the end of the trip. There were no customs lines; someone always handled staff passports at the points of entry. Police escorts were provided for the president and many times for the press from and to the airport. Autos and drivers were available for staffers. State dinners, meetings with prominent individuals, and the opportunity to see the world were added benefits of the grueling work schedule. More often than not, staff had to build private time around their official duties, and this usually meant odd hours, such as visiting Red Square at 2:00 A.M. during Bush's Moscow visit in 1990.

Presidential travel is not all ceremony marked by state dinners, press conferences, and motorcades through crowded streets lined by waving crowds. Just a month into office, Bush took a whirlwind tour of Asia. On February 23 he left for Japan to attend the funeral of Emperor Hirohito. During the five-day trip he also visited South Korea and China, logging thousands of miles across various time zones and leaving the staff exhausted and ragged. During his trip to Japan in January 1992 he fell ill during a state dinner, vomiting on Prime Minister Kiichi Miyazawa and then collapsing. Touched by the flu and tired out, he had refused to have the event canceled. Indeed, earlier, feeling nauseated, he excused himself from the receiving line at one point to find a restroom. Feeling better after emptying his stomach, he returned and resumed his protocol duties. He felt that he had a duty to fulfill and a need to show respect and appreciation to an ally and host, and George Bush was not about to shirk that responsibility.

There also are real dangers that can be encountered on presidential travel. During Bush's trip through South America in December 1990, the traveling party encountered a coup, illness, security threats, and a harrowing flight across the Andes. On December 3, while the group was in Brazil, during the first leg of the trip, a coup broke out in Argentina. Rebellious military personnel took over a number of key points throughout the capital, Buenos Aires: fifty officers took over the military headquarters; thirty took over the Patricios military base, and an undetermined number took over a tank farm at the city's outskirts. Argentine president Carlos Menem declared a state of siege, and roadblocks were set up around the affected areas.

Of immediate concern was whether the president's trip to Argentina should continue as planned. Menem called Brazilian president Fernando Collor de Mello to urge him to let Bush continue as planned and to reassure everyone that all was well in Buenos Aires. By the afternoon, however, the situation had worsened. The White House advance people on the ground in Buenos Aires were hearing gunfire and staying indoors. There were reports of rebel tanks and armored personnel carriers moving to within fifty kilometers northwest of the capital, and there was a takeover of a coast guard facility by one hundred rebel supporters.

The question of whether or not the president should proceed to Argentina was now urgent. Equally important, a decision had to be made on whether or not the press plane should proceed since it was scheduled to arrive ahead of the president. On presidential travel, the White House press corps usually accompanied the president on a separate plane that accommodated all of the various news organizations. The press was scheduled to arrive in Buenos Aires on the evening of December 4 from Uruguay, while the president stayed overnight in Punta del Este with only a travel pool covering him. For the press office, there were two concerns: the safety of the press and whether or not insurance would be available for the Pan Am press charter in a danger zone. Pan Am personnel assured Fitzwater that insurance would be available. He now had to deal with the press. Initial soundings indicated the press leaned toward a plan to fly into Buenos Aires the morning of December 5, thereby allowing more time to see how things were proceeding there. Fitzwater's concern was also that the press had made their own individual lodging arrangements in Buenos Aires; they were not at a single location but scattered throughout the city. If there was more trouble and a speedy evacuation was necessary, it would be difficult to round up the individual reporters.

An additional concern, interwoven into the fabric of presidential and press safety, was how any decision would impact Menem's domestic political standing. In particular, the traveling National Security Council staff feared that canceling the president's or even the full press's arrival could weaken Menem's domestic standing and undermine his administration. A quick call to the U.S. ambassador in Argentina revealed that the situation on the ground was not very bad.

Fitzwater then called representatives of the White House Correspondents Association—Charles Bierbauer of Cable News Network (CNN), Terry Hunt of AP, and Gene Gibbons of Reuters—to his office to review the situation. The press representatives still leaned in the direction of proceeding to Buenos Aires as scheduled but left to poll their colleagues. By 9:00 P.M. they were back, reporting that the consensus was to proceed as scheduled. They made it clear, however, that it was their advice to the Press Office, apparently leaving the ultimate decision in the hands of the White House. To cover himself, Fitzwater went to the briefing room and announced that the White House Correspondents Association's view was to proceed to Buenos Aires and that, as a result, the flight would take place. It all became a moot point by 10:00 P.M. By then reports started coming out that the last of the rebels had surrendered. The military threat was over.

By the time the traveling party arrived in Buenos Aires, the press was getting ornery. The feeling in the press was that Bush's trips were not newsworthy.

Frank Sesno of CNN dubbed it "suitcase diplomacy" and claimed the trips did nothing for the president and might actually backfire on him with the American public. By the time of the 1992 campaign, foreign policy, indeed, had taken a backseat for the American public, as domestic issues came to the fore. That day in Argentina foreshadowed the challenge that Bush would have back on his home turf. Following a news conference with Menem, Bush addressed the Argentine congress. During the introduction, he was heckled by a legislator, who was promptly removed.

Problems continued to mount during the trip. A White House stenographer, who transcribed the president's remarks, was taken ill in Uruguay with gastroenteritis and dehydration. She came down with a fever and could not keep down any food. She was taken to a hospital and put on an IV, but the fever could not be controlled so arrangements were made to fly her back to the United States. One press photographer had his thumb broken when the Argentines slammed the doors at a presidential photo opportunity, and another cut his head on an exposed screw in a press pool helicopter. And then the White House got word about security threats at the Santiago Holiday Inn in Chile, where the staff was scheduled to stay upon arrival. The trip proceeded, with the customary advice that everyone be extra careful in controlling their baggage to prevent any foul play.

The flight over the Andes from Argentina to Chile added to the anxiety. The press plane was tossed side to side as well as up and down. There were about two or three free falls, as if the plane had stopped and started to fall down with such force and speed that everyone was almost lifted out of their seats. The turbulence was caused by westerly winds coming in from the Pacific Ocean, and the pilot maintained the slowest speed possible to ride out the turbulence. This was not an isolated incident; the traveling press encountered many dangerous experiences. In a flight out of the Los Angeles airport to Asia, the press charter blew an engine and had to return to Los Angeles. It was a quiet flight back. There were equal dangers and fears on the ground. During the Thanksgiving visit to the troops in Saudi Arabia in 1990, the press corps was issued gas masks in the event there was a chemical attack by Saddam Hussein.

From Santiago, the entourage was off to Caracas. While in Venezuela, the State Department announced that once all Americans left Iraq and Kuwait, the embassy personnel in Kuwait would withdraw but that the embassy would remain "open." The statement caught the president and Scowcroft by surprise, underscoring the lack of communication that sometimes characterizes government departments and the White House. En route to the Caracas Holiday Inn, where the president was to address the Venezuelan-American Chamber of Commerce, the staff motorcade came to a halt. Deputy Secretary of State Eagleburger's car had stalled out, so he and everyone in the cars behind his had to pile out and walk the extra hundred or so feet to the entrance.

The entourage then headed home, flying from Caracas. That city has many high hills and houses ranging from brick shanties to multistory apartment dwellings that hug the sides of the hills and dot the peaks. There was laundry hanging out to dry on window ledges, on balconies, on poles sticking out of windows, and on many large potted plants. Toward the center of the city, many of the streets are narrow and filled with street vendors selling fruit from trucks—a crush of people and traffic all vying for space. In the plane, the press sat back; they were going home. The wheels up would also bring a sense of relief and joy to the staff as well as a feeling, however fleeting, that the travails of a trip were behind them. It made the waiting pressures of Washington seem light years away. Presidents themselves are not immune from this feeling of exuberance, no matter how ephemeral it might be.

Walker's Point

The strain and stress of the presidency can take its toll on anyone who holds the office. Presidents, therefore, need to recharge themselves in order to maintain the high levels of commitment and energy needed for the job. For Bush, family was a great source of strength and renewal. In addition to family, Walker's Point in Kennebunkport, Maine, was his oasis.

All modern presidents have had an escape from the turmoil and political squabbling of Washington. FDR escaped to the Catoctin Mountains in Maryland, where he found solace at what he dubbed Shangri-la, a facility established in 1942 and maintained by the U.S. government. President Eisenhower renamed the facility for his grandson David in 1953, and Camp David has served as the official presidential retreat since FDR's first visit. It sits on 140 acres about seventy miles from Washington and provides all manner of recreation, including hiking, biking, and movies. However, FDR also found his way to Warm Springs, Georgia, for vacations, and other presidents have also had their own private retreats. Richard Nixon would go to San Clemente in California, and Jimmy Carter would make his way to his hometown of Plains, Georgia.

Walker's Point is an eleven-acre peninsula that juts into the Atlantic outside Kennebunkport. Its main house is a rambling structure with six bedrooms and large dining and living areas. Except for two bedrooms and the kitchen, the house is unheated, emphasizing its nature as a getaway, a place to renew one's energy and spirit, rather than as a permanent residence. Every spring and fall, Don Rhodes makes the trek from Houston to open up and to winterize the house, respectively. Rhodes is a longtime associate of Bush. He started out in Bush's congressional campaign in 1966, worked in his congressional office, and has been the go-to fellow for various administrative needs in Bush's postpresidential office in Houston.

The Walker family acquired the property in 1902, when George Herbert Walker and his father, D. D. Walker, bought it, thus giving the name to the peninsula. The original house was completed in 1905 but was destroyed by a storm in 1978. In 1981, Bush purchased the property from his aunt, Mary Walker.

Bush has spent a part of almost every summer at Walker's Point. The one summer he missed was in 1944, when he was away in military service. Much of Bush's emotion is anchored in the memories of family, which provides a special strength. Bush has moved twenty-nine times during his business and political careers, including his last move, from the White House to Houston, yet Walker's Point is the one spot to which he always returns. Since boyhood, he has boated, fished, and walked every rock of the peninsula. He nourished his hopes and nursed his disappointments in the isolation of the peninsula. For Bush, therefore, the place holds a certain magic that Barbara has come to share. "This is a place where we really enjoy ourselves—but more than that, kind of refurbish our souls and get our batteries all charged up and enjoy life really to the fullest," Bush explained to the Kennebunkport Chamber of Commerce in 1989. "It's a point of view. You can feel it in the land and in the water here." And, in remarks to dinner guests in Kennebunkport in July 2005, Bush summed up the feeling when he said, "You feel liberated here."

For Bush, the Point serves as a kind of anchor for the family. "It's where my family comes home, and it's our anchor to windward," Bush explained to the press in May 1991. "It has great meaning in terms of family." Scattered around the United States, the extended Bush family considers Walker's Point the one place with which all can identify and where they can gather to renew bonds, recharge the spirit, and reinforce each other. Bush takes great pride in seeing the extended family and the new generations participate in the traditions of the Point that he himself experienced. The scattered toys, the noise and bustle, and the constant activity across the lawn over the years have come to be a source of enjoyment and strength.

There is something soothing about the salt air rushing through the rooms, the lapping of the waves along the rocks, and the isolation that the peninsula provides. The fringe of rock sits apart from the daily rush, making one feel removed from the problems of the world and of one's own life. It was the one place where Bush could be himself and be one with his past and youth, which was why the trappings of the presidency created so much consternation for him and Barbara. With Bush's election as president, certain security measures needed to be put in place. While many were instituted, there were plans for two measures that both George and Barbara particularly disliked. One was a twenty-five-foot section of chain-link fence by the entrance to the grounds;

Barbara thought it would make the whole compound look like a prison. The other was an outdoor bulletproof screen off the living room that she feared would obstruct the view of the ocean. Neither plan was carried out. The Bushes' protests were not intellectual but emotional. They wanted to retain at least the outward appearance of their home the way they enjoyed it. All the changes were violating the one place that both regarded as personal and really their own. Bush, for example, sought to preserve the privacy of Walker's Point, at least in his own mind, by refusing to refer to the Point as the "summer White House." In this manner he sought to maintain its role as a private family compound, and avoiding the term also underscored Bush's respect for the presidency and his view that there is only one White House—and it is in Washington, D.C.

It was, therefore, with great emotion that Bush viewed the damage done to Walker's Point by a storm in the fall of 1991. The storm literally tore the house asunder, scattering furniture and priceless memorabilia out into the ocean. What was not swallowed by the ocean was left water logged and beyond saving. What the fury of the ocean could not bury in the depths of its waters were the memories and experiences that Bush had of the Point.

As president, Bush would spend the month of August at Walker's Point. It was an action-filled month. Days were filled with golfing, boating, fishing, and games of horseshoes, and the sea lured Bush like a magnet. In his later years, power walks and jogging have given way to more leisurely strolls, and his balance is no longer quite good enough to permit him to move across the slippery stones amid fast-moving waters of streams and rivers as he fishes. But boating continues to be a passion. Bush is on his fourth cigarette boat, *Fidelity IV,* which he obtained in the summer of 2008. He loves the challenge of maneuvering among the swells, riding the waves, and running his boat at maximum throttle. The thrill in Bush's face is only matched by the angst of his guests, who have a white-knuckled grip on the boat as they are bumped from wave to wave and who often disembark feeling more as if they had ridden wild broncos than had a pleasant boat ride. Refreshed by his recreational activities, President Bush's afternoons and evenings were dedicated to various social and working sessions. Whether it was a picnic for the traveling press or a meeting with a head of state, Bush made sure that each day was filled with activities.

The summer visit of 1989, however, was particularly frustrating. The press, needing a story, finally settled on the long drought in Bush's hooking of a fish. Fishing is Bush's favorite sport and is something that he learned at the age of five along the shores of Walker's Point. Given this background, the fishless streak was especially frustrating. Each day, Bush would go out in his boat, fish, and come back empty handed, and the press office staff would be faced with the inevitable questions: "Did he catch a fish?" "What's the president feel about his future?" Bush brushed off all the media attention with humor. "When I see it on national television, I know we've got to put an end to this monkey business," he joked with the press. "So, we will prevail. And besides that, everyone knows fishing is a team sport." Finally, the drought came to an end, but by then the fish watch had developed its own logo and press following. All this underscored Bush's view of the office. The office is so important that anyone holding it makes news no matter how minor or mundane the issue.

In the environment of Walker's Point, Bush always felt invigorated. At his whim, he could engage in myriad activities. It was also a place where he could relax and shed even the minimal trappings of being president. Gone were the necktie and suits and the formal meals. In this informal atmosphere Bush believed he could establish closer bonds with his visitors and strengthen the personal links he was so skilled at developing. Just as it served as a soothing inspiration for him, Bush believed that the compound worked the same magic on others. Moreover, being invited to the president's house could buttress a foreign leader's standing at home by publicizing a close personal relationship with Bush, thereby also further strengthening the bond between Bush and his visitor. Referring to a steady parade of foreign visitors, he told the Kennebunkport Chamber of Commerce that it was a place where "you could converse and you could relax and you could really get to know each other in a wonderful setting." The visitors were many, from different ends of the world. During one of Brian Mulroney's visits, Bush and the Canadian prime minister relaxed in casual wear, going sockless with their Dockers. The president of France, François Mitterrand, was more of a challenge; he was formal in his conduct and appeared to have no interest in the outdoors. There was concern and some hesitancy about how to get him to shed his tie. The French leader seemed to surprise everyone by donning a sports shirt and sweater during his visit in late May 1989, and he accompanied Bush on a tour of the Point. Walker's Point was also the scene for dealing with some of the momentous foreign policy events of Bush's presidency. Bush first got word of the Tiananmen

Square crackdown by Chinese authorities while he was at Walker's Point on a stopover while returning from a trip to Europe. The coup against Gorbachev in August 1991 happened while he was vacationing at the Point.

And it was at Walker's Point where Bush held some of the early consultations with Arab states regarding Saddam's invasion of Kuwait. In mid-August 1990 Bush hosted the Saudi foreign minister, Prince Saud al-Faisal, and Saudi Arabia's ambassador to the United States, Prince Bandar. That same day he also hosted King Hussein of Jordan. Saudi Arabia was key to generating Arab support for the eventual military action. It was also important as a staging area for U.S. forces preparing to dislodge Saddam's troops from Kuwait. Saudi Arabia from the outset exhibited a willingness and a desire to cooperate with the United States. Jordan was hesitant, with King Hussein believing that the Arab world might be able to find a solution by working with Saddam. The king explained his reasons for not joining the coalition against Iraq and thus sought to assuage the president's concerns. Bush, while frustrated by the king's position, was very understanding and forgiving. His years of friendship with the king would not allow Bush to have a policy dispute turn acrimonious. Bush was willing, according to one participant at the meeting, to "cut the king some slack."

During a visit in August 1991, John Major, the British prime minister, was hosted at the River Club, down the road from Walker's Point, at the outskirts of Kennebunkport. It is a place Bush knows well and recalls fondly. Standing on piers, the club casts a dark shadow on the waters below, creating an inviting lure for any young boy. In his youth Bush rowed his dinghy below the building, examining the stones and watercourse. After dinner at the club with the prime minister, Bush escorted the entourage across the road to the club's auditorium for an evening of entertainment, which included a brief piano performance by his sister, Nancy Ellis.

For Bush, it has always been important to entertain his guests, not ostentatiously, but warmly, leaving them with a sense of friendship and belonging. Such socialization has left visitors with warm memories of their hosts, of their stay, and with a reservoir of goodwill. The crashing waves and cool ocean mists have thus become part of their own lives and have extended the reach and influence of George Bush.

Six

DELIVERING THE MESSAGE

COMMUNICATION IS probably the most powerful tool in the president's leadership arsenal. At a moment's notice, the president can garner national and international media attention, and those executive pronouncements can have an immediate impact. How the president communicates can be just as important as what the president communicates.

Unfortunately, for President Bush message delivery was not necessarily a strong suit. He had a tendency to run on past his applause lines and was saddled with the nervous grin that seemed to flash across his face at inopportune times during the course of his delivery. Bush's looseness of speech and gaffes have become legendary. In 1988 he referred to September 7—not December 7—as Pearl Harbor Day. Bush's speaking style was marked by a faulty syntax, leading him to speak in half sentences and random thoughts, all of which tended to detract from the thrust of his message. He gave his speeches the way he spoke—sometimes rambling, interspersing the text with broken sentences, and welling up with tears in emotional moments. When you came to hear George Bush speak, you got George Bush. "I was not much good at rhetoric," he admits. "Rhetoric is not my strong suit." He took refuge in his work ethic. "People saw I worked hard and was able to make the decisions on hand," he declares.

On paper, however, Bush was able to express his emotions and expose his concerned and caring side, which was not visible to the casual observer. As a prolific letter writer, Bush was able to pen his moods in a detail that has

III

surprised many. This side of him became clear after the publication of *All the Best, George Bush,* a book of his letters and diary entries. Bush notes this dichotomy about himself: "I was not a very good speaker or communicator. I tended to keep a lot of things inside of me that I didn't talk about. However, I enjoyed corresponding from an early age and was able to write some fairly good letters. I suppose I was able to express myself better in writing."

Bush's difficulties with formal speaking contrasted with his private speech in one-on-one and group sessions. On a regular basis Bush met with representatives from various groups, including those working for business, minorities, and the environment. Usually, these sessions took place in the Roosevelt Room. On his own turf, sitting across from the Oval Office, Bush made strong and lasting impressions on his guests with his knowledge of the relevant subject matter, his easy manner in engaging in conversation, and his straightforward exchange of views. "He was very engaged and animated," recalls Bobbie Kilberg, who was head of the White House's Office of Public Liaison. The result was that invariably his guests left with the feeling that, while they may not have agreed with his views, they nonetheless had received a fair hearing and developed a genuine fondness for him.

While much of Bush's emotional side was hidden during his public life, now, with the pressures and constraints of public office removed, Bush's skills as a public speaker come through. While he may mangle his syntax occasionally, he is more relaxed and articulate in his delivery. He has also shown an ease with being more extemporaneous and for injecting humor and story-telling into his presentations, all of which elicit a warm response from the audience. Barbara Bush is dismissive of the view that Bush was not a good communicator during his term in office. "People were delighted to hear him speak," she states matter-of-factly in support of her husband. She is quick to point out that the press played a big role in this negative perception of Bush's speaking ability. "The press ground into him," she notes, echoing the views of many Bush supporters.

Part of Bush's communication dilemma was that he succeeded to the presidency after Ronald Reagan, the "Great Communicator," who could deliver stirring presentations, be one with the crowd, and speak in an articulate manner—all of which were in contrast to Bush's own style. Bush recognized his inability to measure up to the Reagan model, and he neither tried nor wanted to compete with that model. Instead, Bush sought to play to his strength, that being his in-depth knowledge of the issues. The press generally gave Bush high marks for his knowledge of the issues, something Reagan was not afforded, being viewed by many in the media as a nice man but limited in his range of knowledge.

Bush could discourse on both foreign and domestic issues, and he chose an avenue that made him comfortable and further distanced him from Reagan. Bush felt most comfortable in informal settings where he could interact with the press and, thus, demonstrate his knowledge of issues. That setting was also more suited to his rambling style, his ability to banter, and his low-key, informal manner. At the beginning of his administration, B. Jay Cooper, a deputy press secretary, drafted a press plan for Fitzwater, noting that Bush was considered more congenial than Reagan in dealing with the press but that he was not good at formal speeches or press conferences. The recommendation, therefore, was to present Bush in less formal settings, such as one-on-one interviews and appearances in the White House Briefing Room. These press encounters required nothing more than a short opening statement; there was no need for a formal presentation. This approach also had the added benefit of cultivating the press; even though Bush was suspect of the press, he knew the importance of dealing with the media.

Bush and the Media

Bush's communication problems also stemmed from the changing nature of the media. The media is an integral part of American society. It touches every aspect of our lives—social, political, and economic. It greets us in the morning, tucks us in at night, and, in between, through television, tickers, radio, wire reports, and now the Internet, gives us the state of the world and of our community. It is a source of information, a medium for shaping our views, and a vehicle—through its stories and the advertisements it carries—for creating and channeling our wants and desires. No other institution is so present in so many different forms and touches every aspect of our lives.

The press corps that Reagan and Bush faced was not the stereotype of the 1940s and 1950s, depicted in films by a grizzled, unshaven old-timer with a felt hat, pencil stuck behind the ear, pecking at a typewriter while talking on the telephone and taking an occasional puff on a cigarette to rest his fingers. By the late twentieth century, reporters were usually college educated, had a social conscience, and were better paid, and many women had joined the ranks of reporters. Some reporters have become media stars in their own right, writing books and opinion columns and appearing on television and radio talk shows. The late twentieth-century generation of reporters had been weaned on the Vietnam War and the Watergate scandal, which instilled a sense of cynicism regarding government and an instinctive questioning of government actions. With these traditions, the national press corps may be as much social crusaders as they are journalists. For them, it is important not only to report the news but also to shape it by serving as a voice for social justice and by uncovering political and economic corruption. As a consequence, such a reporter regards government as an important tool in furthering various social, economic, and political justice issues. In this environment Bush, with his conservative view of government, was at a disadvantage.

The situation was further complicated by the great explosion in media outlets that cable television and other technology ushered in. In the 1980s, cable television, specifically CNN, introduced the twenty-four-hour news cycle, which requires constant searching for new stories or different twists on the same story. This, in turn, forced the traditional print media to become more sensationalist in order to compete with the various other news outlets. *The New York Times,* considered a staple of staid and sophisticated readership, over the years has shifted its coverage to include more human-interest stories on the front page. In 1997, it introduced color photos on its front page in an effort to make the newspaper more attractive and more competitive in a saturated media market. The Internet has added yet another news dimension. Personal Web sites report and editorialize on the news. These "Web logs" and the "bloggers" who run them have become almost as powerful as more traditional news outlets but often carry a hard edge that pushes a certain political or ideological line.

Overall, news stories are increasingly injected with views that once would have been reserved for the editorial page. There always have been and will continue to be newspapers with a liberal or conservative bias, and they are readily identifiable as such. But the reported news has become more overtly editorial. Traditionally, a newspaper or television station could control a story by determining the amount of and level of coverage devoted to it. Now, news stories are not only presented but often include an analysis of why events unfolded as they did and sometimes with predictions of what may happen as a result. This expansion in the scope of "news" has shifted simple reporting toward news entertainment and advocacy reporting as the media compete for advertising dollars. Bush himself lamented this development, much of it out of the frustration that he was the target of the media. "There's a new wave of journalism where the journalists themselves slant the stories," he stated during the presidential campaign of 1992. "And this isn't a charge, this is a fact. And you say how to do it? I would like to see more objectivity in the news columns and let them slug me in the cartoons and the editorials and the columns and these nuts that come on there on these talking heads."

Bush's political career has made him a skeptic when it comes to the media. "I have a very negative view of the media," he readily admits. "The media has become more hostile, aggressive, and adversarial. The media is totally biased and unaccountable. Some of this is due to the leadership of *The New York Times* and its tendency to mix editorial views with the news."

Television has had a special role in these new developments. While newspapers are still read and radio is listened to, television gives an added dimension and edge to the news. Through television, a bombing in Saudi Arabia, a riot in Bosnia, or the announcement of a budget deal in Washington brings a certain reality to what we read or hear and is more likely to spark emotions, be they of sympathy or anger.

This aspect of television has sparked a debate on how and to what degree news now drives policy makers. In all offices of government, twenty-four-hour news shows are a constant companion of analysts, press people, and policy makers. In many cases government first learns of a situation through the news media. Scowcroft first learned of Saddam's Scud missile attacks on Tel Aviv during the Gulf War from television reports. His office became the White House command center dealing with the situation, with three television sets beaming their various reports. Bush himself was an avid viewer of CNN during the Gulf crisis. His attention to detail was great: at one time he complained that a photo being used of him by CNN was transposed. He watched the opening of Operation Desert Storm on CNN.

Some would argue that policy makers now react to news events in formulating many policies since it is difficult for them to dismiss the public's outcry in the face of human tragedy brought into everyone's living room. The question is debatable, but there is no doubt that the footage of human suffering that television brings into homes cannot but strike a chord of sympathy and caring. In such situations, there may be a greater propensity for policy makers to respond with some form of action. On the second floor of the White House residence, President and Mrs. Bush would relax before dinner, enjoying a cocktail as the evening news played on the television. Toward the end of 1992 the tragic story of a devastated Somalia unfolded on the screen with scenes of starving children, their hands and eyes pleading for a handful of food. The president was moved to do something by his conscience and the greatness of the United States in helping others. He directed that troops be dispatched to Somalia with the mission to end the starvation. "I had a wonderful feeling in my heart that we really helped people," Bush says in retrospect.

Others would argue that the only change news coverage has made in the work of policy makers is that the time frame for decision making has been collapsed, that the direction policy makers take has not been affected. Be that as it may, television has become a tool for policy makers, if only as a medium for generating public support or for sending messages to foreign as well as domestic audiences.

When it came to using television for specific ends, Bush understood how it could serve as a policy tool. This was most evident in the foreign policy area. Whether there was a need to send a signal, reassure an ally, or demonstrate U.S. resolve, Bush grasped the importance of television, most notably during the Gulf War.

In the period leading up to the Gulf War in 1991, the administration used CNN as a vehicle of diplomacy to send messages of resolve to Iraq and the allies. From the White House podium and in statements by the president and Secretary of State Baker, the administration sought to persuade Saddam of its intent and appeal to reason and at the same time reassure its coalition partners that the United States was committed to ousting Saddam from Kuwait. On September 12, 1990, Bush taped a television address in the Oval Office to the Iraqi people, explaining the United States and the international community's opposition to Saddam's aggression against Kuwait. On September 13 Iraq made the commitment to broadcast the address unedited, in its entirety. The program aired on September 16.

When Saddam Hussein offered during the war to withdraw from Kuwait, the initial reaction was that Iraq had ostensibly agreed to fulfill all of the United Nations resolutions. Careful review of his statement revealed that it fell short of UN demands, but the impression of capitulation was left hanging out there, leading U.S. allies to wonder if the war should be brought to a conclusion. In an effort to quickly inform the coalition members and the rest of the world, Bush decided to make a statement to the press, rejecting Saddam's proposal as inadequate. The statement was carried by CNN worldwide, and thus, all relevant governments learned of the U.S. position instantaneously. Diplomatic communication would have taken hours if not days to relay to the various governments.

During the uprising against Soviet president Gorbachev in 1991, President Bush's public statement of support for Boris Yeltsin and the latter's public opposition to the coup undoubtedly played a role in weakening the coup plot and in strengthening the resolve of the opposition. The president made his remarks at a hastily arranged press conference in Kennebunkport after a telephone conversation with Yeltsin. As usual, CNN covered the president's news conference and beamed his remarks around the world.

At times, however, the president was the subject of a CNN report. When President Turgot Ozal of Turkey heard a CNN report regarding Senate opposition to any effort on the part of the president to go to war against Saddam Hussein, he called Bush for clarification. Bush explained that the debate was only part of the democratic process in the United States and not an indication of what would actually occur.

The Bush White House realized the challenge and the opportunity that the new technologies posed. The main opportunity was through satellite technology. The White House was able to leapfrog the traditional White House press corps and get its story into the regional markets. The White House press corps is extremely competitive and focused on immediate headlines and in exposing what it would consider shortcomings or failures on the part of an administration. Regional media tend to be more straightforward in their reporting, since they cater to individual markets, where local events take precedence over the daily political battles in Washington. Taped interviews by the president and White House press releases usually get aired and reported without much comment. Furthermore, outside the Washington area the arrival of Air Force One is a major news item. It draws large crowds that normally would not have a chance to see a president. The thrill of such a visit is an honor for city officials, and every effort is made to make the city and the president look good. The pressing issues of the nation's capital over which the national press corps obsesses are largely irrelevant in such an environment. What the president says about the city and local leaders dominates the local news cycle. In this process the president's message is also incorporated, all without the editorial filter that the national media can attach to the process.

Bush had a hard time adjusting to the changing technological and social conditions that were beginning to sweep the country in the late 1980s and early 1990s and that were greatly affecting how the public was receiving its news and the type of interest the public had. He maintained a traditional, highly respectful view of the presidency and did not want to do anything that he believed could diminish the aura surrounding the office. Bush tackled the dilemma in a diary entry in June 1992, ruminating over his inability to get coverage for his campaign policies over the traditional airwaves. He noted the possible need to go the route of the "new fad" of call-in talk shows and morning shows. He wrote, "I want to respect the office of the president, keep its dignity . . . we've got to do it all with a certain sense of dignity, a certain sense of propriety." In like manner, he explained to the American Society of Newspaper Editors in 1989 why he refused to answer questions over the sound of the helicopter when he was departing from or arriving at the White House. "I want to treat the press with the dignity to which it is entitled," he explained. "And if you have to get your question answered by screaming at me when I don't want to answer it, you don't look very good. And I don't think it's very good for the White House."

Throughout his career, Bush had ascribed many of his problems to the press. There was always a feeling that the press did not provide accurate or fair coverage. Bush had ample reason to be leery of the media.

En route to Kennebunkport at Thanksgiving time, in the wake of his re-election defeat in 1992, Bush was somewhat wistful aboard Air Force One. He strolled to the back of the plane, where the staff sat, carrying with him a wire story that spoke of the country's economic rebound. Most of the seats were empty; the staff, in the wake of the defeat and the family nature of the holiday, had opted to bypass the trip. Mostly lower ranking staff were on board. Sean Walsh, a young press aide, quietly took in the president's lament. Throughout the campaign, Bush noted, he had stated that the economy was much stronger and getting better. Unfortunately, he continued matter-of-factly, fully aware that there was nothing one could do about the situation now, the press had not paid attention.

Bush believed there were many instances in which media behavior was reckless. During the action to capture Panama's dictator, Manuel Noriega, Bush believed that the media compromised the mission by broadcasting news of the departure of planes from Pope Air Force Base in North Carolina. Bush was also annoyed by the dire—and, as events proved, erroneous—warnings by the press that the Gulf War would lead to thousands of U.S. military casualties. He also did not appreciate the press's tendency to drive events and to color its reporting with opinion. Bush believes that he was the victim of such an effort when the Berlin Wall came down in November 1989, bringing an onrush of freedom in Eastern Europe and the eventual reunification of Germany. Bush was at the White House on the day the wall came down. There was a clamor from the press for a response to the momentous event. It was decided that the president would meet with a press pool in the Oval Office. Bush, however, was not going to be stampeded into any rushed announcements or judgments.

Seated behind his desk in the Oval Office, Bush greeted the press in an almost nonchalant manner. The removal of the Berlin Wall was a seminal event: the demise of a glaring symbol of the cold war. The end of the wall was the result of a great desire for freedom, and it foreshadowed the actual spread of freedom. It also signaled that the Soviet Union was tottering. In this sea of vast changes the Soviet empire was slowly losing its grip on its constituent parts, and under Gorbachev's policies of glasnost and perestroika, the Soviet Union itself was also undergoing change.[1] It was a time of joy but also a time for greater opportunity. Many hard political issues remained to be addressed: the actual reunification of Germany in NATO and the continued collapse of the Soviet Union itself. How the United States responded to the demise of the Berlin Wall could well have an impact on how future events would unfold.

Bush was criticized for his lack of enthusiasm and unwillingness to declare victory with the removal of the Berlin Wall. In hindsight, Bush has expressed his dismay at the press's shortsighted approach: "The stupidest, dumbest idea I've heard," he has stated, was "to stick a finger in Gorbachev's eye when things were moving peacefully."

By his restrained comments, Bush gave Gorbachev some space in which to save face and maneuver in the midst of the reactionary forces in the Soviet Union. By doing so, Bush left the lines of communication open and signaled that the United States was a trustworthy partner in the changes that were sweeping Eastern Europe and not an adversary willing to exploit events at the expense of Moscow. As a result, Bush was able to guarantee a continued U.S. role in the developments unfolding in that part of the world, which meant that events would move forward in an evolutionary and manageable manner. Furthermore, the event could speak for itself: Gorbachev himself could see what was happening without having Bush point it out to him. Events proved Bush correct. On December 1, the Communist Party gave up its sole leadership in East Germany. On December 7, Lithuania ended the Communist Party's monopoly on power. On March 13, 1990, the Soviet Union's Communist Party monopoly on political power ended.

In addition, during the time that the wall came down, the United States, together with the Soviet Union, had already announced the meeting between Bush and Gorbachev, which was scheduled for Malta in early December 1989. The United States did not want to do anything that would jeopardize this meeting. Also forgotten in the excitement of November was Bush's address on May 31, 1989, in Mainz during a visit to West Germany. At that time, Bush, recounting the barriers that were falling in Hungary, emphatically stated, "Let Berlin be next—let Berlin be next!"

The issue of German unification had major ramifications for foreign policy. Not only was there the question of what impact unification would have on the Soviet Union but there were also parallel issues: unification within NATO, the stationing of NATO troops in the eastern part of a unified Germany, the removal of Soviet troops, and allaying the concerns of European allies, such as Britain and France, who had historical memories of a resurgent Germany. Through careful consultation, prodding, and reassurances, Bush was able to help meld the divergent personalities and interests of German chancellor Kohl, Gorbachev, British prime minister Thatcher, and French president Mitterrand into a successful policy that gave birth to a united Germany within NATO. His reaction to the demise of the Berlin Wall was one of the key steps in this process.

One press incident, in particular, left Bush with a raw feeling. On the domestic side, the press chose to portray Bush as aloof and out of touch with the American public. A *New York Times* story about a grocery store price scanner epitomized this view of Bush. In a visit to the National Grocery Association in Florida in February 1992, Bush expressed interest in how a scanner National Cash Register had recently developed was able to read even damaged universal product codes. Andy Rosenthal of the *Times*, who was not even present at the event but based his story on a press pool report written by another reporter, wrote a story depicting Bush as out of touch with mainstream America. In complimenting the company and the brand-new technology, Bush was portrayed as being out of touch with American lifestyles. Protests by Fitzwater and even letters from National Cash Register outlining the erroneous nature of the story did not dispel the impression that had been created. Bush himself wrote to the *Times* publisher requesting that a retraction be printed, but none was forthcoming. Reporters who covered the event did not file stories along the lines that Rosenthal did. Unfortunately, the *Times* story got the attention and was picked up by other news outlets.

Bush's disdain for the press did not, however, undermine his civility. While he was suspicious and viewed the press as biased, he treated its members, individually and as a group, as he did all others. He bantered with them, on Air Force One or in informal news sessions, hosted them at a barbecue at Walker's Point, and held numerous press conferences in the White House Briefing Room. He knew most of them by name. Overall, despite the friction between Bush and the press, members of the media held him in high regard. As a person, the press genuinely liked Bush. Ken Walsh of *U.S. News and World Report* has covered many presidents, and his view sums up the media's general impression of Bush. "I liked President Bush best," he says, "because he is such a genuine and decent man to the people around him."

Bush has a visceral aversion to leaks and to reports of White House and government agency infighting appearing in the press. He had witnessed this problem frequently during the Reagan years and was adamant that his administration would not be marred by the spectacle of such public infighting. The administration did have a harmonious working relationship for the most part, although there were occasional detours. At the start of the administration, a gentleman's agreement was in place that the lead spokesman on foreign policy would be Secretary of State Baker. This arrangement appeared to work well during the first year. However, with the botched U.S. role in the abortive anti-Noriega coup in Panama in October 1989, the finger pointing started. State Department officials readily took the initiative, with the press following up, to fix blame on the White House.

It had been a longtime aim of U.S. policy to see Manuel Noriega ousted from his place as Panama's dictator because of his blatant suppression of political freedom and his involvement in the illicit drug trade. In 1989 Noriega was indicted in the United States on drug charges. In May of that year Noriega stole the presidential election, and his followers bloodily beat one of the vice-presidential candidates. These actions only whetted the United States' appetite to remove him from power. On October 1 the United States received word of a planned coup by an army major and longtime Noriega loyalist, Moses Giroldi. Initial doubts by the United States about a planned coup were reinforced by the fact that the coup was postponed for a few days. When the coup plotters moved, the United States ordered troops to block certain points to assist the coup plotters. However, the lack of coordination between the United States and the plotters led the coup to collapse, and Giroldi was executed. The botched coup led Congress to criticize the administration for not being forceful in its support of the coup. The experience led the administration to tighten its crisis decision-making procedures, and Noriega was eventually captured and taken into U.S. custody in December 1989. At that time U.S. forces invaded Panama in the wake of the killing of a U.S. marine by Panamanian troops and the harassment of a U.S. naval officer and his wife.

That October night, however, in the wake of the failed coup, Scowcroft sat slouched and dejected in his West Wing office. Stoically, and without comment, he took in the reports of what State Department officials were telling the press. In particular, Scowcroft was being fingered for the lack of coordination of the administration's effort. Out of this experience Scowcroft created the Deputies Committee at the NSC to help coordinate the interagency process during future administration efforts.

Equally important, the White House from then on took a more active role in presenting foreign policy issues to the press, with Scowcroft taking to the airwaves more often. This public relations activity was intended to gain ground on internecine policy struggles among the principals and the bureaucracies. Much of the friction revolved around the Defense Department, since at this time, as the cold war was winding down, the Pentagon was unsure of how its equipment and weapons needs would be handled in the future.

Bush himself, however, was not lax in sending his own signals to the press. At one point, when the press was speculating as to whether Baker or Scowcroft was more influential in the foreign policy process, Bush invited Baker and his wife Susan to Camp David for the weekend. It was a clear signal to the press that such speculation was fallacious and unwarranted: the secretary of state was in charge.

Bush as Communicator

For Bush, the policy process was the result of negotiations and personal contact; it was the ability to explain and persuade on an individual basis, which suited his personal style. In the White House environment, giving speeches was a necessary part of the president's job, but it was neither the essence of nor the proper tool for accomplishing goals. In fact, speeches could be regarded as possible detriments. They could be viewed as seeking to bypass the individual and personal contacts on which Bush relied.

With this view, Bush failed to grasp and to fully utilize the strength of the bully pulpit and the importance of presidential rhetoric in stirring and persuading the public. In the patrician world that he came from and in the gentlemanly conduct of his character, you did not take your disagreements out into the public. Bush also refused to take the traditional "loneliest job" photo in which the president is posed, alone, staring into the distance, shoulders seeming to bear the weight of the world. He ascribes his rejection of this view to Reagan. "I learned a lot from Ronald Reagan," Bush told the press in March 1989. "One thing I learned from him is, I never once in eight years, no matter how difficult the problem, heard him appeal to me or to others around him for understanding about the toughest, loneliest job in the world." Indeed, Bush is quite proud that he avoided such a pose. For reasons like these, Bush also felt uncomfortable with using the first-person singular pronoun "I." He would routinely excise the word from speech drafts and replace each occurrence with "we." The speechwriters wrestled with this dilemma yet wound up losing this tug of war over words many times. The low priority that the White House put on the written word was seen in the fact that Sununu organized a smaller speechwriting staff than had existed during the Reagan administration.

Bush not only avoided highlighting himself but also had a tendency to acknowledge people in the audience at the beginning of his speeches. He insisted on this practice, and these comments were, at times, extensive. The acknowledgments were predominantly shaped by Bush. To the ones provided by the speechwriters Bush would add more individuals to single out, and he would personalize many of the acknowledgments. In addition, he was wont to ad lib acknowledgments depending on whom he spotted in the crowd. The practice was an extension of Bush's courtesy, delivered usually in a friendly, rambling way but one that made him appear as if he was backing into his speech. As a result, some of the impact of his words was lost.

By his own admission, Bush never felt comfortable with the "flowery language" his speechwriters employed. He believed that such language was not a true reflection of himself as an individual, that his use of such language would make him uncomfortable and make him appear to be trying to be something that he was not. During the campaign in 1988, while en route to a campaign appearance on Air Force Two, Bush objected to proposed language for his planned speech. Campaign chairman Jim Baker and pollster Bob Teeter, back at campaign headquarters, had decided to throw into the remarks a lot of hyperbolic and critical language about his opponent. They believed it was important to ratchet up the rhetoric of the campaign. On board the plane, the remarks were being supervised by media adviser Roger Ailes. The move raised Bush's disdain and discomfort with anything too hyperbolic, matching his aversion to flowery or self-aggrandizing rhetoric.

Tom Collamore, staff secretary to the vice president, brought the cards bearing the proposed remarks to Bush in his cabin at the front of the plane. Left alone, Bush quickly set to reading through the remarks. As he read, his face furrowed into a frown, and he hurried through the remaining few cards. He called for Collamore.

"I'm not going to say these ridiculous things," stated Bush in exasperation as he tossed the cards to Collamore. Collamore understood. He had worked with Bush long enough to know that the words did not fit the man. Without a word, Collamore turned and quickly went to Ailes, who was seated in the staff section. Collamore explained the problem to Ailes.

"You better let campaign headquarters know," Collamore concluded, leaving Ailes to his work. As the plane landed, a new set of cards with a revised text was ready. Collamore took them to Bush in the cabin.

"How you doing?" asked Bush with a smile, seeking to take the edge off his earlier irritation. "You know I'm not yelling at you." Then he got to the heart of the matter. "Did Roger get the message?" Collamore smiled and nodded at the cards in Bush's hands.

Given his aversion to flowery language, the staff had to work hard at times to persuade Bush to incorporate certain language in his presentations. Preparing for the fiftieth anniversary commemoration of the attack on Pearl Harbor, Bush balked at some of the language in the speech he was to give at the

USS *Arizona* Memorial because he believed it was somewhat "over the top." The speechwriters pushed for their version and finally turned to Scowcroft for assistance. Scowcroft backed the speechwriters, Bush relented, and the language remained. The speech turned out to be a stirring presentation, worthy of the occasion and capturing the spirit of the event.

The speech process, however, did not always work so smoothly. In late 1991, Dick Darman, director of the Office of Management and Budget (OMB), and Sununu persuaded Bush to use the forthcoming State of the Union address as a springboard for the coming reelection campaign in 1992. The approach was wrapped in secrecy, thus isolating valuable sources of information and news. Peggy Noonan, working with both Darman and Teeter, was tasked with drafting the address. Noonan had worked as a speechwriter for Reagan and for Bush during the campaign in 1988; she had crafted Bush's convention speech that year. The speechwriting office was not aware of all the details of this parallel activity and thus continued to labor on a speech without much guidance from Sununu, who eventually resigned in December.

About a week before the address, the speech office was told that the draft by its speechwriter, Tony Snow, was inadequate. Snow, who served as press secretary to President George W. Bush, was a young, idealistic editorial page writer for the *Washington Times* turned speechwriter. He came to his job in the speech bullpen at the White House with a burst of excitement and enthusiasm. He learned the travails of White House intrigue during the State of the Union incident. Snow dutifully tackled the task of drafting the address but encountered roadblocks almost immediately. His repeated calls to Darman to get a sense of the direction the speech should take proved fruitless.

A few days before the address, a meeting in the Oval Office raised hopes that, finally, some concrete guidance and policy initiatives would be laid out so that Snow could work them into the draft. The gathering was small, the main participants being the president, Darman, Snow, and communications director David Demarest, among others. The president was attentive but noncommittal to the exchange that was taking place. Finally, Darman came to the point.

"I know that Tony's been working hard," Darman stated. This was not going to be a compliment, Snow thought as he tensed up, anticipating the proverbial drop of the other shoe. "But this speech is just not up to it," Darman concluded.

No one said anything, but Snow could see some of the heads nodding around the room. He felt as if he were at an arranged execution.

"Of course it won't do," Snow blurted. He admitted that the speech draft was inadequate; indeed, he did not like it himself. "We have no idea what we are supposed to be doing," he concluded in defense of himself and the speechwriting staff.

The president sat quietly. He was taking in the exchange and the facts as best as they could be gleaned. No one offered any encouragement or advice to Snow. The parallel plan had already been well under way.

Noonan's speech was first provided to the speechwriting office that weekend before the State of the Union, and the office was reduced to the role of fact checking the text. Demarest, boxed out of the process, wound up watching the address from his West Wing office. Some initial reviews of the speech were favorable; however, the whole message eventually fell flat. The lead-up to the speech raised expectations that were not met, and the address fell short of the vision that Darman had hoped would stimulate the campaign at its outset.

The whole incident weighed on the president. Two days after his address, he cornered Demarest. This was not a situation for small talk. Demarest felt uncomfortable as he anticipated what the ensuing conversation would entail. But he also knew George Bush. If anyone could handle the matter, it was Bush.

"Are there any hurt feelings?" the president asked, getting to the heart of the matter. There was no need to elaborate. Both men knew what the issue was.

"Yes," said Demarest candidly. He then proceeded to elaborate. Yes, he was hurt and felt he had been misled by those around the president, but he tried to soften his comments by stating how his goal had always been to do the best possible work for the president.

Bush listened attentively. He did not like encounters in which he or staff members had to be put in uncomfortable situations, but he also knew that this was a special circumstance that warranted his attention. He valued teamwork based on a congenial atmosphere, and he wanted to reaffirm this model. The president appeared apologetic.

"I hear what you are saying," Bush stated. He reassured Demarest that he believed it had all been wrong too. Bush's personal attention to the matter helped to rebuild bruised egos and put the issue behind the staff.

Bush's discomfort with public speaking did not fit into the changing nature of politics. Just as the nature of the media was changing, politics was changing with it. Politics was adapting to the new media and also being shaped by it. The result was that politics was becoming more of a media show. Candidates were being judged on how telegenic they were, on their ability to present pithy yet articulate snippets for the cameras, and on the eye-catching and stirring backgrounds in which they were pictured. Bush did not fit this world. Indeed, this world seemed to magnify any personal shortcomings, such as his one-sided nervous grin or broken syntax, all of which combined to undermine his public image. With this new aspect of politics in the media spotlight, the natural next step was for the media to concentrate on any such idiosyncrasies, further undermining how Bush projected himself and how he was viewed by the public.

Bush was, in essence, a victim of television. Following the third and final debate of the campaign in 1992, the panel of questioners quickly left the hall for a group dinner away from the site. They wanted to avoid the inevitable rush by their press colleagues for views on how the debate went and who they thought had won. Over dinner the consensus developed that Bush had put in a strong performance and that he had command of the facts and appeared most presidential. Reuters White House correspondent Gene Gibbons, who served as one of the panelists, could only conclude that Bush had won the debate. The public consensus, as portrayed by media coverage, however, was that Clinton had emerged on top. Several weeks later Gibbons viewed a tape of the debate and was struck by the different perception he had in seeing it on a television screen. Clinton came across as filling the screen, showing a commanding presence and a knowledge of the facts equal to that of Bush.

Presidential debates were a particular nuisance for Bush. He detested them, viewing them more as entertainment than substance, and therefore he did not regard them as being productive. "In the end," Bush said in his Gauer lecture, "debates have very little to do with one's qualifications to be president of the United States." In addition, Bush hated the staging he was put through and all the media attention given to the debates. His discomfort with the debate format and the fact that he did not perform well in them undoubtedly fed his dislike.

The television screen is not a neutral filter. While it can bring real-time events to everyone's attention, it can also magnify and enhance, giving a distorted impression of individual qualities for better or worse. In Clinton's case it played to his advantage. Clinton showed a commanding presence, and with his facial expressions and gestures of empathy and articulate responses, he struck a chord with the public.

Paralleling the old cliché that all politics is local is the mantra that all politics is personal. The ability to persuade and even to compromise as well as the personal relations and rapport that one can establish are key to success under this rubric. This was the tradition of American politics, reflected in the door-to-door campaigning, the personal contact of candidates and voters at picnics and church functions, and the stump speech, geared mainly toward entertaining a crowd and developing a rapport with it. This was the world of politics that Bush felt comfortable in; it reflected his own personality and the roots he had established in West Texas, where a man's word and neigh-borliness were valued. The television age was largely alien to him. While he realized its importance, he could not master it nor did he feel comfortable in its setting and the demands it placed on him—the need for articulate and concise statements, staging, and talking to a camera rather than a person.

Furthermore, Bush's personal, fast-paced approach to life made him im-patient and frustrated at attempts to orchestrate or choreograph his appear-ances. His preparation for press appearances, for example, was almost non-existent. The normal procedure was for the Press Office simply to provide a list of questions, which was brought into the Oval Office for his review prior to meeting with the press. Joining the Press Office staff would usually be the chief of staff and the national security adviser. The president would lean back in the chair behind his desk and glance at the list of questions. He would look at each question and nod, a signal that he knew how to address it. Very seldom would he look up for assistance, and in those instances it was mostly to glean more information from the attendees.

The whole process would last about two to three minutes, and then he was off to meet the press. During his administration, Bush had only one formal East Room press conference. The rest were held in the White House Briefing Room or in other, more informal environments. All of this was in keeping with his penchant for plainspoken, unpretentious appearances. That one time that the president had an elaborate, formal East Room press confer-ence he was no different in his preparations than for those he held in the Briefing Room. Just prior to the East Room press conference, Bush and his advisers gathered in the Oval Office to review the issues and questions that might arise during the press conference. The president's principal advisers were present to participate in the briefing. Fitzwater methodically posed each question to the president. The president easily parried each one. Occasionally, a staffer would suggest an addition to the answer Bush offered.

Like any public official, Bush was held hostage by demands on his valuable time and by the demands of the media. As president, he needed to use his time efficiently for maximum impact. This need favored structured events, well planned and orchestrated. In the media age, there was also the need to present settings that were photogenic, once again putting Bush in situations that were largely alien to his nature. "I did not like staging," admits Bush. "I was not interested in doing something that was not quite real. I did not want to do it just because someone asked me to do it." This personal dilemma was evident in the campaign of 1988. During the Iowa caucuses Bush made formal appearances, using a podium, rope and stanchion, and a background curtain. His opponents put much emphasis in face-to-face encounters, such as meetings in voters' homes. Bush's poor showing in Iowa led the campaign to switch tactics in New Hampshire. It was decided to let Bush be himself, and he shed many of the trappings of the vice presidency. Bush wound up having breakfast with patrons of a fast-food outlet and making visits to a truck stop and a lumber yard. Through these opportunities, people who were familiar with Bush in his role as vice president came to know him as a person.

Staff, however, know that even the most natural appearances need planning and coordination. To make sure that events went off smoothly and, at the same time, did not make Bush feel as if he was being manipulated, staff usually resorted to clandestine steps. Part of the strategy involved not giving Bush a formal briefing on the sequence of events, thus making it appear as if events were unfolding naturally.

Bush, however, could be extemporaneous. During his visit to Budapest in July 1989 he discarded his prepared text. "The speech was very boring," he has said about the move. "That is true." But equally important, the day was rainy and icy cold. He felt for the crowd, which had enthusiastically assembled long before his appearance. He did not want to subject the people any longer than necessary to the inclement weather. To further underscore his concerns, he graciously offered the raincoat he was wearing to a rain-soaked elderly woman standing by the podium. Unfortunately, the raincoat was not his; it belonged to a Secret Service agent who, true to his profession, demanded that Bush wear it against the weather. Bush made sure later on that he replaced the agent's coat.

Some staffers, such as Bobbie Kilberg, noticed Bush's ability to perform better without a script and sought to have Bush speak without a prepared text. Others felt very strongly that Bush needed to be exact and therefore should use a text. There was a logical reason for this latter approach; it was important that the president be specific when making any domestic or foreign pronouncements so that his remarks would not be misunderstood. This was particularly true in the foreign policy arena, where the world of diplomacy and state relations hinged on words and the impressions or lack of impressions they could convey. Furthermore, policy pronouncements were not given to being short; many involved detailed presentations of facts, thus making it difficult for anyone to attempt a spontaneous presentation without a script. Whether he liked it or not, a text was the mainstay of Bush's public appearances.

According to Bush, he held 268 press "availabilities" during his administration, making him one of the most accessible presidents. Bush also delivered approximately 1,300 speeches and statements from behind a podium—including those in the White House Briefing Room. In the majority of cases, Bush accepted the written word and recommendations of his speechwriters. He showed his hand in approximately 10 percent of the speeches, mostly through some serious editing, including recommendations in the margins and insertions into a text. He did pen a few speeches on his own.

Previous presidents, such as FDR, Nixon, and Reagan, had been closely involved with the speechwriting process. Reagan, for example, was involved in the preparation and editing of his speeches; he understood that every public utterance counted and could have an impact. Bush seldom got involved in the overall process. However, when he did, he was very energetic and engaged, and his actual performance in delivering the speeches was much better.

On the foreign policy front, Scowcroft had major fights with the speechwriters. Scowcroft insisted on having the NSC draft the president's foreign policy speeches. The draft would then be given to the speechwriters, whose task Scowcroft viewed as putting the remarks into the president's language. The speechwriters objected to this sequence. They wanted to write the first draft and then hand it to the NSC for corrections. Scowcroft was concerned that the speechwriters were interpreting policy rather than limiting themselves to crafting the words of the remarks.

Bush's interest in the speechwriting process was greatest when foreign policy issues were to be addressed, and he would usually send suggestions to his speechwriters. During the Iraq crisis, the speechwriters would arrive in their offices at about half past six in the morning and already find page after page of text typed by the president at his portable typewriter the night before. Bush's speech to the annual conference of the Veterans of Foreign Wars on August 20, 1990, was one such example, showing both his thought process and handicraft. When Curt Smith pulled the typed pages from his box, all that was left for him to do was to editorially clean up the draft and type it. Similarly, Bush penned the address he gave to the American Legion's annual convention on September 7, 1989, leaving mostly editing duties for Smith.

Bush put particular effort into what is known as the Hamtramck speech, in which he introduced his policy toward Eastern Europe and, in particular, outlined specific economic steps to recognize the changes taking place in Poland and to encourage additional market reforms in that country. Realizing the historic nature of the speech, to be delivered at the city hall in Hamtramck, Michigan, in April 1989, he worked on the text personally and, in order to convey the importance of its content, he practiced the delivery. The president was also very much involved with the writing of his nomination acceptance speech in 1988 and his speech in 1991 on the concept of a just war; both speeches were sound performances.

The same clear determination was lacking on the domestic policy side. In foreign policy, the speechwriters were usually given good guidance regarding what the administration was attempting to accomplish. In many cases the guidance came directly from the president. On domestic issues, however, the speechwriters often found themselves adrift. Bush was, as Smith recalls, "erratic domestically" but "steadfast globally." Bush's involvement in foreign policy speeches is understandable: these were clear issues, such as freedom in Eastern Europe or in Kuwait. On the domestic side, the sheer number of issues, spanning the full range of social, economic, and environmental policies, makes it impossible for a president to delve into the crafting of each set of remarks; a president who tried to do so would become a full-time speechwriter.

Bush, however, was not oblivious to the domestic side. The American Legion speech revolved around fighting domestic crime, the anti–drug trafficking effort on the domestic and international fronts, the march of freedom in Eastern Europe, and the need for a strong national defense.

During the budget negotiations in 1990, the speechwriters were whip-sawed, preparing various versions, including contradictory ones, of intended remarks—all in the same day. This type of problem became most glaring and troubling during 1992, when the reelection campaign was taking place. Chief of Staff Skinner and Bob Teeter would meet with the speechwriters for strategy sessions that left the latter clueless as to what needed to be accomplished. Skinner and Teeter would confront the writers with the need to develop an agenda and a plan, yet left no guidance as to what the administration sought to accomplish.

Bush realized his own shortcomings when it came to speeches and tried to rectify this through practice and some coaching. Bush practiced the address he was to make at the memorial service for the forty-seven sailors killed in an explosion aboard the USS *Iowa* in April 1989. Bush traveled to Norfolk, Virginia, for the service, well aware of his tendency to get emotional in such circumstances. In order to control the emotions that he sensed would grip him on the occasion, he practiced the delivery of his text. All of his practicing, however, did not prevent him from choking up.

Bush would also sometimes practice the delivery of major speeches, such as the State of the Union and an occasional Oval Office address, such as the one announcing the National Drug Control Strategy in September 1989. For these practice sessions a videotape was made, and Roger Ailes, the media consultant, was brought in to view and critique the performance. Along with Demarest, Ailes would edit the text and review the president's body language and make recommendations as to where the president should place emphasis. Mrs. Bush herself took a keen interest in how the president was coming across on television and offered her advice.

In addition to these efforts, an attempt was made to provide a comfort-able environment whenever possible in order to help Bush relax and be more natural in taping sessions. In February 1991 Dorrance Smith joined the staff. Smith was a former ABC-TV producer, a childhood friend of the Bush family, and the president's frequent tennis partner. Everyone expected that Smith's involvement would be a great comfort for Bush. Smith, aware of Bush's aversion to being handled, devised the strategy that put the emphasis on making the videotaping sessions routine. He made sure to use the same make-up person, the same staff people, and the same technical procedures, all with the intention of increasing Bush's comfort level so that the whole process would become second nature to him. Unfortunately, all of these efforts did not seem to have much impact. The president would sometimes require ten to fifteen takes, and at other times sessions were rescheduled. Still, his overall performance did not seem to improve appreciably. Whether in television broadcasts or video sessions, Bush could not relate to a camera; he stiffened, and the warmth and ease that he exhibited in personal contacts disappeared.

Staff also tried creating an environment in which Bush could personally interact with his audience when he was delivering remarks before a live audience. Bush was best when he could relate directly to people, such as in one-on-one or small group sessions, so efforts were made to make sure that Bush would be able to see the first two rows of his audience despite the glare of the stage lights. This sometimes led to differing views with the lighting crews. The crews needed the bright lighting to present the president in the best possible manner, both to the crowd and to the television cameras; Bush needed the dimmer lights in order to be able to make eye contact with the audience. To a large degree this was a moot point; he still had to read a text, which was not his strong suit.

Seven

~~

BUSH AND THE WORLD
OF DIPLOMACY

USH OPENLY admitted to his keen interest in foreign policy and was
often accused—unfairly in his view—of favoring foreign over domestic
policy. His enjoyment of foreign policy is clearly seen in his memoirs,
written after he left office. *A World Transformed,* jointly authored with Scowcroft, deals exclusively with the international issues his administration faced.
No similar memoir on domestic policy has appeared. His next book, *All the
Best, George Bush,* was a compendium of personal and official letters and diary
entries, underscoring the importance of personal relations in his life and career. He defended his interest in foreign policy as being for the national good,
and he sought to deflect the criticism regarding his allegedly one-sided interest. His retort to critics, stated in remarks to the Disabled American Veterans
national convention in 1992, was that "when the Sunday strategists say that
I've spent too much time on foreign policy, let me just put it this way: I will
never apologize for a single minute spent keeping America strong, safe, and
free."

Observers attribute his predilection for international issues to his foreign
policy–related positions during his years of public service prior to becoming
president. The actual reasons are a bit more complex.

Bush, after all, ran two unsuccessful campaigns for the U.S. Senate and was
a two-term member of Congress from Houston. All these campaigns hinged
predominantly on domestic issues such as civil rights, welfare reform, revenue
sharing, and abortion, among others. Bush proved himself adept at under-

standing and arguing these and other issues. What frustrated him was the changing alliances, the uncertainty of support, the need to form a consensus among disparate voters, and the need to constantly be attuned to the mood of the public. The world of foreign policy is largely devoid of such cross-pressures. It had its own pressures, but it operated largely on the basis of bipartisanship and a known enemy—the Soviet Union—during most of Bush's public life. "Working with Congress is the most difficult part of presidential leaders," Bush claims. "You can make something happen in foreign affairs more easily than with domestic affairs without the acquiescence of Congress. A lot of people don't understand that." It was this freedom of movement that Bush enjoyed. "Congress did not control foreign policy and that's why I liked foreign policy," Bush openly admits. "Presidents have a lot more flexibility in foreign policy than in domestic policy. On domestic policy, I was slammed all the time. I could not get anything done."

Bush's frustration regarding the various domestic players and, in particular, the Congress, came to the fore in a conversation he held with his secretary of housing and urban development, Jack Kemp. Kemp, venting his own frustration over the economic policies of the administration, particularly with regard to Bush's willingness to abandon his "no new taxes" pledge, beseeched Bush to be more active on the economic issue.

"You majored in economics at Yale," Kemp reminded Bush. "Why don't you take a more active interest?"

Bush did not hesitate in his response.

"Well," he stated, "I can't get much done with a Democratic Congress. In foreign policy I can be an activist. I can call Major, [Israeli prime minister Yitzhak] Shamir. I can get things done. I feel like an executive."

Bush paused. He sighed and then added, "Congress is so obstinate."

On another occasion, while addressing the press during a trip to Rio de Janeiro in 1992, Bush stated his view succinctly. "In foreign affairs, fortunately," he said, "I don't need a congressional acquiescence every step of the way."

In addition, Bush's world was one in which personal relations helped everything move smoothly. From his postings and from his many trips overseas, Bush had developed a web of personal contacts, which played to his strong suit of dealing with issues on a personal basis. In this regard, he could deal directly with a foreign leader, unlike on the domestic side, where he would have to deal with the various layers of leadership and committee interests that characterize Congress. In addition, foreign policy presented a more structured process that was easily understandable in terms of the actors involved and the chain of command. The president, under the American system, is the sole representative of the United States overseas and is empowered to negotiate treaties, appoint ambassadors, and be commander in chief of the armed forces. While the Senate plays an important role in all of these functions, such as approving ambassadorial appointments and treaties, they do underscore the preeminent role of the president.

On the domestic side, Bush preferred to give direction and then rely on his chief of staff to run with the agenda. There are so many competing interests in domestic policy that it would be difficult for a president to handle all of them. That is why there is a White House staff dealing with Congress, state and local governments, interest groups, and the media. It is the chief of staff's responsibility to oversee and use this vast resource of experts. Dealing with a hostile Congress controlled by Democrats also did not help Bush in achieving his full domestic agenda. Furthermore, Bush believes there is a connection between domestic and foreign policy, so he did not regard the respective issues as totally separate. Besides the obvious importance of maintaining national security via a strong defense, the economic interconnections of the world have important domestic consequences for the United States. To prevent global conditions from having a negative impact on the nation, it is important for the United States to demonstrate world leadership, particularly in helping to bring down trade barriers and maintain exports. These factors did not mean that Bush avoided domestic policy. "I think we've got a good domestic agenda," Bush stated on May 30, 1992. "I do not plead guilty to neglecting it." In 1992 Bush claimed that, as regards time, "much more of it has been spent on domestic matters."

Bush's World View

Bush had a clear world view and a set of guiding principles for U.S. behavior on the international front. Overall, Bush's views are like those of many Republicans in the post–World War II era: a focus on a strong defense in foreign affairs, with domestic affairs left more to the operation of private-sector forces. Domestic policy was shaped by the Republican philosophy that domestic issues, particularly the economy, were mostly outside government control.

Foreign affairs, however, was the domain of the government and thus warranted strong involvement and attention.

Like all presidents before and since, George Bush saw America as a special place, a country that is unique among nations, with a special role based on the idea that U.S. policy abroad should be guided by the principle of spreading democracy and freedom. For the nation to keep this special status, it was necessary to maintain a strong defense with a military and technological edge. Bush is a firm believer in "peace through strength."

Beyond this fundamental belief, Bush's understanding of the uniqueness of U.S. power underlay his approach to international leadership. He realized that America's power—military and economic—overshadowed that of all other states, and with that power came a certain responsibility. The responsibility included using power judiciously and in a transparent fashion. This meant, among other things, making sure that decisions were as multilateral as possible, thereby giving other states input and a stake in decisions. As a result, Bush set two criteria for the commitment of force: other states should participate in the action, and the action should take place, if possible, under the authority of the United Nations. In the Gulf War to liberate Kuwait, Bush saw to it that other states shared the burden both militarily and economically, thus inoculating the United States to a certain degree against any widespread international criticism of the action. For Bush, it was important for the world not to view the United States as an arrogant power. Indeed, through a multilateral effort, Bush saw U.S. power being augmented, both morally as well as militarily. The United States, Bush was emphatic, should not be the world's policeman, responding unilaterally to every challenge the world might pose.

Bush saw the world as a set of interacting players, some more powerful and important than others, but all essential to the smooth functioning of the whole. He realized that any one state could unbalance the system by challenging it—as had the Soviet Union for many decades—or by acting alone in pursuit of its goals. Thus, a unilateral course of action by the United States ran the risk of isolating the nation diplomatically, creating unfavorable international perceptions and, ultimately, undermining U.S. goals. He understood the ephemeral nature of raw power and the need to project it in a fashion that was not threatening or even appearing to threaten the world. Otherwise, the United States would be seen as a state using its power at the expense of others. As a result, Bush, in addition to carrying out a diplomacy that was as inclusive as possible, sought to ensure that as many diplomatic steps as possible were carried out before the United States acted. Bush's approach also emphasized not placing a state in a position in which it had no diplomatic escape or would not be able to save face. As he did personally, he sought a national stance that avoided gloating or taking too much credit for any action.

The need to work with international organizations increased as U.S. policy witnessed successive achievements. The end of communism, the Gulf War, and the emergence of new democracies required an international effort aimed at managing these new developments. Therefore, consultation, both bilaterally and multilaterally, as in the United Nations, played a key role in Bush's leadership on international issues. His ideas were crystallized in the concept of a new world order, built on the twin pillars of democracy and economic freedom for all states and committed to settling issues peacefully. He formally presented this concept to Congress in an address on September 11, 1990. He believed in the possibility of a world order based on justice and fair play and in which weak states were protected against the strong. And he looked to the United Nations as the vehicle for helping the world move in this direction. "My vision of a new world order foresees a United Nations with a revitalized peacekeeping function," Bush explained in February 1991 to the Economic Club of New York. While the United Nations performed its economic and social functions well, it had fallen short on the political front due to cold war animosities that crystallized over the U.S.-Soviet conflict. The changing nature of the Soviet Union during his administration, Bush believed, opened the doors for cooperation and, hence, a strengthened political and peacekeeping function for the United Nations. He believed, as he stated to a joint session of Congress in 1991, that the new world order was "a world where the United Nations, freed from cold war stalemate, is poised to fulfill the historic vision of its founders. A world in which freedom and respect for human rights find a home among all nations." This multilateral vision, however, did not include the sacrifice of U.S. sovereignty. Bush was clear that he would "not give one ounce of our sovereignty."

While Bush was clear in his own mind regarding his world view and goals, he encountered the same problems with the press that he had in presenting his domestic policy to the public. On taking office, Bush had announced a ninety-day foreign policy review to be conducted by the National Security Council. As the weeks went by, however, the press became anxious for action.

The process, therefore, became the story. With the fast-changing world scene, such as the Soviet withdrawal from Afghanistan in February 1989 and the Soviet announcement of troop cuts in December 1988, the press started to portray the United States as lacking initiative and being bogged down. The failure of Bush to get Republican senator John Tower of Texas confirmed as secretary of defense in March 1989 also was taken as a signal of a foreign policy in disarray.

At a news conference on February 21, 1989, Bush was faced with the accusation that he did not have a foreign policy and that, specifically, he was allowing the Soviets to take the initiative in world affairs. Bush parried by stating, "We have a foreign policy." He outlined the administration's review process but offered no real specifics, promising that they would be coming in due time.

In March, the press, sensing that Bush was on the defensive, continued to pursue the issue, claiming that the administration was adrift and even in a malaise. In a news conference on March 7, Bush brushed aside the stated concerns, claiming that the administration was moving ahead, tackling various domestic and foreign issues. He emphasized, however, that he would not be railroaded into putting forth dramatic foreign policy initiatives.

Despite the criticism, the foreign policy review continued, and eventually the outlines of the administration's positions began to unfold. In his speech on April 17, 1989, at Hamtramck, Michigan, Bush unveiled an assistance program to help further Polish reforms; at Texas A&M University the next month, Bush outlined his broad approach to dealing with the Soviet Union. And, later that month, at the NATO summit, Bush gave his first concrete proposal: the limiting of conventional forces in Europe and accelerating the timetable to achieve an agreement on conventional forces in Europe.

In a commencement address at Oklahoma State University in May 1990, Bush coined a phrase that was little noticed but had deep ramifications for U.S. policy and, indeed, should help identify his presidency. He dubbed the times as the "age of freedom," an apt phrase to describe the yearning for freedom and democracy that had been unleashed throughout the world. He summed up the historic year: "The cry for freedom—in Eastern Europe, in South Africa, right here in our precious hemisphere to our south—was heard around the world in the Revolution of 1989."

The theme of freedom was woven throughout the various commencement addresses the president presented in the spring of 1990. At the University of Texas he proclaimed, "Today, as perhaps never before in history, freedom is prevailing throughout the world because freedom works. . . . And it is because of the indomitable spirit of man that the day of the dictator is over." Bush had actually struck this theme even earlier in his administration. In his inaugural address he stated, "For in man's heart, if not in fact, the day of the dictator is over. The totalitarian era is passing, its old ideas blown away like leaves from an ancient, lifeless tree." And, in a news conference in December 1989 reflecting on the changes throughout the world, Bush stated, "I think democracy and freedom are on the move around the world."

During Bush's term, the Soviet Union imploded, Eastern Europe moved toward freedom, U.S. forces helped set Panama on the course of democracy with the capture of Manuel Noriega, and U.S. resolve helped democratic forces win the election in Nicaragua that displaced the leftist Sandinista forces in 1990. Also on Bush's watch, U.S. support thwarted an antidemocratic coup in the Philippines, apartheid met its end in South Africa, and Iraq's aggression against Kuwait was turned back.

Bush viewed these developments as the result of U.S. policy and the beacon of freedom that the United States held out to the rest of the world. He also believed that continued growth of freedom depended on the role of the United States. He took every opportunity to talk about the march of freedom and democracy and the role of the United States. Bush realized that a certain force had been unleashed and that there was no stemming the tide. The goal was to manage and shepherd the change to achieve peaceful and positive outcomes.

During his term in office the world witnessed the greatest spread of freedom since the end of the colonial period in post–World War II Africa. This march toward national freedom was matched by the simultaneous movement toward democracy, and this move, while imperfect, was unparalleled in world history as so many nations started to remove the shackles of authoritarian rule. The list of achievements extends beyond the spread of freedom and democracy: the Middle East peace talks held in Madrid, which joined Israel and all its Arab neighbors in face-to-face talks for the first time; the repeal of the United Nations resolution equating Zionism with racism; the signing of the Strategic Arms Reduction Treaty (START), which cut in half the most dangerous Soviet long-range nuclear warheads; the first ever international drug summit, in Cartagena, Colombia; an increase of 152 percent in funds—from $304 million to $768 million—for the international fight against drugs; and the negotiations that led to the North American Free Trade Agreement (NAFTA), passed by Congress in 1993, which enhanced economic trade and cooperation with Mexico and Canada.

Of all his roles, Bush valued most his role as commander in chief. He regarded it as the most important function of any president, given the impact the role has on the lives of Americans and people around the world. Bush's experience in the military helped color his perspective on it and the military decision-making process. Foremost, the decision to send troops into combat is one that only the president can make. Bush did so on three occasions: the Panama action in 1989, the Gulf War, and the humanitarian mission in Somalia in 1992. Bush readily admits that the "toughest decision a president makes is when he sends someone's son or daughter into battle." This sense of responsibility was reinforced in Bush's mind by his own near death after being shot down over the Pacific. "I saw men die before my own eyes," he told a conference audience at the Bush Library Center in October 2003. "Like everyone else who experienced death this close up, I'm sure that experience will stay with me until the day I die."

As president, therefore, Bush was always sensitive about his responsibility of sending someone's loved one off to battle. When he did so, he worried a great deal. Outside of this emotional stress and concern over sending troops into battle, there were two other things that guided Bush as commander in chief: he made sure he was not an "armchair general" and he believed in clearly defining a mission. He allowed his generals to draw up the plans and run the wars. In this regard, he gave his military commanders what they needed. He believed in his generals' ability to define and request the resources they required to accomplish the mission. He was cognizant of the fact that the military needed to feel secure in itself, and if this meant providing reassurance beyond what one would normally think was required, Bush would do so. Bush in no way wanted to appear as not being supportive of the military. He provided what the military needed to accomplish its goal. For the humanitarian mission in Somalia, Gen. Colin Powell stated he would need 28,000 troops to meet the objective. Bush authorized the request without question. "You got it," was Bush's immediate response when Powell gave the number.

Bush realized that his support would help the military bounce out of the lingering "Vietnam syndrome," in which it felt it had been shortchanged by the country's political leadership. In this regard, Bush also made it clear what the military mission would be in each instance. Bush was adamant that U.S. forces should always have the means necessary to meet the task and that a clear and viable strategy be in place. In his address at West Point in 1993, Bush stated that "in every case involving the use of force, it will be essential to have a clear and achievable mission, a realistic plan for accomplishing the mission, and criteria no less realistic for withdrawing U.S. forces once the mission is complete." Bush was personally averse to and feared "mission creep," that is, he strongly believed in setting a mission and adhering to it. In this way the military had confidence in proceeding and also realized when its responsibilities would be at an end.

While Bush was clear in his determination regarding commitment of forces and in defining a mission, he, like other presidents, had the dilemma of actually defining what the national interest was in any particular case. Every state has the dilemma of defining its national interest in the gray areas, not just in the black-and-white situation of an attack on its territory. A student of the Bush School of Government and Public Service once asked Bush under what circumstances a president should put U.S. forces in harm's way. Bush unhesitatingly stated that it could be done when the "national interest" was at stake. On further reflection, Bush readily admitted the difficulty of defining this concept, stating that, in the final analysis, it was a subjective decision. This is the crux of leadership: the ability to make the right choices. More importantly, it is the ability to make the right choices in the face of competing interests and pressures. Every president faces this challenge.

Personal Diplomacy

Bush tackled foreign policy with relish. His enthusiasm was driven, in part, by the personal contacts and friendships he had formed over the years. As in domestic policy, Bush relied on the personal approach to allay fears, persuade the doubting, and build bonds. Reading a briefing paper or discussing an issue with Scowcroft, Bush, struck by a particular point that needed clarification, would reach for the telephone to seek out the information or get an explanation directly from the particular foreign leader involved. Much of his telephone diplomacy, therefore, was self-initiated. This habit was a continuation of how he conducted himself during his tenure at the United Nations. During those days, Bush tended to wander the halls of the world organization, talking and chatting with any ambassadors or other representatives that he would come across. As president, he substituted the telephone for his wanderings.

This habit had built up a reservoir of foreign personal contacts and relationships as Bush moved through the U.S. bureaucracy in various capacities. Thus, once he became president, Bush was already acquainted with many world leaders and found it easy to interact with them. His first address to the United Nations General Assembly in September 1989 underscored his breadth of foreign contacts. Seated in the audience were a number of officials with whom he had established friendships during his days at the world body. These included representatives from Mongolia, Honduras, Madagascar, Monaco, and Venezuela as well as Secretary-General Javier Perez de Cuellar of Peru, who had been his country's United Nations representative during that period. In addition, Bush recognized a number of foreign ministers and members of the world body's Secretariat.

The telephone was an easy yet important part of Bush's diplomatic tool kit. It not only served to reassure individual world leaders with the sense that they were part of any presidential decision making but also was a source of information for Bush. He used this tool effectively in the weeks before his summit with Gorbachev in Malta. He made telephone calls to Mitterrand, Mulroney, Kohl, Thatcher, and Prime Minister Giulio Andreotti of Italy. There was concern that the United States would use the summit to negotiate the future of Europe at the expense of the European states. Touching base with all of these leaders helped to solidify European confidence in the leadership of the United States during those uncertain times of Soviet change.

Telephone diplomacy was a two-way street: not only did Bush use it to lobby and inform his foreign counterparts but it also proved useful as a medium for up-to-date briefings by foreign leaders on various issues. When Gorbachev stopped in Canada en route to the United States, Bush got an update from Prime Minister Mulroney. Mulroney detailed Gorbachev's plans and also offered his own recommendations. "It was very, very helpful," Bush says of the exchange.

In his relations with foreign leaders, Bush sought to identify their interests and see if he could mesh them with U.S. goals. He thus played on the common bonds that would help establish a close personal relationship that could then translate into trust and cooperation in areas of mutual concern. This practice was relatively successful, and he was able to establish good personal and working relations with many world leaders, such as Kohl, Gorbachev, Mulroney, Major, and President Hosni Mubarak of Egypt.

Two world leaders whom Bush admires were Gorbachev and Deng Xiaoping. "Gorbachev was a leader because he changed the direction of his country with his policies of glasnost and perestroika," says Bush. "Deng Xiaoping singlehandedly deserves credit for moving China in the direction of economic reform. History will remember both of them. Gorbachev, in particular, has not been given the full credit that he deserves." One leader with whom Bush was unable to establish a close rapport was British prime minister Margaret Thatcher. "I admired Thatcher but I was not very close to her," Bush recalls. "She brought about enormous change to the British political system, leading a progressively conservative and successful agenda. Overall, I would say she was a strong and admired leader." Thatcher had enjoyed a close relationship with Ronald Reagan. This, undoubtedly, affected Thatcher's and Bush's respective views of each other. "I think Thatcher had a problem with me because I wanted to speak for myself," Bush recalls. "She and President Reagan had a very close relationship and she often spoke for him at NATO meetings. At my first NATO meeting, I think it took her aback that I was going to make my own remarks." Thatcher perhaps missed the kindred spirit of Reagan, while Bush, in an effort not to be viewed as Reagan's understudy, remained somewhat aloof. Reagan and Thatcher also had a knack for speaking their minds—as witnessed by Reagan's characterization of the Soviet Union as an "evil empire"—which ran counter to Bush's more diplomatic and nuanced approach. In addition, Bush's relationship with Mitterrand was good but mostly formal. The strain in their relationship was the issue of German unification, which was also an issue for Thatcher. Both Mitterrand and Thatcher favored a "go-slow" approach on the issue, attributable to the political differences and military clashes Britain and France had had with a powerful Germany. Bush, however, favored a more rapid approach and worked closely with Kohl, probably fueling unwarranted suspicions among the French and British regarding the United States–German cooperation and the role of a reunited Germany in Europe.

Bush's standard efforts to limit the trappings of office extended to his interactions with various leaders. He sought to deal with them in casual settings that provided a more friendly atmosphere, one that would help break down barriers and build trust and understanding. "It is hard in foreign policy to build a relationship if there is no personal trust," Bush states. When Russian president Boris Yeltsin visited the White House in June 1992, the two leaders shed their suit jackets and toured the grounds in shirt sleeves. At Camp David, visitors were usually treated to a golf cart ride, with the president at the wheel. When Kohl visited the presidential retreat in the winter of 1990, the two men bundled up against the cold with heavy coats and hats. The two then took a stroll through the grounds, aides and security in tow. One stretch of the path is a little steep and gave the robust chancellor a bit more of a challenge. In his honor, Bush dubbed that particular stretch of the path the "Helmut Kohl Hill."

A certain fondness and friendship developed between Bush and Gorbachev that extends beyond their tenures as leaders of their respective states. Gorbachev reciprocated these feelings of friendship. He and Bush worked together at a crucial time in world history and it was with Bush that Gorbachev, at the Malta Summit in December 1989, declared that their two nations no longer considered each other enemies. In the time since their respective departures from office, the friendship has continued and grown. They have made joint appearances, and Gorbachev has been presented the George Bush Award for Excellence in Public Service in recognition of his role in bringing reform to the Soviet bloc and furthering peace and understanding in Europe. Speaking at Bush's eightieth birthday celebration in Houston in 2004, Gorbachev rated Bush "as an outstanding statesman and also as a wonderful person, as an authentic person." He then highlighted the particular strength of character that Bush brought to the arena of international diplomacy. "Of all my counterparts on the world arena, George Bush was the best," Gorbachev continued. "He was a reliable partner; he had balanced judgment, and he had decency. He had qualities that were and are critical to trust, and trust is what makes it possible to solve any international problem."

It was this relationship of trust that helped the two sides handle the slow political demise of the Soviet Union. Therefore, it was no surprise that Gorbachev was very much in mind in the final days of the Soviet Union. The day the political bonds of the union broke, Scowcroft was sitting back in his chair in his West Wing office, his shoulders drooping, his chin resting in his hands. It was very quiet that Christmas night, 1991, in the West Wing, the outside darkness only reinforcing the stillness and the quiet, contemplative mood in which he found himself.

Bush was scheduled to address the nation at 9:00 P.M. to announce U.S. recognition of the independence of twelve former Soviet republics and the establishment of diplomatic relations with six of them, with diplomatic ties with the remaining six pending until certain goals were met.

Bush, who was spending Christmas at Camp David, returned to the White House at 7:25 P.M. Scowcroft had arrived at his office a little past 8:00 P.M., at which time an aide joined him and they reviewed the day's events before Scowcroft fell into his introspection. He finally broke his contemplation and, lifting his chin from his hands, he summarized for his aide in a quiet voice the day's events as "historic." And historic they were.

At noon Gorbachev had resigned, formally putting an end to the Soviet Union, the cold war, and his own political career, thus setting the stage for the president's speech. Earlier, at 10:00 A.M., he had called Bush to inform him of his intended resignation. And about a half hour before the president's speech, a letter from Gorbachev via the Soviet embassy arrived in the Situation Room. It spoke of Gorbachev's desire to keep the path of reform going and the need for the United States to continue the partnership with his successors. He sent regards to the president and Barbara from himself and his wife Raisa.

It undoubtedly was an emotional and frustrating time for Gorbachev. The man who had set in motion the process of Soviet reform was now being superseded by that very success. Ironically, even as the reforms were gaining popularity over the years, Gorbachev himself was losing popular support.

During Gorbachev's visit to Washington in May 1990, Bush had invited him to Camp David. As Marine One glided smoothly over the Maryland suburbs for the half-hour ride, Gorbachev leaned forward in his seat, peering intently out the window. Below him rows of single family homes stretched almost endlessly. Finally, Gorbachev could not contain himself.

"There are many large homes down there," he stated in amazement.

The president leaned over to him, saying, "These are what we here call suburbs," Bush stated.

Gorbachev looked up at the president. "How many families live in each one?" he asked.

The president realized the learning curve he was dealing with. A home in suburbia is something to which almost every American family aspires, but the size of the homes Gorbachev saw from the air was positively alien to the Soviet culture.

"One," the president responded.

"You mean one family in a house that big?!" shot back Gorbachev before the president could continue.

"Yes," Bush stated, and once again, before he could continue, Gorbachev volleyed another question.

"How can one family afford such a big house?" asked Gorbachev, incredulous at what Bush had told him.

Bush then launched into an explanation of the house financing system, sounding more like a real estate agent or banker than president. "Well," the president started, "people save money to make a down payment. They then qualify for a loan and go to a bank."

Gorbachev listened politely, but it was doubtful he was fully grasping what the president was trying to explain. The president, however, continued, intent on explaining the whole process. "They then get a mortgage," Bush stated, "and pay so much per month over twenty to thirty years. At the end of the payment period, the people own their house."

Gorbachev just blinked and nodded. He looked out the window, amazed and thoughtful, the realization possibly sinking in regarding the wonderful world that had developed outside the Soviet system.

It was with such wonderment that Scowcroft himself now sat, recalling the decades-long conflict between the United States and the Soviet Union. It had marked his whole adult life and the lives of those who had come to steward U.S. foreign policy since World War II. For them, the relationship had a permanence; it was a fixture of everyday life, and, as such, it was something that was taken for granted. Decisions were made, options weighed, and strategy formulated based on the expected actions of Moscow. The Korea conflict, the Berlin airlift, the Cuban missile crisis, Vietnam, the development of sophisticated weapons, and the creation of NATO and other alliances all hinged on U.S. attempts to stymie the spread of Soviet influence. Now, that world had dissipated. Intellectually, Scowcroft could not conceive of the Soviet collapse without a shot being fired, a development that only sharpened his amazement and the historic nature of the day.

Scowcroft gathered up his papers. It was nearly time for the president's address, and he wanted to spend some time with him before the speech. His aide walked with him, and as they crossed the West Wing Lobby, they bantered about the dramatic changes they had come to witness. As they passed into the corridor off the Roosevelt Room, his aide peeled off toward the Press Office, while Scowcroft headed straight toward the Oval Office. At that moment, his aide congratulated him on the success of the day and his management of the country's foreign policy during this historic time.

Scowcroft whirled around and, with a smile and in mock shock, stated, "For what? For standing back and watching everything unfold around us?"

U.S. Policy toward the Soviet Union

In the waning days of the Soviet Union, many Americans considered U.S. policy toward Moscow to be a mixture of happenstance, wishful thinking, and reaction to events beyond the control of the United States.

The underlying reality, however, was quite different. U.S. policy was an amalgam formed by historical forces and personal experiences. Moreover, it was the product of leaders who understood the dynamics of the international system and diplomacy and who were able to help guide events in an almost imperceptible fashion. Bush's early interactions with Gorbachev, such as their initial meeting in 1985 and the meeting on Governors Island with President Reagan in 1988, gave him insights and a belief that the United States had an opportunity to influence change in the Soviet Union. These experiences gave him a certain advantage over others, such as Baker and Scowcroft, in viewing events in a more positive light. Of the latter two, Scowcroft was more negative and cautious while Baker was much more optimistic about events in the Soviet Union. Bush held the belief that the Soviet Union wanted change and was changing. This view was instrumental in shaping the administration's strategy toward the Soviet Union.

During his speech at Texas A&M University in May 1989, Bush laid down the five thresholds the Soviet Union needed to cross in order to establish a better working relationship with the West. They were: (1) reduction of Soviet forces; (2) self-determination for Eastern and Central Europe; (3) working with the West for diplomatic solutions to regional disputes; (4) permitting pluralism and protecting human rights at home; and finally, (5) working with the West to solve global problems, such as dangers to the environment and the international drug threat. By the time of Gorbachev's resignation, these goals had been mostly met or, as in the case of the last point, were in the process of being addressed by the emerging Russian state.

The collapse of the Soviet Union and the end of the cold war cannot be ascribed to any single act or administration. Bush would be the first to admit this. The U.S. policy of containment, starting with President Truman, reaching a horrifying apex with the Cuban missile crisis under President Kennedy, and pushing the Soviets to extremes during Reagan's military buildups against the "evil empire," spanned decades and included both Democratic and Republican administrations. American military strength and the willingness to commit forces and resources to the decades-long struggle led to the eventual collapse of the Soviet Union. Bush's expertise guided the cold war to a peaceful end, with minimal loss of life and without a direct confrontation. Bush himself sloughs off any credit.

"A lot of tumultuous history-making events took place during my four years," Bush readily admits. But just as quickly, he brushes off claims of responsibility. "I'm not saying we did it, but the cold war ended, the Soviet Union actually came apart at the seams, the Berlin Wall came down, and Germany was unified. Big major things happened, but it's more with gratitude in my heart that I was lucky to be there. We had a superb team. All these people came together as a team to cope with, manage, and solve some huge international problems."

The central figure on this team was Jim Baker. Baker and Bush had established a strong personal relationship before Bush entered politics. Their strong ties were formed by a mutual love of politics and by their competitive natures, as seen by their winning doubles partnership in tennis at the Houston Country Club. George and Barbara gave emotional support at the time when Baker's first wife, Mary Stuart, was dying of cancer. And Bush introduced Baker to the world of politics when Bush ran unsuccessfully for the Senate in 1970 and Baker coordinated the campaign in Harris County, which encompasses Houston. From these various roots sprung a strong and lasting bond. Baker admired Bush for his competitive spirit, for being a person who strove to succeed in everything that he tried, and for his overall character. "He is a man whose word was good," Baker explains. "He is the most kind and considerate man I have known and a man who had the most profound impact on my life." For Bush, Baker is someone whom he can trust without question. Barbara Bush shares in her husband's high regard for Baker. "I adore him," is her simple summation of how she views Baker. While Baker ran the State Department, his close association with Bush guaranteed him access to and a hearing by Bush.

At the White House itself, Bush had Brent Scowcroft. As the president's national security adviser, first to Gerald Ford and then to Bush, Scowcroft had witnessed and dealt with many international issues. But none may have been as dramatic and historic as the impending demise of the Soviet Union. As the president's foreign policy adviser, Scowcroft had formed a close personal working relationship with Bush, and foreign policy was what both sparked and maintained that relationship.

At first sight, the two seem an unlikely pair. Bush stands tall, with an athletic body, while Scowcroft is diminutive, with a thin, frail build. Scowcroft does not share Bush's patrician background from the Northeast. He is a Mormon from Utah who went to West Point. His career as a fighter pilot was derailed when he injured his back in an airplane crash during a practice mission. In the field of international politics, Scowcroft is a long-term practitioner with an intellectual bent and was content to play a background role, whereas Bush, an affable politician, was willing to enter the public limelight. After Bush first met Scowcroft, he readily came to respect his work ethic and knowledge of the issues. During Bush's tenure as president, the friendship deepened. The two men spent much time together in person and on the telephone. Bush would often invite Scowcroft, who tended to work late in the office, to dinner at the residence. He would also telephone Scowcroft in the morning and at night regarding news stories and other matters related to foreign affairs.

Both men, however, shared some similarities. Close in age, they witnessed the horrors of World War II and the tensions of the cold war. As an assistant air attaché in Belgrade, Scowcroft experienced the potential explosiveness of nationalism. Through their service in and outside government, both men came to appreciate the importance of a strong defense and good planning in managing U.S. policy. As a result, whether trolling for fish while at Kennebunkport, in the many briefings in the Oval Office, or in quiet dinners in the president's private quarters, Scowcroft and Bush discussed, philosophized, and planned the U.S. role in the world. Scowcroft was perfect for the role the president envisaged for his national security adviser. He wanted someone who would be well versed in foreign affairs and who would see himself as an honest broker of the policy process, without a personal agenda. The national security adviser also needed to be someone with whom the president would feel comfortable. "He was the ideal head of the National Security Council," Bush claims, calling Scowcroft "an honest broker, bringing to the president opinions of various departments and intelligence provided by the CIA and then offering the president, quietly, advice."

In August 1990 one particular discussion in Kennebunkport between the two men led to a major turning point in both U.S. policy and in Bush's hope for a new world order based on peace and cooperation. Saddam Hussein had just invaded Kuwait. The United States was faced with the challenge of devising a strategy to roll back the invasion, but, equally important, Bush realized the opportunity that was being provided to revamp the world. The day started as any other for Bush—early to rise and a flurry of calls and memos and then off to do some fishing. Scowcroft joined Bush on the *Fidelity* as the president guided the craft out of the cove at Walker's Point and out into the open ocean. The engines roared as the boat began to pick up speed, eventually gliding from wave to wave. The thud of the waves added to the deafening roar, jolting Scowcroft's body but releasing a new burst of energy in Bush, who enjoyed the thrill of the boat's speed. Racing alongside, the Secret Service craft tried to keep pace. Just as suddenly, Bush brought *Fidelity* to a stop, and as the boat bobbed uncontrollably at first and then settled into a gentle rock, the two men began to fish.

Bush, tossing a graceful left-hand cast, simultaneously carried on the conversation. For Scowcroft, fishing was more a duty than a pleasure. He did it slowly and consciously, as if not to break his trend of thought.

For four hours they fished and trolled for bluefish without a nibble. The line cut easily through the summer waves, an occasional jolt of the boat falsely suggesting a bite. But nothing was at the end of the line. The minutes turned to hours. The growing frustration with the excursion, however, was overcome by the evolving conversation. Scowcroft's attention to his line turned mechanical; he was engrossed in the discussion and bluefish were not part of his agenda. The president continued for a time with his usual intensity. Eventually, Bush's interest waned as he began to realize that this may be an unsuccessful day on the boat. He became fully engaged in conversation.

The lack of success at fishing helped shape the contemplative mood since there were no distractions. The conversation was free flowing, philosophical at some points and pragmatic at others as both men recognized the opportunities the changing world was offering. That change was occurring was indisputable to both of them; the challenge, as Scowcroft saw it, was how to shepherd that change and what steps the United States needed to take. Both Bush and Scowcroft saw that the relationship between the United States and the Soviet Union was changing, rather quickly and dramatically, from enmity to one of cooperation. What visibly brought this to mind and, indeed, helped stimulate the discussion was the Soviet Union's condemnation of Iraq earlier in the month. This was the first time since World War II that both the United States and the Soviet Union were on the same side of a conflict. Based on this development, the president surmised that the United Nations could probably now operate as envisioned at its creation. If the United States and the Soviet Union could reach agreement and continue to cooperate, then the chances for ending world conflict could be enhanced. Bush formally unveiled his thoughts on the new world order the next month in a speech to a joint session of Congress.

Scowcroft provided intellectual and analytical support for the president. Bush's interest in foreign policy always had him leaning forward, questioning and examining. It was Bush who constantly pushed Scowcroft to be bold on ideas and to push forward. It was the president's initiative, for instance, that helped the United States push forward on German unification and, indeed, to stay ahead of events. Scowcroft provided the caution and intellectual grounding. Together, they balanced each other and made a powerful combination.

Under Bush and Scowcroft's tutelage, the U.S. approach to the Soviet Union had taken an intellectual and pragmatic turn. Bush sought to make his mark as a new administration and not be viewed as a continuation of the Reagan era. At the same time, Bush realized the changing nature of the international environment; he wanted to make sure that there was a full understanding of the changes taking place and that the United States was positioned to take advantage of those changes.

Since World War II, U.S. policy had been based on containment. The policy had been geared toward maintaining a strong defense and responding assertively to any Soviet actions. The two mainstays of this policy were arms control and dealing with the weak links in the Soviet chain. Thus, throughout the post–World War II decades, the U.S. relationship with Moscow focused

on limiting and controlling the development of the respective nuclear arse-
nals. In Scowcroft's view, this focus on military rather than political issues was
a derailment of what the cold war was all about. The cold war was a political
conflict; it revolved around ideology and the makeup of the Soviet Union and
what it stood for. He considered it important to return to this concept and to
challenge the Soviet Union on political grounds. Gorbachev was espousing
glasnost and perestroika, which provided the United States with the opportunity to address this political situation. Until then, on the political front,
the focus was on dealing with the problem states in the Soviet sphere, such as
Yugoslavia and Romania, in an effort to keep Moscow off balance.

With the start of the Bush administration, steps were taken to move beyond this policy. Scowcroft put a greater emphasis on the political front. He
shifted the focus to states, such as Poland, that were flexing their political
muscle by seeking internal reforms that, if carried out, would lead to a break
from the Soviet grip. Solidarity, the unsanctioned labor union, was at the
forefront of the Polish reform effort under the leadership of Lech Walesa.
Through its tireless efforts it was able to chip away at the government's armor,
leading eventually to discussions for Solidarity to participate in the political
process. Success was realized in early April 1989, when Solidarity became part
of Poland's political system by being allowed to stand candidates for the Polish parliament. This growing reform in Poland prompted Bush to give his
Hamtramck speech, rewarding the Polish steps by offering various forms of
assistance. After Poland, Hungary, with its growing reform movement, and
Czechoslovakia, its movement spearheaded by dissident playwright Vaclav
Havel, were pushing against their autocratic governments.

Realizing that the Soviet Union was undergoing changes, as witnessed
by Gorbachev's policies of glasnost and perestroika, the administration now
had a policy that focused on helping to facilitate and take advantage of those
changes. Scowcroft tasked an interagency review of U.S. policy toward the
Soviet Union to formulate an approach taking into consideration this philosophical shift. The report that was produced was, according to Scowcroft,
"abysmal." Reflecting the president's disappointment, Scowcroft lamented the
lack of originality. The review reflected the traditional interests and approaches
of the foreign policy bureaucracies and failed to provide any understanding
of the changing world. Scowcroft believed it was important to think of how
the world would evolve over the next twenty years and how the United States

should be positioned so as to influence the changes. Frustrated, Scowcroft brought the entire review process into the White House. He tasked his NSC staffer, Condoleezza Rice, to draft the new strategy based on the ideas and goals that he had formulated. This work produced a blueprint for dealing with the Soviet Union as it began tottering under Gorbachev's reform policies. This was the fruition of a process that had begun during the Christmas holidays in 1988, when, as president-elect, Bush was given use of Camp David by Reagan. During those days, Scowcroft and Bush took long walks around the perimeter of the camp, discussing in an unstructured fashion the state of the world and how the NSC system should be set up. It was the beginning of the bond that soon developed between the two men and established the pattern for their philosophical discussions about the state of the world and the U.S. role. In May 1989 during a commencement address at Texas A&M University, Bush voiced many of the ideas that came forth from these strategy review sessions. While western policy had been characterized by containment since World War II, Bush now saw a new era of "beyond containment" in which the Soviet Union could become an integral part of the international community. "In sum, the United States now has as its goal much more than simply containing Soviet expansionism," Bush stated. "We seek the integration of the Soviet Union into the community of nations. . . . Western policies must encourage the evolution of the Soviet Union toward an open society."

However, even within the administration there were differences of opinion on the strategy that should be pursued regarding the possible breakup of the Soviet Union. Overall, U.S. policy looked toward Moscow and the republics to work out their relationships. The State Department's view was shaped by an inordinate focus on Russia. The focus on Russia did have some merit on the face of it. Russia, after all, is a big country that, even in the wake of the dissolution of the Soviet Union, would continue to wield considerable influence. And, at the time, there was little room for argument. Baker had established a close working relationship with the Soviet foreign minister, Eduard Shevardnadze, and through his tireless diplomacy had helped to bring Moscow to play an important and positive role in international affairs.

Scowcroft's views closely mirrored those of the president. Scowcroft saw the need for working closely with Gorbachev, because he, like Baker, recognized the fact that the West was achieving a great deal thanks to Gorbachev's reforms. Privately, Scowcroft, while he was hoping for the breakup of the Soviet Union, did not intellectually believe that it would really happen. He claims that no one at that time, including himself, could have foreseen that Gorbachev would bring an end to the Soviet Union in so quick and peaceful a manner.

An overall caution marked Scowcroft. Although sympathetic, he was reluctant to push the national cause of the individual Soviet republics too much to the front, fearing that it could alienate Gorbachev without appreciably helping the republics. This reluctance characterized his approach to the Baltics, when at first he did not want to have the Baltic leaders visit the White House. As a result, Scowcroft at times appeared to vacillate, pushing for greater dealings with the republics while at the same time supporting Gorbachev. Scowcroft feared a possible Soviet crackdown if the pace of change was too rapid.

Secretary of Defense Cheney was probably the strongest advocate of support for the republics. It was Cheney who sponsored the first visit of a high-level representative of independent Ukraine, the most politically, economically, and militarily important former Soviet republic after Russia, when Defense Minister Konstantyn Morozov visited Washington in April 1992 for a round of consultations at the Pentagon and the White House. At the Pentagon, Morozov was greeted with full military honors, and Cheney hosted a dinner for him at Blair House. The Ukrainians themselves realized the support that the Defense Department provided Kiev and often commented favorably about Cheney and his subordinates.

A common denominator, however, was that U.S. policy makers realized that the Soviet Union the world had known was not going to last. Furthermore, while the Soviet Union was undergoing vast political changes, no one knew where these changes would ultimately lead. The question the United States faced was what would emerge in its place. At that time it appeared that some new union would replace it, and the issue at hand was how to manage the changes. It was natural, therefore, to be supportive of Gorbachev since he represented the forces of reform and had a proven track record of cooperation with the West. Over time it was becoming evident that Gorbachev, however, was growing politically weaker at home.

The End of the Soviet Union

In July 1991 Bush visited Moscow, where he and Gorbachev signed the START treaty. The atmosphere of the signing ceremony contrasted with the mood in the streets. The signing took place in the ornate St. Vladimir's Hall in the

Kremlin, which one reached by a long flight of red-carpeted stairs. At the top
of the stairs one was greeted by a huge painting of Lenin haranguing a crowd.
The signing desk was white with gold trim, as were the two podiums for the
presidents. The signing pens were made from the metal of an SS-20 and a
Pershing II missile that had been banned under the INF Treaty (Intermediate-
Range Nuclear Forces Treaty, signed in 1987). The two presidents pocketed
the pens after the signing. While those present were impressed by the historic
nature of the event and the increased cooperation that the West could come
to expect from Gorbachev, the people in the street were thinking differently.

In the streets of Moscow, White House staff in discussions with vendors
and others heard the Russian people expressing their support of Boris Yeltsin,
who was emerging as Gorbachev's political competitor. People were coming
to speak about the inequalities of life they were experiencing.

Scowcroft believed that Boris Yeltsin, who had been elected president of
the Russian republic in June 1991, was a demagogue. Yeltsin, however, helped
bring a peaceful dissolution to the Soviet Union and established a good working relationship with the United States and the West. Scowcroft complained
after their first meeting in September 1990 in his West Wing office that Yeltsin
spoke so much that he did not seem to stop to take a breath or let Scowcroft
get a word in edgewise. What impressed people most about Yeltsin was that
Yeltsin was most impressed with himself. As a result of this and the rumors of
his drinking, it became very difficult to take Yeltsin seriously. The great fear
was that the conflict between Gorbachev and Yeltsin was a struggle for power,
one that, if Yeltsin won, would be a threat to the peaceful reform that Gorbachev seemed to be riding. As a result, there was a policy rationale, right or
wrong at the time, behind the U.S. support of Gorbachev. The cautious view
of Yeltsin did not change much even after the failed coup against Gorbachev
and the increasing realization that Gorbachev was losing power.

However, paralleling this support of Gorbachev was the hesitancy to get
directly involved in Soviet affairs. For one superpower to support the dis-
mantlement of another could only create a backlash and lead to direct political conflict. This, to a great extent, influenced Washington's "go slow and
let events unfold" policy toward the recognition of Baltic independence.
Washington looked toward Moscow to acknowledge the Baltic states' independence; that acknowledgment would likely guarantee the survival of those
resurgent nations. In the same way, the moment and sequence of recognition

of Ukraine and the other republics was eventually designed to avoid pushing events and building resentments in Moscow that could backfire against the United States.

But there were also concrete reasons for supporting Gorbachev and his policies. Under Gorbachev, the two Germanies were moving toward unification, arms control was proceeding, and the Soviet Union had not blocked the U.S. military action against Saddam Hussein. Furthermore, Gorbachev was experiencing reactionary pressures against his more liberal policies. He undertook a number of shifts, such as a change in economic policy, at the end of 1990 to quell these criticisms. But his actions underlined the fragility of the Soviet reform process and the stake that the West had in dealing with and supporting him. Indeed, if the Soviet Union did fall apart, there was concern that ethnic strife could erupt and that the status of the nuclear weapons would be jeopardized, leading to the proliferation of weapons and the possibility of them getting into the hands of terrorists. The Soviet breakup threatened not only to unleash Russia's vast store of nuclear weapons but also to create three new nuclear states—Belarus, Kazakhstan, and Ukraine. Therefore, to many Washington policy makers, at a minimum, the continuation of some form of union was appealing while, at a maximum, a slow pace of change was favored.

Late at night on August 18, 1991, many of these concerns intensified as an anti-Gorbachev coup occurred, with the plotters announcing that Gorbachev had resigned due to health reasons. Yeltsin leapt to the forefront in opposition to the coup plotters. One of the motivating factors for the military and KGB coup plotters was the new union treaty, which they believed would weaken their authority since it could lead to a decentralization of power from Moscow toward the constituent republics. Bush was vacationing in Kennebunkport at the time of the coup. The next morning, August 19, 1991, Bush held a news conference at which he called the coup an "extra-constitutional" move and a "disturbing development." Reflecting the pragmatism of keeping options open and spurred by the possibility that the coup might not be successful, Bush stated at the news conference that the situation in Moscow was still "unfolding" and that "coups can fail."

By the time of the news conference, Scowcroft had already been having doubts about how well the coup was proceeding. It was not until about half past four that morning, that information had been received indicating the type of troop movements that one would associate with an unfolding coup. A former military man himself, Scowcroft felt himself begin to have doubts. The troop movements appeared to be taking place very late after the announcement of Gorbachev's alleged resignation, thus signaling possible disagreement and disarray among the coup plotters. This feeling was increasingly being confirmed by the time Bush was on Air Force One headed for the White House later that Monday, where he would review the Moscow situation before returning to Kennebunkport.

Bush, reflecting the uncertainty of the situation on the ground in Moscow, had sought to tread softly in his news conference comments. For Scowcroft, the concern was that if the coup succeeded, the United States would have to deal with the new Soviet leadership whether or not the United States liked the outcome. There was no doubt in Scowcroft's mind that the success of the coup would be a setback for reform in the Soviet Union, a view he later shared with the press aboard Air Force One.

On Air Force One it was decided that someone should meet with the press pool in the rear of the plane if there were follow-up questions from the news conference; doing so would show the administration's active involvement in tracking the coup. Since Bush had already held a news conference, it was left to Scowcroft to meet with the pool. Scowcroft, already having more doubts about the coup, was more negative about the plotters than the president had been.

At the White House, Bush met with an interagency group in the Roosevelt Room and received an update on the situation. The views expressed around the table continued to shed more doubt on the eventual success of the coup, based on the observation of Soviet troop movements and the unfolding political opposition in Moscow spearheaded by Yeltsin. Eagleburger was representing Baker, who was en route to Washington from a truncated vacation. He tried to lighten the mood by pointing out that there might be a certain benefit with Gorbachev off the scene.

"At least now, Mr. President," huffed Eagleburger, who, due to his heavy smoking habit, habitually seemed to be forcing out his sentences, "you cannot be criticized by political opponents for always siding with Gorbachev."

"No matter what the situation," Bush replied wryly, "there is always political criticism."

After the meeting, the White House released a written statement by the president that was stronger in tone than his comments in Kennebunkport, reflecting the assessment that the coup might not succeed and that support of Yeltsin was important to stave off the coup plotters. Bush condemned the "unconstitutional resort to force" by the coup plotters and termed the coup a "misguided and illegitimate effort" that undermined Soviet law and the will of the Soviet people. The president called for the reaffirmation of the post of Soviet president Gorbachev, thus echoing a demand made by Yeltsin to the coup plotters, and demanded continued reform as well as a "process of peaceful reconciliation between the center and the republics." He also stated that the United States would "not support economic aid programs if adherence to extra-constitutional means" continued. Western allies, such as Britain, were already taking steps to discontinue economic assistance to the Soviet Union. Finally, the statement said that the United States would avoid any steps that could lend "legitimacy or support" to the coup. The coup quickly failed, but it signaled the beginning of the end of the Soviet Union.

Even before the coup attempt, Yeltsin, as president of the Russian republic, was already carrying out policies separate from the other republics and undermining Gorbachev's authority. Yeltsin had his own foreign minister as well as emissaries to foreign states. His successful rallying of the people against the coup plotters only served to enhance his stature and to diminish Gorbachev's, particularly after the failure of the coup.

By October it was becoming increasingly clear that Gorbachev was losing control. Yeltsin was taking greater powers unto himself, including the purse strings. At the Middle East peace conference in Madrid at the end of October, Gorbachev presented himself as a fading figure, yet intent on publicly declaring his importance to the political life of the fast crumbling Soviet Union.

Many events were affecting the way the United States handled the breakdown of the Soviet Union, but the personal relationship that had developed between Bush and Gorbachev was critical in this regard. Gorbachev had always been somewhat of an enigma. His twists and turns in policy always left concerns about his ability to follow through on his stated objectives and about the objectives themselves. His showmanship in announcing grand proposals put the United States on the defensive many times, raising questions about his sincerity and intentions. But over time, Bush grew to appreciate Gorbachev. He said that when he first met Gorbachev in 1985, there was no way that anyone could have predicted the changes Gorbachev would institute. But in 1991 Bush was saying that Gorbachev "just inspires great confidence in you." Bush had established a close personal working relationship with him, so one cannot ignore the fact that he wanted to treat Gorbachev with the dignity and friendship that his assistance over the years warranted. The fact that Bush wanted to follow a logical sequence of events regarding the demise of the Soviet Union helped him fulfill the personal side of the policy as well. Events were moving beyond Gorbachev's control, but at least he could be treated with dignity.

This concern for Gorbachev's dignity was evident by the fact that, on that Christmas Day in 1991, some hours before Bush's address to the nation, the White House issued a statement from the president about Gorbachev: "As he leaves office, I would like to express publicly, and on behalf of the American people, my gratitude to him for years of sustained commitment to world peace and my personal respect for his intellect, vision, and courage."

Bush had managed the U.S. response to the demise of the Soviet empire, brought a unified Germany into NATO, and at the same time had used the support of the crumbling empire in his successful strategy against Saddam Hussein. It was a remarkable feat. In the end he dismissed it by acknowledging the leader of the regime the West had stood in conflict with for so many decades. It was vintage George Bush.

Eight

⟨decorative swash⟩

DEALING WITH CONGRESS

THE SUCCESS of any president's domestic agenda depends on the support of Congress and the initiative a president demonstrates in presenting legislation. The relationship with Capitol Hill underscores a president's negotiating skills and ability to form consensus and reach compromise—essential elements for the success of a legislative agenda. Successful legislative programs also reflect on presidents' skill in fashioning public support for their programs and in parlaying that support into pressure against any opposition in Congress.

Sununu believes that Bush's domestic accomplishments will be judged favorably by history. "George Bush's domestic results and performance [were] more than any other president['s] in the postwar era except for Lyndon Johnson's Great Society legislation," claims Sununu. The former chief of staff continues, "I am absolutely convinced that when history starts to do the scorecard, this president's accomplishments on the domestic side will be seen to be as significant as what he was able to accomplish in leading the free world to respond in exactly the right way to the dissolution and the crumbling in the Soviet Union and to the international changes that he was the leader of during one of the most critical international periods in history."

Bush's initiatives ranged over a wide gamut and included education, the environment, crime, energy, trade, civil rights, child care, agriculture, and others. Much of his legislation was forward looking, breaking new ground, as in the reform of child care. That legislation revolved around the principle of parental choice and provided for the single largest increase in resources for poor families.

During the campaign of 1988, Bush differed with his Democrat opponent, Michael Dukakis, on the issue of child care. Dukakis favored granting funds to child care providers, while Bush advocated tax credits, which gave parents a choice of leaving children with a provider or relatives. The latter approach fit Bush's philosophy of maximizing individual choice and stemming the role of bureaucracy and government in dictating individual choices. After the election, Bush was successful in getting his bill passed.

Other legislative action originating in the White House helped stabilize the savings and loan industry in the wake of its collapse, safeguarded depositors, and helped calm the financial markets. The Immigration Act of 1990 enhanced border enforcement, expanded the number of legal immigrants, and provided for adequate documentation for illegal workers. The HOPE Act—Home Ownership for People Everywhere—helped provide affordable housing. In education, Bush was able to provide the first national education goals when he convened a historic summit of the country's governors in 1989 in Charlottesville, Virginia. Additional measures included the Clean Air Act amendments, which reduce acid rain, smog, and other types of air pollution; the Civil Rights Act of 1990; the Transportation Act of 1991, which provided $151 billion for the repair and construction of the nation's roads, highways, and bridges; the Americans with Disabilities Act (ADA) of 1990; and the balanced budget agreement of 1990. Bush also put through a landmark farm bill in 1990 that was protective of conservation areas. Through that bill and by the creation of fifty-seven new wildlife refuges, Bush designated 500,000 acres as wetlands. He increased the acreage of parks, forests, wildlife refuges, and other public lands by more than 1.5 million acres. Underscoring his own commitment to the environment and recognizing the need to tackle this issue in a concerted and a long-range approach, Bush proposed the creation of a Cabinet-level Department of the Environment.

In the wake of the oil spill caused by the *Exxon Valdez* tanker off the coast of Alaska in March 1989, the administration prosecuted Exxon and championed the legislation that placed liability on tanker operators and instituted the requirement that all new tankers be built with double hulls. In an effort to reduce ocean pollution, Bush provided $400 million per year to major cities such as Los Angeles and New York for secondary sewage treatment.

He also enacted a ten-year moratorium on drilling for oil off the coasts of California, North Carolina, Oregon, and Washington, and in the Florida Everglades and Georges Bank, off the coast of New England. Other initiatives included bans on large-scale driftnet fishing, a ban on ivory imports, and, under the Basel Convention, a ban on the illegal disposal of hazardous wastes in developing countries. In 1992, Bush participated in the Earth Summit in Rio de Janeiro that concluded a framework convention on climate change.

Bush also increased research and development funds for the National Institutes of Health and the National Science Foundation and ensured future space exploration by supporting the International Space Station against congressional opposition. Bush also established the National Space Council in March 1989 and named Vice President Quayle to head it.

During Bush's tenure inflation and interest rates reached their lowest levels in two decades, assistance to local law enforcement organizations was almost tripled, and the active antidrug program cut drug use by 13 percent, including a 27 percent decrease among adolescents.

To these initiatives, Bush would have added numerous others, but they were stymied by Congress. These included efforts for the proposed Family Savings Plan, product liability, crime control, and a comprehensive health care plan. Many of these measures were enacted in subsequent administrations. President George W. Bush's No Child Left Behind Act of 2001 has its basis in the education initiatives of his father's administration. The Roth IRA legislation of the Clinton administration was patterned on the Family Savings Plan.

Bush was heavily involved in pushing this very active domestic agenda. Roger Porter spearheaded the agenda, but he did so in close collaboration with Bush and made sure that he was not out in front of him; he always stayed within the parameters that Bush set. Porter, with an easygoing manner, had a style that dovetailed with Bush's low-key personality, and the two worked together comfortably. Porter had first met Bush as a White House Fellow during the Ford administration. The contacts continued during the Reagan administration, in which Porter held the position of director of the White House Office of Policy Development for almost five years. Porter found Bush to be very intelligent and knowledgeable on all the issues he addressed and easy to be around. In addition, Bush made a lasting impression on Porter. "He is a man of integrity," recalls Porter. "He never cut any corners. I never knew him to do anything that was deceptive or misleading." Porter had access to Bush and consulted with him as needed. Behind the scenes, Bush was very active. In addition to working the Hill through his informal visits, he was in touch with members of Congress by telephone.

Perceptions of a Failed Domestic Agenda

Despite his role, Bush has not been recognized for his effective stewardship of the domestic agenda. His own self-effacement prevented the administration from gaining recognition. Unwilling to talk about his role and successes, his public perception suffered. The stagnant economy also came to overshadow the whole domestic agenda, creating the impression that Bush was inattentive to people's needs. In line with this, the budget agreement of 1990, which broke Bush's "no new taxes" pledge, also stymied his maneuvering on domestic initiatives due to spending caps that were put in place. In addition, the momentous international events, such as the Gulf War, and Bush's very visible role in them led to a further impression that he had no interest in domestic policy. The press quickly seized on these events to weave a portrait of a president detached from domestic realities.

But there were additional considerations, some endemic to the administration and others purely partisan. Sununu has his own interpretation. He ascribes much of the failure to the White House Press Office. He believes that the Press Office was exceptionally skilled in dealing with the administration's foreign policy issues but that when it came to domestic policy the Press Office demurred and let the responsibility for communicating the administration's policies fall to the individual Cabinet agencies. As a result, there was not a coherent approach, and statements from the agencies lacked the authority associated with statements that came directly from the White House.

Specifically, the administration appears to have misplayed opportunities to highlight a domestic agenda. Much of the problem hinged on political judgments that, in hindsight, proved inaccurate, such as downplaying the domestic side in favor of foreign policy, which was viewed as Bush's strength heading into the campaign in 1992. The high point of the domestic policy agenda was in 1990, which was the passage of the ADA, the budget agreement, the child care act, and the Clean Air Act amendments. Subsequently, the administration appeared to go into a dormant stage, with the chief of staff deeming there was no need to push the agenda forcefully. Typical was the imbroglio over the health care initiative.

After the budget agreement of 1990, Darman set his sites on health care. The belief was that this was the next big issue that the administration needed to tackle. Darman had two concerns. First, he believed that the number of uninsured Americans was a big social and policy issue. Second, he believed the explosion in health care costs was eating deep into the federal budget. For reasons of quality of life and sound economic practice it was incumbent upon the administration to tackle health care. As a result, from the time the administration had come into office, staff had been examining the issue. After the budget deal, however, Tom Scully, who served as associate director of human resources, veterans, and labor for the Office of Management and Budget, was tasked to work the details, and by March 1991 the outlines of a plan were in place. Sununu, however, believed that the administration, in the wake of the successful Gulf War, was in great political shape and did not need to introduce new initiatives. The concern was that any such action could serve as a lightning rod to draw criticism and thus detract from the overall positive standing Bush was enjoying in the wake of the war. Furthermore, Sununu believed that health care was more of a Democratic Party issue that would not help the administration. As a result, the plan, which provided for 98 percent universal coverage, was put aside until the fall of 1991. At that time, former attorney general Dick Thornburgh lost the special Senate election in Pennsylvania to Harris Wofford, who made health care a major issue in the campaign.

James Carville, the Democratic Party strategist, viewed health care as an issue that the Democrats should push and urged Wofford to make it a key element of his campaign. Wofford had himself come to the same conclusion. A Philadelphia ophthalmologist whom Wofford knew had made it a point to push the issue. The ophthalmologist's reasoning was simple yet appealing to the groups he addressed: you have a right to an attorney, should you not also have a right to a doctor if you are ill? Carville was dismissive of such a simple approach, doubting its effectiveness. Wofford, however, adopted the mantra and pushed the health care issue, surprising Carville and many political pundits with his victory.

The political debacle in Pennsylvania shocked the White House; it did not, however, ruffle the civility and decency of Bush. One month after the election Bush entertained guests at the White House in the traditional series of Christmas receptions. Attending one was the newly elected senator from Pennsylvania, Harris Wofford, along with his wife, Clare. Standing in line to greet Bush, Wofford was set for his first encounter with the president and was a little apprehensive as to how it would unfold. Senator William Cohen (R-Maine), was wondering the same thing. His curiosity got the better of him, and with a smile and some jesting as to his reasoning, he let Wofford move ahead of him in the line. As Wofford and Bush greeted each other, Wofford was struck by Bush's graciousness and kindness. Bush congratulated him on his victory and acknowledged the toughness of political campaigning. He recommended that Wofford and his wife set off for a vacation to get some rest and relaxation before he undertook the full work of the Senate when it convened in January. From that day an affinity developed between Wofford and Bush, with Wofford holding a deep sense of admiration for Bush, and their friendship developed over the years. Wofford went on to serve as a board member of the Points of Light Foundation.

The election setback revealed the political vulnerability of the administration on the health care issue. A day after the election, an energized Sununu instructed that the dormant administration plan be reviewed and prepared for introduction. However, by this time Sununu was in political trouble himself over his use of government planes for private use, and by mid-December 1991 he had resigned. Sununu's troubles only served to delay the work on the health plan, and so it was not until February 1992 that the plan was unveiled.

The hurried and uncoordinated nature of the exercise was underscored by the fact that Scully wound up briefing the president on the plan on February 4 aboard Air Force One while Bush was en route to and from Orlando, Florida, to address the meeting of the National Grocers Association. It was there that Bush viewed the checkout scanner and the now infamous but inaccurate story of his amazement at the scanner broke, accusing him of detachment from everyday life. Two days later, on February 6, Bush unveiled his health plan at the Greater Cleveland Growth Association, but the scanner story only served to divert media attention from the plan.

In addition, the plan did not receive a warm welcome. The aim of the plan was to make health care more accessible to low- and middle-income families by making health insurance more affordable via tax credits, but it ran into two key criticisms: the administration refused to provide a price tag for the plan, which some believed could be $100 billion a year, and the plan did not make provisions for insurance companies to cover individuals with pre-existing conditions. Democrats, rather than focusing on the merits of the plan, criticized the president for acting too late and for not having been attentive to the issue early in his term. In the wake of the Wofford victory, it had become a political issue and undermined the likelihood that Bush's plan would receive a fair hearing.

Bush's Congressional Experience

While the administration created some of its own difficulties, the health care initiative also underlined the main problem that Bush faced in furthering his domestic agenda: a Democrat-controlled Congress. Equally important, the political environment on the Hill had changed considerably from the time when Bush served in the House. Bush's relationship with Capitol Hill was colored by his own experiences. As a two-term member of Congress from 1966 to 1970, Bush had learned the culture, befriended many members of both parties, and learned the mechanics of the legislative process. He quickly learned that Congress operated mainly on a bargaining principle largely based on personal relations and credibility. This suited his personality, and he soon had established friendly relations with a number of members, including Democrats Lud Ashley of Ohio, a former Yale classmate, and Sonny Montgomery, that continued beyond his own congressional and presidential terms.

As a member of Congress, Bush had tackled his responsibilities with relish. He enjoyed his work, his committee assignments, and interacting with constituents and other members. He took in all aspects of the job, devoting his full energy to both mundane paperwork as well as committee assignments. He was in the office by 7:00 A.M. and invariably stayed late. On Saturday mornings he would bound into the office and grab a handful of constituent questionnaires, read them, write responses, and mail them out, all of which upset his staff since they did not know what he was writing or possibly to what he was committing himself.

In his work, Bush never forgot the human element of politics. It was what drove him to respond to mail, meet with young people, and to be ever cognizant of the travails of those around him. His caring and deeds resonated in a wide circle. Following his unsuccessful run for the Senate in 1970, which had caused him to leave his House seat, Bush received an upbeat letter from a constituent. At the time, the letter may have provided some solace, but with the passage of time it proved prophetic. The letter congratulated Bush on all the good that he had accomplished but noted that this was not the end of his career. It concluded by stating that there were great things in store in his future.

During the 1960s, Texas was still a solid Democratic Party stronghold. George Bush was one of the few Republicans able to crack the barrier and win a House seat. In addition, many of the committee chairs at the time were held by Texas Democrats. As a result, Bush's arrival received much attention within the halls of the Capitol.

The Republican Party seized on this novelty, and Bush became a freshman member of the powerful Ways and Means Committee. It was an attempt both to bolster a potential rising star of the Republican Party and to garner much-needed publicity for the Republicans in an effort to extend the party's public appeal. The committee is very powerful. It oversees all revenue legislation and exercises oversight authority on such issues as Social Security, international trade, and general economic policy. His friend and colleague, Lud Ashley, dismisses the notion voiced by some that Bush's father, a retired senator from Connecticut at the time, had a hand in arranging this appointment. "By that time, his father had been retired from the Senate for a few years," notes Ashley. "Furthermore, there is no way that he would have been able to pull strings on the House side. That would have been unacceptable from the House side."

Bush made a favorable impression during his congressional tenure. Typical was the friendship that he struck up with David Abshire in the spring of 1970. Abshire was the assistant secretary of state for congressional relations at that time. He later went on to serve as ambassador to NATO and as special counselor to President Reagan during the Iran-Contra investigation. As the Department of State's congressional liaison, Abshire would attend midweek morning meetings on the Hill to brief members on various issues. On a particular spring morning in 1970, the briefing was on the Middle East. Abshire was told of the outstanding young representative from Texas, George Bush, whom he should get to know, and so he made a point of sitting next to Bush at the meeting. Abshire was impressed. Bush proved to be well informed, posing penetrating questions, particularly on Syria. From that meeting a lifelong friendship developed, and Abshire went on to handle Bush's congressional hearings after his appointment as ambassador to the United Nations.

The political culture of Capitol Hill during Bush's tenure there was quite different from what it was during his presidency. Many members in the earlier period had shared in the experiences of World War II. It was a camaraderie that bound them and crossed party lines. The Hill was at that time like a club; it was marked by gentlemanly conduct, and though political differences existed they were not allowed to interfere with personal relations or sour the political discourse. Democrats and Republicans were fond of each other and socialized a great deal. However, as a married man with children, Bush was on the periphery of much of this social activity. Bush skipped the "let's go for a drink" occasions that single members usually participated in and that helped build the camaraderie of the members. Bush, however, was an avid athlete, and through tennis and racquet ball he formed many of the friendships that continued beyond his stay on the Hill.

Institutionally, Congress was a very structured and conservative body. This aided greatly in the largely smooth functioning and relationships between the post–World War II members and the older and more senior prewar members. Reinforcing this atmosphere was the manner in which the press operated. The press was seen as and operated as a record keeper: it reported on the status of legislation and on how it could affect the public. It confined its opinions to the editorial page.

This world started falling apart in the early 1970s during the closing years of the Vietnam War and the Watergate scandal. Both, stimulated and fed by a more emboldened and skeptical press corps, helped inject greater partisanship into Washington and the national political debates. Bush readily recognized this development. "There has grown a certain divisiveness," Bush said in his inaugural address. "We have seen the hard looks and heard the statements in which not each other's ideas are challenged but each other's motives. And our great parties have too often been apart and untrusting of each other. It's been that way since Vietnam."

The "gotcha" politics that evolved out of Vietnam and Watergate—the sharp partisanship, press entrapment, and exposés—was alien to Bush's character. He had been exposed to the increasingly vitriolic politics of Washington during his tenure at the Republican National Committee during the Watergate scandal, but he could not accept it. Bush's instinct was not to be confrontational but rather to rely on the friendships he had on both sides of the aisle, to cultivate support via personal relations. He started his outreach to Congress the old-fashioned way—he signaled his personal interest and willingness to cooperate.

"I have always believed in dealing with people in a fair and personable manner," Bush likes to say. "This has a lot to do with how a problem is solved. How you go about dealing with people leaves a lasting impression and is more important than what you do. In this manner you can make a decision without incurring anyone's anger." In large measure, he met disappointment.

There were also two sound empirical reasons for Bush's personal approach. The foremost was the Democrat-controlled Congress. The Republicans were a decided minority in both chambers. In the Senate, the Republicans held 43 of 100 seats. In the House the number was 175 of 435 seats. In both cases President Bush had the smallest margin of party supporters of any twentieth-century president. The Democrats increased their margin in the midterm election of 1990. "It is a terrible burden to have the opposition party controlling both houses of Congress," Bush states. It is an experience that has left a vivid impression. "For four years I was up against a Democratic House and a Democratic Senate," Bush said. "The president thinks he's elected to get certain things done his way. Then the reality hits you that every program you send up on domestic policy is declared by a hostile Congress 'dead on arrival.' And so, the president is left singing from the other guy's sheet of music, dealing from the other fella's agenda."

In addition, Bush had run behind the winners in the vast majority of congressional districts. This exposed a certain political weakness on the Hill, where he could neither claim a mandate nor risk confrontation; compromise and conciliation would be the guiding principles.

Bush got a rude awakening from his idyllic memories of Congress when he submitted to the Senate for confirmation as secretary of defense former Texas Republican senator John Tower. A respected senator from 1961 to 1985, Tower had the knowledge and experience to serve in the post at the Defense Department. Unfortunately, issues related to his personal life, intertwined with partisan politics, soon doomed the nomination and introduced Bush to the bareknuckle politics that had taken hold in Washington.

Tower was rejected by the Senate committee about a month into Bush's administration, and the full Senate followed suit in early March. For Bush, the Tower nomination had become a test of loyalty rather than a rational political process. Bush was aware that Tower, accused of alcohol abuse and womanizing, was facing a Democrat-controlled Senate and would be in a difficult position. Bush, however, felt confident about the nomination, believing that Congress would not turn its back on one of its own. Bush stuck by his nominee even as Democratic senator Sam Nunn of Georgia, chairman of the Senate Armed Services Committee, clearly showed his displeasure with Tower. With the nomination doomed, Bush turned to a current member of Congress, Rep. Dick Cheney of Wyoming, who was quickly confirmed.

The winds of political change, however, were already beginning to blow, and the Democrats were missing the indications of a Republican front that finally swept to a majority in Congress in 1994. Early signs seemed to be inconsequential: growing numbers of local, state, and national officials switching from the Democratic to the Republican ranks and the increasing Republican activism on the state level. In the 1980s, for example, Florida, a key electoral state, started to see increases in its Republican ranks. In June 1989, Bush hosted a number of Democrats who had made the switch to the Republican Party. "The switch is on to the party in sync with the American principles," he announced. "The switch is on to the Republican Party." For the Democrats, Bush saw a party on the decline. "The Democratic Party is leaving droves of voters behind as it moves over onto the more liberal side, the left side of the political equation," Bush stated. "And now many of those stranded voters have made a move on their own—to the Republican Party, our party of family, faith, and the future."

Bush set the target of good relations with Congress immediately after his election by instructing his staff to schedule meetings with the Democratic and Republican leaders. Moreover, he offered to make the trip to the Capitol himself to meet with them. His aim was to symbolically extend his hand in cooperation, to signal that he would be cooperative and accessible. Also, on his first full day as president, Bush wrote to Speaker of the House Jim Wright, a Democrat from Texas, and the other congressional leaders to reaffirm his commitment to working with Congress on a deficit reduction plan and the need for a bipartisan foreign policy. He ended his note with a plea for a "spirit of bipartisan cooperation." At his first congressional meeting, on January 24, 1989, the leadership presented Bush with Texas hot sauce and pork rinds as their own gesture of cooperation. On February 9 Bush also addressed Congress, using the opportunity to present his administration's plans for the country. In a news conference on January 27, 1989, the president was asked to summarize the message of his first week on the job. "Reaching out to Congress," he stated without hesitation. "And so, I'd like to signal an era of real openness with Congress." To highlight his desire to work with Congress, Bush hosted small groups of congressional members at the White House during the first weeks of the administration. These informal gatherings were held on the residence floor and involved all members.

The White House instituted a two-track process for its work with Congress. The White House congressional office focused on domestic issues while the NSC congressional office, headed by Virginia Lampley, dealt with the foreign policy issues. Lampley's knowledge of the government bureaucracy, particularly at the Pentagon and on the Hill, helped play an invaluable role in shepherding foreign policy issues in Congress. There was close coordination and cooperation between the two offices. Scowcroft, in particular, was very active with Congress members. His reputation as a foreign policy expert, his closeness to the president, and the many friendships he had formed with Congress members over the years made him a highly respected advocate for the administration. In addition, since the national security adviser is not under any legal mandate to testify on the Hill, Scowcroft's contacts were that much more appreciated and valued by the members. In structure, Bush held regular congressional meetings, alternating between the Republican leadership and a bipartisan leadership session in the Cabinet Room. In addition, depending on the issue, such as defense or the budget, other relevant congressional leaders would join the meeting. Quayle was also instrumental in the legislative strategy and spent a great deal of time on the Hill, where he had many friends and contacts in both chambers and on both sides of the aisle. He was helpful to the president on many issues, including the Clarence Thomas hearings, the budget agreement of 1990, the Senate vote in support of Operation Desert Storm, and outreach to conservative Republican members of Congress.

In terms of organization, the White House used an ad hoc approach, organizing internal working groups led by Roger Porter to shepherd a proposed piece of legislation through the Congress. Throughout the process, White House staffers consulted with Congress members and congressional staffers regarding the status and prospects of individual pieces of legislation. On a weekly basis, Fred McClure forwarded a memo to Bush outlining the previous week's activities and the status of various pieces of legislation and what could be expected in the forthcoming week. These reports, submitted through the staff secretary, came back to McClure with Bush's comments; it was left to McClure to follow up with additional information. For Bush, there were two key questions that he posed and that guided his review of legislation. First, he looked for a general status report. Second, Bush was interested in an assessment of whether the administration's efforts were sufficient to get the necessary votes on each proposed bill. He did not look for an elaborate presentation but rather the simple facts, and he seldom got involved in the detail of draft language. Bush did, however, get involved with the drafting of the congressional resolution supporting the United Nations' call for the use of force against Saddam Hussein. Bush penned a draft over the Christmas holiday in 1990 at Camp David and forwarded it to Sununu, Scowcroft, and McClure for handling. A working group was put together to produce a draft resolution along Bush's guidelines that was then vetted informally on the Hill; virtually all of Bush's points were eventually reflected in the actual resolution. In addition, McClure submitted to Bush a weekly report regarding congressional correspondence addressed to the president or McClure on various issues and pending legislation.

From his first days in office, Bush cultivated Congress through personal involvement. He lunched and used the recreational facilities on the Hill. "I played paddle ball in the House gym and once in a while in the Senate gym," Bush says. "Some of the members I played with in the House were Lee Hamilton [D-Indiana], Sonny Montgomery, Bill Archer [R-Texas], and John Dingell [D-Michigan]. I would also go swim in the Senate pool and work out in the Senate gym."

Bush wrote to individual members, commenting on news reports that he had read or explaining U.S. policy on certain issues. His efforts did not prove as fruitful as he hoped. He soon found that personal cultivation did not always translate into policy cooperation.

This emphasis on personal relations also exposed a weak spot in Bush's political armor. Bush believed that decent treatment and personal attention would translate into political support or, at a minimum, a return of decency on the political front. The failure to realize this type of quid pro quo was a source of irritation and bewilderment to Bush, and he openly shared this reaction with those around him. On one occasion, Bush interrupted the departure of an Oval Office guest, a journalist whom Bush had known for many years. Sitting behind the desk, his manner changed from the friendly tone of conversation that he had been engaged in to one of befuddlement, his face skewed in wonderment regarding the actions of a certain senator.

"Did you see what he said about me in today's *Washington Post?*" Bush asked in disbelief. He focused on his visitor as if awaiting an explanation that would take away the hurt.

"What do you expect?" retorted his visitor. "It was a cheap political shot. He's a Democrat and you are a Republican. You have to expect these kinds of things."

"Yes, but darn it all," complained Bush, shaking his head in apparent disbelief, "I just had him and his wife over for dinner about a month ago."

It was this same type of wonderment that marked his relationship with Democratic senator George Mitchell of Maine. Relations with Mitchell had started out on a good note but soon soured. Bush thought he could work things out with Mitchell. He offered him rides on Air Force One whenever he went up to Maine. At one time, due to a misunderstanding, Bush believed that Mitchell had not been invited on the Maine trip. A staffer remembers him being visibly angry. "He was mad as a wet hen," recalls the staffer.

Bush and Mitchell were able to partner on a few policies, such as the Clean Air Act. However, partisanship ultimately got in the way, and Bush's staff regarded Mitchell as bent on blocking the president every which way in an effort to undermine his reelection. "I would take Mitchell up to Maine on Air Force One," said Bush. "We'd go play tennis in Kennebunkport. He'd smile, enjoy it, and then go back and cut my heart out on Monday as he led from a very different agenda than what I felt I was elected to do by a rather substantial victory. He was highly partisan and everyone in our administration and, indeed, in the Senate knew this too." It was particularly frustrating for Bush in view of the effort he put into cultivating Mitchell.

Bush, however, was no stranger to the politics versus friendship dilemma. As the vice-presidential candidate in 1980, the Reagan camp dispatched Bush to campaign on behalf of a Republican House candidate who was running against his friend and Yale classmate, Democrat Lud Ashley, in the Toledo area of Ohio. Bush conducted the pro forma visit, carrying out his Republican Party duties with a tight check on his enthusiasm. At the end of the stop, he did an interview with the *Toledo Blade* during which the questioner sought to exploit his personal dilemma. The questioner put him on the spot by inquiring whether people should vote against Ashley. Bush's retort was sharp and short. He did not say that, he parried, and he reiterated his call on behalf of Republican candidates. Ashley, who had first been elected to the House in 1954, went down to defeat in the Reagan landslide. His defeat was aided by his split with organized labor in the district, which further undermined his public support. Both he and Bush understood the politics of the situation and it did not impair their friendship, which continues to be strong to this day, with Ashley serving as a board member of Bush's Presidential Library Foundation.

The letdown over policy matters is something Bush never forgets. De-cades after his stay at the United Nations, Bush still recalls how he felt over a switched vote by the Cypriot delegate on the issue of dual representation for China, which the United States lost, and which led to the expulsion of Taiwan from the world body. "He exercised his ambassadorial authority and he voted against us," Bush recalls. "I remember getting up from the chair and walked over and said, 'What the hell are you doing?' We knew he had his instructions to vote with us. 'How do you think you get away with this? Why do you do this?' I was furious at the guy." It does not matter that the United States itself was moving in the direction of establishing contact with China behind the scenes. What matters to Bush is one's word.

Bush was careful not to become engaged in any fights with Congress. He did not believe in personal confrontation or in burning his bridges. House majority leader Dick Gephardt (D-Missouri) was critical of the president, claiming that he was not a strong leader in the face of the evolving situa-tion in the Soviet Union. Bush dismissed these attacks, refusing to engage in any criticism. When Senator Nunn was in the forefront of opposing Senator Tower's nomination, Bush was reluctant to be confrontational with Nunn or the Senate. "I don't see any point in making this personal," Bush told the press. As usual, he was focused on process and the facts, which he believed outweighed everything else: "I want to talk on the merits here and encourage senators, all of them, to take a look at the facts, not at the rumors, not at the innuendo; and, therefore, there's no point getting into a fight. We're going to have to work together on a lot of other issues." At another time he stated, "I mean, I try not to measure my presidency by personal pride or in personal wins or personal losses—who's up, who's down, victory or defeat."

When Tower's nomination went down to defeat in the Senate, the White House issued a statement on the president's behalf, putting the issue to rest and looking to the future. "The Senate has made its determination. I respect its role in doing so, but I disagree with the outcome," the president's statement read. "Now, however, we owe it to the American people to come together and move forward."

Bush had a mixed experience with individual members of Congress. "I was not close to Gephardt or Mitchell," Bush recalls. "They had big majorities and were fiercely partisan." Irrespective of such individual cases, Bush believed that he had a good personal relationship with many members on both sides of the aisles of Congress. "I enjoyed working with a number of congressional members," Bush says. "Dan Rostenkowski was someone I could talk with frankly." Rostenkowski, a Chicago Democrat and chairman of the House Ways and Means Committee, was one of Bush's favorites; he valued his friendship and advice. They worked closely on the budget deal in 1990, and the Bushes entertained the Rostenkowskis in the residence of the White House.

"I liked and enormously respected Bob Michel [R-Illinois]," Bush further recalls. "I had great respect for Bob Dole. He was the best leader a minority president could have. Sonny Montgomery was close to me and helped a lot. Jack Murtha [D-Pennsylvania] was very good to work with. I had great respect for Tip O'Neill [D-Massachusetts]. I wanted to make him ambassador to Ireland, but his wife, Millie, was ailing and, so it could not be worked out."

Congressional Strategy

Facing a Democratic Congress as a block to many of his initiatives, Bush sought to circumvent Congress by advocating various steps that the administration hoped would resonate with the American public and expose what he believed was the ineffectiveness of Congress. A key debate with Congress was over the president's desire to have a line item veto. Forty-three governors have the line item veto. Bush and his predecessors for over a century had also sought this authority, which would give presidents the power to veto what they viewed as objectionable parts of a bill. The concern on the Hill, of course, was that the president would veto the pet projects of individual members, thus undermining their ability to deliver special projects to their constituents. As a result, in 1990 Bush introduced a proposed amendment to the Constitution granting the president the line item veto.

In his own dealings with Congress, Bush exercised the veto forty-four times and it was sustained forty-three times. Most of the vetoes were aimed at preventing government overspending and overregulation. The veto was an important governing instrument for Bush. Faced with a heavily Democratic Congress, the veto—or threat of a veto—was key in his attempts to keep Congress in check. While Bush could not necessarily get his programs through, he could at least thwart Congress from pushing its own agenda.

Closely tied to his use of the veto was the effort to revise the rescission authority enacted by Congress in 1974 under the Congressional Budget and Impoundment Control Act. Under this legislation, presidents can "veto" any appropriated federal program by informing Congress of their desire to do so. Congress then has forty-five days in which to act. It can approve the move with a simple majority vote by each chamber. It could disapprove by so voting or by simply taking no action, thus parrying the president's desires by inaction. It was this latter alternative that proved most frustrating for presidents since it provided no accountability on the part of either chamber or individual members. Bush sought to create some accountability, and he saw the line item veto and a revised rescission authority as important tools for restoring fiscal responsibility and discipline to the federal government. The padding of bills with wasteful spending had grossly raised the deficit of the government and was a threat to the long-term economic well-being of the nation.

In addition to these attempts at promoting fiscally sound government practices, Bush also sought constitutional amendments to restore voluntary school prayer and to prevent desecration of the American flag. For Bush, these were value issues—issues of morality and patriotism aimed at reinforcing personal as well as civic responsibility. Neither of these efforts, like the effort for a line item veto or a revised rescission authority, was successful. Critics saw all of these efforts—particularly the issues of prayer and the flag—as political opportunities for the president to cater to certain parts of the electorate and to isolate political opponents. The flag issue had been an important one during Bush's presidential campaign against Michael Dukakis. Bush was viewed as having wrapped himself in the flag in an effort to portray Dukakis as outside mainstream America. Dukakis had, in fact, vetoed a Massachusetts state bill that made it mandatory for schoolteachers to lead students in the Pledge of Allegiance. The critics, however, failed to realize or appreciate the deep beliefs Bush's stand represented. These were beliefs on which he had been raised and that he saw as important values to pass on to succeeding generations. He held these positions, even in the face of setbacks. In June 1990, the Supreme Court overturned a law that deemed burning or defacing the American flag a crime. The court viewed the law as violating the First Amendment right of free speech. Bush, however, remained steadfast in his desire for a constitutional amendment. He had been skeptical that a simple law would be sufficient.

The administration also undertook a strategy of favoring reform of Congress in the hope of shaking it into action and getting public support. None of these efforts at reform to make Congress more responsive met with success. Bush favored term limits, with House members limited to six terms and Senate members limited to two. In addition, he favored various internal reforms in Congress. The bank and post office scandals in the Congress added fuel to Bush's call for electing a new Congress. In the House banking scandal, numerous representatives were guilty of overdrawing their accounts and thus getting de facto loans. In the House post office scandal members exchanged stamps and postal vouchers for cash. The scandals affected both sides of the aisle and ensnared a number of big names in their nets. Dan Rostenkowski got embroiled in the post office debacle and eventually was convicted of abusing the service and various other illegal activities, which led to a prison term and loss of his House seat.

Rostenkowski's downfall, however, did not affect Bush's friendship with him.

"When he went to jail, George called him," says Barbara Bush, "and stayed in touch with him."

Bush also called for the elimination of special interest political action committees that gave incumbents an unfair advantage when they were up for reelection. In addition, Bush favored a balanced budget amendment to the Constitution. There was popular support for a balanced budget amendment—Bush liked to cite that 80 percent of the American public was in favor of it. In addition, forty-four states have some form of constitutional balanced budget restrictions. Bush believed that the amendment was key to limiting congressional spending, to limiting federal spending, and to ensuring long-term economic growth. However, he was not able to generate the requisite votes in Congress. The House vote in June 1992 was nine votes short of the two-thirds vote needed for passage of the bill. The Democratic leadership made a concerted effort to block the action. It forced seven Democratic cosponsors of the amendment to withdraw their support and to vote against the measure. On the Senate side, the measure failed to obtain votes required to invoke cloture. If the measure had been successful in both houses of Congress, it would have gone to the state legislatures for further action. The failure of these various initiatives that Bush championed did nothing to dent Congress's armor or to inspire a wave of popular support for Bush. Bush's frustration increased during the beginning of the election year and was compounded by the lagging economic situation.

While Bush won the New Hampshire primary in February 1992 over his challenger Pat Buchanan, a conservative news commentator who had served in the Reagan White House, the victory was considered a weak showing for an incumbent president. The view emerged that Bush was politically vulnerable, which had all types of ramifications. It emboldened his challenger, opened Bush to further critical dissection by the media, and put a new focus on the Democratic challengers. Another ramification was that it emboldened the Democrat-controlled Congress to drag its heels—no help could be expected from Congress at a time when it sensed a weakening president. This lack of action on the part of Congress further undermined Bush in the public mind since the lack of congressional action stymied his domestic agenda and portrayed Bush as uncaring and ineffective. Buchanan's continued strong showing in the primaries heightened the president's political troubles and intensified his opponents' motivation to defeat him.

In 1992, therefore, Bush sought to run against the Democratic Congress by challenging it to undertake certain actions to aid an economic recovery. In short, Bush took the gamble that if Congress did not give him what he wanted, it would be viewed as obstructionist and parry much of the criticism Bush was receiving over the poor state of the economy. In some ways, this was the type of strategy that some Republicans had urged back in 1990 to avoid a budget deal that involved raising taxes. In his State of the Union address in January 1992 Bush set the target of March 20 as the date by which Congress should pass his proposed incentives for economic growth. In March, Congress passed a bill, but the president failed to get the tax credit for first-time home buyers and other measures he considered important to help stimulate the economy. Instead, Congress gave Bush an act that would raise taxes by more than $100 billion, forcing him to exercise his veto. Bush was opposed to increasing taxes, believing that they would hinder a rebound of the economy, while the Democrats believed Bush's plan favored the rich. Irrespective of this philosophical difference, the deadline strategy did not bring any benefits to Bush. Any benefit that the administration had hoped to garner from portraying the president as being against tax increases had already been undermined by the budget deal in 1990 that forced him to break the "no new taxes" campaign promise. The weakness of the approach was seen by mid-1992, when the Bush campaign was faced with a perplexing dilemma: voters continued to view the economic situation as worsening even as the economy was beginning to improve.

Bush attributes his problem to the opposition he encountered in Congress. He viewed the actions of the Democratic Congress as deliberate. "I think they made a calculation after the war that they were not going to cooperate with the president," he stated on October 28, 1992. The next day he went further and stated, "They made a decision: 'The only way we are going to win the White House is by denying the president success on some of this terribly important domestic legislation.' That is the fact."

The Budget Agreement of 1990

Although Bush complained about the Democratic Congress, it was a reality with which he had to deal, and he therefore viewed the situation as both an obstacle and a challenge. For him, navigating the partisan waters was part of his leadership. "A president has got to learn to lead with opposition," Bush has said. In this environment, compromise was the best approach. For Bush, compromise was not a sign of weakness but a tool of leadership to achieve a greater end. He fully understood the benefits of compromise and was willing to engage in it. "It doesn't hurt to give a little if you can get something in return," Bush has said. Indeed, strength and foresight are needed to compromise; it takes personal strength, a sense of security in oneself, and foresight or an understanding of the benefits that can result from compromise. Compromise does not come easy for many, and for them, the opportunities for leadership are squandered. In hindsight, Bush believed his most successful compromise was the budget deal of 1990. "My most heroic compromise cost me my job," Bush has said about the budget deal. "I was turned on by the right wing of my own party and, yet, we handed President Clinton a growing economy, an economy growing over 5 percent in the last quarter of 1992. So the economics proved to be okay, but the politics killed me."

At the time, there were differing views on what to do. Some Republican voices cautioned that reneging on the "no new taxes" pledge would be politically fatal for the president. It would rob him and the Republicans of a key issue they held over the Democrats. It would level the political playing field, undermining any Republican claims that the Democrats were the party of taxes and spending. Simultaneously, it gave the Democrats the right to charge Bush with hypocrisy and political opportunism. To avoid such a political debacle, some Republicans pushed for Bush to maintain his pledge and to take the fight to Congress. The strategy was to saddle the Democratic Congress with the responsibility to cut spending.

One of the biggest disagreements that Kemp had with Bush was over the tax issue and the budget deal. There were a number of Cabinet sessions that brought the issue to the fore in intense discussion. Kemp opposed, for political and economic reasons, Bush breaking his "no new taxes" pledge. In particular, Kemp urged Bush not to go along with the Democratic pledge of spending cuts in exchange for raising taxes. Kemp favored no tax increase and a freeze on the budget for one year in order for the president to get through the midterm congressional elections of 1990. Darman, together with Sununu, was able to persuade Bush that an agreement on the budget, including a tax increase, was essential to righting the increasingly shaky economy. Bush believed that he could tackle the problem without a tax increase; he was not given the opportunity, however, because of the Democratic Congress. He faulted the Democratic Congress for his inability to get a budget without the tax increases. "I wish I had a Congress who would do it just my way," he explained to the press in November 1990, "because I am still convinced we can get by without having raised anybody's taxes of any kind."

Bush's pledge of "read my lips, no new taxes," included in his acceptance speech at the Republican National Convention in 1988, was a key element of his campaign and one that helped him achieve his victory. However, when Bush broke that pledge in order to cement the budget deal, many conservative supporters and Americans in general came to see the pledge as nothing short of campaign political expediency. Facing a growing budget deficit and worried financial markets, the president was at a crossroads: he could either stick to his "read my lips" pledge not to raise taxes or he could balance the budget with a tax increase and reassure domestic and world markets. In addition, due to the Gramm-Rudman-Hollings Act's budgetary guidelines, OMB was under restriction; it had to implement certain cuts if deficit targets were not met. In the case of defense expenditures, this could have meant a cut of 34 percent at a time when Saddam Hussein had invaded Kuwait and the United States was contemplating a buildup of forces in the region. For Bush, the choice was clear—either stick to a campaign pledge and let the deficit accelerate, further undermining the nation's economy, or get a budget deal and set the country on the road toward prosperity. The former would solidify his conservative base; the latter would alienate his conservative base and threaten his reelection chances.

Bush was criticized for his change of course, lost the support of many conservatives, and exposed himself to a polemical primary campaign by Patrick Buchanan that helped undermine his political capital and contributed to his defeat in the general election. Bush, however, exhibited his usual determination and thought process at a Cabinet meeting a few weeks before he signed the budget agreement. It was a poignant moment, one that crystallized the president's strength of character. "Bush reaffirmed his commitment to the deal," recalls Michael Jackson, special assistant to the president for Cabinet liaison. "He emphasized that, while he realized the political costs of the decision and that it could impact his reelection, it was the right thing to do. The United States was on the verge of war with Iraq and the president noted that neither the troops nor the American people deserved to have the government shut down over a budget crisis."

The Democrats knew the quandary that the president faced. Democratic congressional leaders Tom Foley of Washington and George Mitchell made it a precondition that for any budget deal, taxes had to be included. The budget negotiations with Congress started in May 1990, spearheaded by Sununu and Darman on the White House side, and continued through the summer, with an agreement being announced on September 30 in the Rose Garden. After a breakdown in the agreement in early October, on November 5 Bush finally signed the Omnibus Budget Reconciliation Act of 1990. The bill targeted almost $500 billion in deficit reductions over five years. Of this amount, only 28 percent involved tax changes; the remainder involved curtailed spending, including both entitlement programs and discretionary program caps. Regarding entitlements, the act aimed to save about $100 billion by instituting reforms in such programs as federal housing, student loans, federal employee benefits, and Medicare. In the case of Medicare, it was the providers and not the beneficiaries who were affected. On the discretionary side, the bill was expected to achieve $180 billion in savings.

On the tax side, the bill actually included a tax rate cut for 3.5 million middle- and upper-middle-income Americans. In addition, for those earning up to twenty thousand dollars per year, there was a tax decrease. The tax increases involved excise taxes on luxury items and limits on itemized deductions. In addition, there were limits for higher-income taxpayers regarding personal exemptions.

Bush paid a price almost immediately. In addition to the uproar over breaking his "no new taxes" pledge, he also suffered a setback in the midterm congressional elections that many viewed as the result of the budget agreement. In 1990, the White House had hoped to pick up some Republican congressional seats in the election. It turned out that the Republicans suffered losses in both the House and Senate. Bush took some comfort in the analysis that the overall losses were fewer than one would expect in off-year elections. However, he was realistic in viewing the budget agreement as having negatively impacted the results.

The great failure of the budget deal was in how it was presented to the public, and, in this, Bush and those around him made some missteps, particularly regarding when and how they articulated their views on the process. Little was done to explain why cutting the deficit was important, how an eventual deal would benefit the country, and why the president's reversal on his campaign promise was necessary. Darman, in particular, believed that a number of factors would work to the administration's benefit. First, he believed that the action was early enough in Bush's term that, by the 1992 election, it would have faded from the public's consciousness. Second, he believed that the approaching war with Saddam Hussein would overshadow all other concerns the public might have.

Sununu and Darman, in an apparent effort to maintain the integrity of the negotiating process with Congress, failed to keep other parts of the White House informed. In this regard, they had regular budget update meetings with Bush from which others were excluded. In addition, sometimes when Jim Cicconi requested the briefing papers for these meetings, his requests were deflected or he was told that no papers were necessary. When the deal was announced, however, Sununu called in the staff and instructed that a strategy be set in place for selling the deal. Unfortunately, this move was ineffective: no one knew how the process had transpired. The budget deal was as newsworthy to them as to the general public. As a result, the staff, particularly the Communications Office and the Public Liaison Office, was not in a position to devise a coherent plan to explain the president's reversal on his "no new taxes" pledge.

The problem became evident immediately following the announcement on September 30 of the initial budget agreement. Sununu and Darman intercepted Bobbie Kilberg in the hallway outside the Cabinet Room following the event.

"Now you go out and sell it," Darman told Kilberg. She, like everyone else in the White House, had been blindsided by the Darman-Sununu series of secret negotiations.

"I can't sell this," she stated firmly. She went on to explain her concern.

"You've cut out all the groups that we deal with," she continued. "The business groups that will be affected by this budget deal were not consulted. They have been excluded. I can't sell something to them if they have not been part of the process."

While the task was daunting, Kilberg also knew that she had no choice. Despite her initial frustration, she had to face the challenge.

However, with the deal already public, it was receiving negative coverage, and thus it was difficult to devise a strategy when facing a negative avalanche of media criticism. In addition, the secret negotiations on the Hill isolated numerous members of Congress, thereby creating pockets of resistance to the deal, which fed the public criticism.

Mixed signals from the administration during the process also prevented the creation of a favorable public reception for the budget deal. In a statement released on June 26, 1990, after a meeting with the bipartisan congressional leadership, Bush included "tax revenue income" as one of the elements necessary for a budget agreement. The statement was supported by the bipartisan leadership, but Bush immediately had a political problem. The press started to push him on his willingness to consider tax revenues part of a budget deal with Congress. His response was practical: he saw a problem and it needed to be corrected. "I think the president owes the people his judgment at the moment he has to address that problem. And that's exactly what I'm trying to do. . . . I've got to do what is right," he told the press.

His additional response to the media's pressure was that "everything is on the table" and that he would not discuss details since negotiations were proceeding. The problem was further exacerbated by the fact that White House staff—led by Sununu—sought to allay the concerns of conservative Republicans that the president's position on taxes had changed. And the administration concocted the idea of dubbing the taxes "revenue enhancement" in order to sell the deal to the public and make it more palatable for the president. Bush's further explanation seemed a bit disingenuous. "I'm not changing my view on taxes," he said on June 29 to the press. "I'm just saying everything's on the table."

Furthermore, the initial agreement on the budget that was announced on September 30 fell through in early October, heightening the perception of a White House in disarray. Bush gave a televised address from the Oval Office on October 2 to sell the deal, calling on the American public to express their support of the agreement to their senators and representatives, but his plea fell on deaf ears and did not generate the grassroots support that he sought. Many conservative House Republicans began to hesitate and, on the day of the vote, came out against the agreement. Bush was able to garner the support of fewer than half the Republican members in the House. Seeing the Republican opposition, many Democrats abandoned their leadership and also voted against the measure. It was defeated by a vote of 254–179.

Symptomatic of the disconnect between the White House and Congress was the president's vacillation on the issue of tying a cut in the capital gains tax, something that he favored, to his accepting the idea of raising income taxes on wealthy Americans, something the Democrats sought. In the span of a few days in October following the budget agreement defeat and the negotiations to revive it, Bush sent varying signals. An exasperated press sought to pin him down, but Bush, seeking to keep his negotiating flexibility with Congress, refused to oblige. On October 27 Congress finally passed a budget agreement that Bush signed on November 5. It did not contain the capital gains tax provisions that Bush had sought. The agreement that was passed placed more of the financial costs on wealthier Americans, thereby bringing the support of many Democrats who had viewed the earlier agreement as placing too much of a burden on poorer Americans.

Rep. Newt Gingrich's position also was instrumental in shaping the public reaction to the final deal. A participant in the budget negotiations, Gingrich, a staunch Republican conservative from Georgia who served as the party's minority whip in the House, originally went along with the notion of a tax increase being a part of any deal. His position was that taxes should not be more than half of any final agreement. However, the night before the agreement was announced, Gingrich came to the conclusion that he would be better off politically by not associating with the agreement. As a result, when all the congressional participants gathered in the Rose Garden on September 30 for a photo with the president and the announcement of the bipartisan agreement, Gingrich was conspicuously absent. Just before the announcement, Bush met with congressional leaders in the Cabinet Room. He went through what had been agreed to and then asked if there were any questions or concerns. He paused. There was a stillness; no one said anything. Bush then led the group out into the Rose Garden; Gingrich, however, peeled off and headed for the West Wing Lobby. Much of the political fallout that the president experienced in his own party probably stemmed from Gingrich's public snub. If Gingrich had stood with the president, much of the political damage probably could have been avoided. Other presidents, notably President Reagan, had raised taxes and had been able to weather the ordeal with strong party support.

Bush did not get that party support, as seen by the action of Ed Rollins, who headed the National Republican Congressional Committee. Rollins penned a memo urging the party faithful to take on Bush for breaking his "no new taxes" pledge. The memo helped drive a wedge between Bush and congressional Republicans. The White House was livid; it viewed the step as heresy, but the damage was done.

Despite the political turmoil that the budget agreement initiated, it may well turn out to be the most important factor in stimulating the exceptional economic growth of the 1990s. In terms of size, it was the largest multiyear budget reduction of the 1990s, surpassing those of 1993 and 1997. Furthermore, many features of the 1993 deal were extensions of the package adopted in 1990. This then raises another important point: the budget deal of 1990 laid the tough political groundwork that facilitated decisions on the budget during President Clinton's tenure in office.

The Bush budget also set some other standards. First, it tapped into all the major sectors that comprised the budget, including federal employees, discretionary spending, and taxes. The second thing Bush did was present a balanced approach. While taxes were part of the solution, most of the budget relied on spending cuts. This was unlike the deals made in 1993 and 1997. The former relied heavily on taxes while the latter actually helped increase the deficit. There were other important features as well, according to Robert

Grady, who served as deputy director of OMB and deputy assistant to the president. "The agreement," according to Grady, "succeeded tremendously in capping the growth of domestic discretionary spending at rates far below the inflation rate." The agreement called for mandatory spending caps that could be overridden only by a two-thirds majority vote of Congress. Spending that exceeded the caps would trigger an across-the-board sequester to bring spending back into line and curb Congress's tendency to create expensive new entitlements. According to Grady, the agreement basically instituted "a 'pay as you go' requirement that required new spending to be offset by cuts elsewhere."

While Bush was the target of much political vilification for the budget deal, some experts viewed it as an important juncture. "I think history will show that the 1990 budget agreement was the turning point and was the most important single event in getting our fiscal house in order," stated Robert Reischauer, who served as head of the nonpartisan Congressional Budget Office from 1989 to 1995. "It was so from a substantive standpoint and from a procedural standpoint," Reischauer added, "and it took policy makers who had a lot of courage and willingness to put their jobs on the line to get this done."

The Clean Air Act

In two policy areas—having to do with the environment and disabled Americans—Bush was able to forge a coalition for the passage of major legislation without the rancor and political costs that the budget deal had brought. The Clean Air Act amendments of 1990 constituted a sweeping piece of legislation that Bush was able to produce in cooperation with Senator George Mitchell, who otherwise found himself in opposition to Bush's agenda. Increased public concern about the environment, particularly poor urban air quality and acid rain, also helped stimulate the congressional action. The act aimed at three forms of pollution: sulfur dioxide from power plants, smog, and toxic air pollutants. The act led to a 50 percent cut in acid rain (sulfur dioxide emissions) by using an innovative emissions trading system to do so cost-effectively, and it reduced smog by 40 percent throughout the United States, allowing more than one hundred cities to meet health-related ozone standards. By putting to use new technologies, the act helped cut toxic emissions into the air by 90 percent. Overall, the legislation was projected at the time of passage to reduce air pollution by 56 billion pounds annually, or as Bush pointed out in his signing ceremony, "224 pounds for every man, woman and, child in America."

Bush has a long-term commitment to the environment. His love of the outdoors, particularly fishing and quail hunting, plus his home on the oceanfront instilled a sense of environmental stewardship that he actively pursued during his days in Congress and as both vice president and president. In his approach, Bush was driven by two considerations. "He wanted to combine two things—the conservation ethic, that is, a genuine effort to clean up our air and water and preserve our land," explains Grady, who was part of the team that shepherded the act to a successful conclusion, "with a commitment to using market-based mechanisms to achieve these environmental aims in the most economically efficient and sound means possible."

As vice president, Bush oversaw the phasing out of leaded gasoline, which led to a 98 percent reduction in lead emissions. During the presidential campaign of 1988, Bush made the environment an important part of his platform. In his nominating speech, Bush clearly stated his commitment when he said, "We must clean the air. We must reduce the harm done by acid rain." Under Grady and Robert Zoellick, the campaign's issues director, campaign staffers developed a range of proposals and speeches underscoring Bush's commitment to the environment, including clean air, wetlands preservation, preventing ocean pollution, and reducing ozone depletion. In a meeting at the vice president's residence in midsummer that year, Bush met with Grady and Zoellick to review the various environmental initiatives, and he made a personal commitment to pursuing clean air legislation. This step was a break with his predecessor Ronald Reagan, whose administration had opposed efforts to extend the Clean Air Act of 1977.

The campaign benefited from the growing interest in and support of environmental issues by an important electoral segment—the suburban voter. These voters were conservative on issues such as taxes and crime but were more liberal on other issues, namely the environment and education, which touched on their families' quality of life. In particular, the campaign identified six battleground states—California, Illinois, Michigan, Missouri, New Jersey, and Ohio—with a high percentage of such voters. Armed with this information, Bush was able to make a surprise appearance in his opponent's home state of Massachusetts to highlight Dukakis's failure to provide adequate sewage treatment. Massachusetts was not in compliance with the requirements of the Clean Water Act of 1972 that there be facilities for treatment of sewage discharged into Boston Harbor. Bush showed up at the harbor to point out the sewage that fouled the water. Bush's handling of the environmental issues helped neutralize the Democrats' advantage on the issue.

Once in office, in an address to Congress on February 9, 1989, Bush stated his commitment to pursuing clean air legislation. The administration put together a working group headed by Roger Porter. Joining him were White House counsel C. Boyden Gray; Michael Boskin, chairman of the president's Council of Economic Advisers; and Bob Grady. The group also included William K. Reilly, administrator of the Environmental Protection Agency (EPA); William G. Rosenberg, assistant EPA administrator for air and radiation; Secretary of Energy James Watkins; and Deputy Energy Secretary Linda Stuntz. The administration worked closely with members on both sides of the aisle in Congress and with industry and environmental groups, including the Environmental Defense Fund. The proposed legislation was submitted to Congress in June 1989 and was signed into law in November 1990.

A major stumbling block in getting the legislation passed was reconciling the differences between the midwestern and eastern states. The coal power plants of the Midwest spewed pollutants that caused acid rain to fall on the lakes, forests, and cities of the East, creating various environmental and health risks. The midwestern states viewed the issue as a national rather than a regional problem and thus did not accept the proposition that they would be expected to bear the costs of reducing their sulfur dioxide emissions. The eastern states, in turn, balked at any move that would involve their residents subsidizing a program to make the Midwest's plants more efficient and thus more environmentally sound. Furthermore, the eastern states could point out that their plants were already operating at efficient levels. There was also an employment issue for the Midwest. Pollution controls could impact the job security of coal miners in these states, which depended on coal to fuel many of the region's power plants.

Bush was able to forge a compromise that benefited both regions and that remained true to his philosophy of minimal government regulation and no additional taxation. The solution lay in allowing utilities to trade emissions allowances. The act set a national standard for power plant emissions. Plants that were able to control emissions below the standard could "sell the rights" to excess emissions to other plants. This had the effect of subsidizing those plants that needed to retrofit equipment while maintaining the overall emissions goal, which was to reduce power plant emissions of sulfur dioxide from roughly 20 million tons per year to approximately 10 million tons. Most important for Bush, no taxation was involved.

The Americans with Disabilities Act

Bush's support of the Americans with Disabilities Act highlighted his compassion and commitment to equal opportunity for all Americans. The Americans with Disabilities Act of 1990 is a far-reaching piece of civil rights legislation that broadened the rights and opportunities of disabled Americans and helped them cross a new threshold of opportunity and self-respect. Until 1990, federal legislation for the disabled was limited to the Rehabilitation Act of 1973, which set guidelines regarding the disabled for the federal government, anyone doing business with the government, and institutions that accepted federal funds. In addition, the Education for All Handicapped Children Act of 1975 provided equal education opportunities for the disabled. These bills, however, did not tackle a major concern of the disabled: doing away with the de facto discrimination that existed in society and the workplace regarding access to transportation and accommodations. The act gave the disabled the opportunity to apply their talents and thus become an economic benefit to and participant in society rather than an economic dependent.

The passage of the legislation was made possible through a constellation of forces, both political and social.

The action had broad public appeal. Opinion polls at the time showed the vast majority of Americans favoring the legislation. The support is understandable. In 1990 there were 43 million disabled Americans and hundreds of millions of people worldwide affected by various mental and/or physical disabilities. The problem is an enormous challenge to individual families and an economic challenge to society and government in terms of dormant talents and medical costs. It costs millions annually in public and private funds to support the disabled.

The large numbers of disabled Americans undoubtedly stimulated the broad bipartisan support of the bill. Like the general public, many members of Congress had family members with a disability. Bush's interest in the issue was an outgrowth of his own personal experiences. He and Barbara had suffered the loss of their daughter, Robin, to leukemia; their son, Neil, is afflicted with dyslexia; and Bush's uncle, Dr. John Walker, suffered from polio. President Bush felt comfortable in the presence of disabled individuals and felt a high degree of empathy. This empathy, in turn, was instrumental in helping Bush to realize the pervasive nature of disabilities in American society and the need to address the issue.

Another plus was that there was great interest in Congress for this type of legislation, and the early work toward this end began before Bush actually took office. Bush expressed his support early on, paralleling the efforts that were under way in Congress. In his acceptance speech at the Republican National Convention in August 1988, Bush stated his determination: "I am going to do whatever it takes to make sure the disabled are included in the mainstream. For too long they've been left out. But they're not going to be left out anymore."

The legislation was also a logical extension of the Civil Rights Act of 1964. That act had granted certain protections to women and racial minorities. It stood to reason that protection also be extended to disabled Americans. Finally, the concerns of skeptical groups, mostly the business community, were allayed. The latter were concerned that the new regulations would bring undue economic hardships, particularly for small business owners. To alleviate these concerns, the bill exempted businesses with fewer than twenty-five employees; it also did not make the regulations retroactive. Thus, for example, lifts were not necessary for old buses but only for newly constructed vehicles.

Bush became involved in the disability issue during his vice-presidential days at the behest of his counsel, Boyden Gray. In 1986, on behalf of President Reagan, Bush accepted a report from the National Council on Disability. The report, *Towards Independence,* recommended sweeping measures to end discrimination against the disabled. The issue became part of his campaign platform in 1988. After coming into office, Bush incorporated the issue into his administration's mission and goals list, but there was no coherent plan of action for making progress on the disability issue. It sank into the inertia that seemed to characterize the administration during its first few months as it sought to get itself started. However, numerous groups with a specific interest in the disability issue quickly seized on the administration's stated concern and began a strong effort to put some action behind the administration's intentions.

Much of the work in the White House fell to Boyden Gray and Bill

Roper, the deputy assistant for domestic policy. In addition, Evan J. Kemp Jr., chairman of the Equal Employment Opportunity Commission, and Justin Dart Jr., chairman of the President's Committee on the Employment of People with Disabilities, two friends of the president, were also key players in offering advice and shepherding the legislation.

The political benefits of the issue were not lost on those around the president. Lee Atwater estimated that 4 percent of the votes for Bush in the 1988 victory could be attributed to his support of rights for the disabled during the campaign. By 1992, however, this lesson had been lost on the White House. Bush was advised not to run on the issue out of some advisers' concern that doing so would irritate the business community and sharpen any opposition business leaders might harbor toward his campaign. Others, particularly in the vice president's office, believed it was a strong issue for the president, that the great number of disabled voters would far overshadow any particular opposition by the business community. Vice President Quayle had a particular interest in the issue because he chaired the Competitiveness Council.

The fear of a business backlash was more hypothetical than real. During the negotiations leading up to the passage of the legislation, business did not present a united front of opposition; it did not regard the legislation as threatening in terms of drastically increasing business-related costs. Much of this had to do with the nature of governmental regulations; the intended regulations were forward looking and did not touch on existing procedures, and many of the measures called for, such as wheelchair ramps, were relatively inexpensive to put in place.

The ADA opened new horizons for the disabled on four fronts. In employment, it monitored affected employers in order to prevent discrimination against qualified individuals suffering from a disability. In public accommodations, it ensured access for the disabled. In transportation, it expanded access. In communication, it provided services for those suffering from hearing or speech difficulties. In signing the legislation, Bush stated, "This historic act is the world's first comprehensive declaration of equality for people with disabilities—the first. . . . Together, we must remove the physical barriers we have created and the social barriers that we have accepted. For ours will never be a truly prosperous nation until all within it prosper."

Nine

MANAGING THE ECONOMY
AND THE CAMPAIGN OF 1992

IN ADDITION to the difficulty of dealing with Congress, Bush faced a number of other challenges that tested his personal and managerial skills. The most pressing of these were the economy and the reelection campaign.

Managing the Economy

In the final campaign debate in 1992, Helen Thomas, UPI reporter and dean of the White House press corps, asked Bush to what he ascribed his decline in the polls; he had slid from percentages in the eighties to the forties by mid-October that year. Bush readily attributed his problems to the economy. "Well," he responded, "I think the answer to why the drop, I think, has been the economy in the doldrums."

With the economy in the doldrums, the administration faced a public relations problem rooted in its philosophy. Bush, wedded to the conservative idea of limited government, believed that the economy should be and was indeed driven by individual initiative, and the less government action, the better the result. That was Bush's dilemma—how to explain a plan for the economy when, philosophically, he viewed the economy as something that the government should not—and could not—easily influence.

In his State of the Union address in January 1992, he stated, "Let me tell you right from the start and right from the heart, I know we're in hard times.

But I know something else: this will not stand." The effort to draw a parallel to his resolve in the Gulf War, when he said Saddam's aggression would not stand, suffered from the lack of a coherent plan. What Bush had to offer in the address was, basically, a warmed-over listing of all the points that he had been advocating throughout the years. And many of these points did not resonate with the average American, such as an alternative minimum tax, a 15 percent investment tax allowance, a cut in the capital gains tax, and making the research and development tax credit permanent. An unemployed man hearing this "plan" would have difficulty seeing how it would help him. Furthermore, the president had a tendency to explain the economic situation in a manner that appeared to lack any empathy for the worker and that seemed defensive rather than forward looking. A month before the general election in 1992, Bush explained the economic situation by stating, "I know America has had tough economic times, but understand, we're being affected by a global economic slowdown. Our competitors in Europe, every single one of them, would trade places with us in a minute." In a campaign stop in early September 1992 in Pennsylvania, Bush got a question regarding his plan for aiding middle-aged and older unemployed workers. He responded that "the fundamental thing is, get the economy stimulated so young and old will be able to have jobs in the private sector." This is not necessarily inspiring rhetoric for anyone who is unemployed, but it did help fuel the notion among the press that Bush was adrift on economic issues.

In retrospect, Bush readily admits that he fell short on this score. "I focused my attention on doing my job as president," Bush explains. "I felt an obligation to the American people to do my best. In this context, I did not believe personal or inner feelings should play a role. I guess I kept many such feelings inside. In hindsight, I should have been more open and displayed more emotion. It might have helped. When I stated that the economy was recovering, and it was, people regarded this as being out of touch. They did not see the deep care and concern I had for everyone's well-being." Bush further undermined his image by a somewhat surprising statement during the first debate of the campaign. At that time Bush made the comment that he would put Jim Baker, who in August had become White House chief of staff, in charge of coordinating an economic plan for the nation during his second term. While he tried to use the statement as an indication of his seriousness about tackling the economic issue by having his closest associate spearhead the effort, it only served to portray Bush as incapable of managing his office and the economy.

Nevertheless, as the economy began to improve, Bush had a deep faith that the public would recognize the improvements that were taking place. "I knew the economy had problems, but the recession had long since ended and the economy was improving," Bush explained in retrospect in his Gauer lecture in 1997. "I believed the facts would lift people out of their doubts and fears. So I was determined not to do anything that might jeopardize the healthy economic recovery that was picking up steam."

Bush had come into office in the wake of a successful "Reagan-Bush economy," one that saw a decrease in inflation from 12 to 4 percent, interest rates cut in half, and the lowest unemployment in fourteen years. Moreover, in his acceptance speech at the nominating convention in 1988, Bush had pledged to create 30 million jobs in eight years. These were the statistics that the American public expected him to live by. However, circumstances beyond his control quickly intruded and negatively influenced the economic momentum in the short term. During his administration, Bush was able to navigate the economy on a steady course that created 2.5 million jobs. While this may have been the lowest job creation number among recent presidents to that time, the raw numbers failed to illuminate the context in which the administration was operating.

While presidents have a limited ability to affect many elements of the economy, they can, through bail-out programs, budget decisions, loans, and other actions, sometimes affect the course of the economy. This was evident in the cases of the savings and loan crisis, the budget crisis, and financial crises in Mexico and Brazil, all of which Bush's administration handled in a way that helped prevent major dislocations in the U.S. economy and prevented world economic instability. In addition, Bush was correct about the worldwide economic slump that was affecting countries such as Canada, Britain, France, and Germany. Moreover, in 1990 there was a substantial increase in world oil prices. This affected the growth of the U.S. economy. The result was that in the fourth quarter of 1990, there was a decline in U.S. economic output and the country was in a recession. Early in 1991, Michael Boskin announced that the United States was in a recession. In January 1992, in a sign of the worsening economic situation, the government announced that the unemployment figure in December 1991 stood at 7.1 percent.

By the end of October 1992, however, there were indications that things were moving forward. In April, the Federal Reserve dropped the interest rate by a quarter percent; for the first quarter of the year the economy grew at 2.4 percent and continued to grow so that by the third quarter of 1992 the economy was in its sixth straight quarter of growth. Yet press coverage continued to be negative. Bush complained during a news conference in October that more than 90 percent of the coverage of the economy was negative, and he accused the "talking heads" on television of "telling everybody how bad it is."

The economy had actually started improving in March 1991. In June of that year, Boskin spoke to Bush about this positive change but cautioned that it would be a while before the public would become aware of the improvement. Boskin had first met Bush during the campaign in 1980, when he helped prepare Reagan for the debates. Afterward, Boskin joined the faculty at Stanford University, but at the request of Bush's chief of staff, Craig Fuller, he started meeting with Bush in the late 1980s to discuss economic matters at the latter's office as well as at the vice president's home on the grounds of the Naval Observatory. Through these meetings Boskin and Bush developed a rapport, and Boskin eventually became active in Bush's own presidential campaign. Viewed through Boskin's economic lenses, the economy was improving, but it still had a long way to go. He saw it as being the slowest economic recovery since World War II. At the daily senior staff meetings, Boskin repeated his mantra that the economy was improving, a view that eventually proved correct. The electorate, however, was looking for more inspiration and a sense of commitment from the administration.

The administration's economic spokesmen were not too helpful in explaining the economic situation the country faced. The effort was spearheaded by the trio of Nick Brady, Boskin, and Darman. Even though the economy was improving month by month in 1992, the administration's economic team could not devise a method to make the public appreciate the improvement; the public perception remained that the economy was lagging.

Part of the message problem was due to a split in Bush's inner circle regarding the economy. Sununu and Darman sought at first to ignore the bad economic news. Boskin, however, urged the president to formulate an approach to tackle the economic slowdown and to convey Bush's concern and understanding of the economic problems to the public.

As the public perception of the economy continued to be negative and Bush's favorable ratings began to decline, Darman and Sununu switched from ignoring the economy to urging an upbeat message. This argument only served to compound the problems for Bush. Darman, who opposed any form of tinkering with the economy, believed that dealing with the economy was an issue of public relations, that an upbeat and optimistic message could overcome a negative public attitude. Boskin, concerned about the president's credibility and accuracy, was continually fighting to inject a sense of realism and patience into the president's remarks.

In mid-1991, Boskin sought to implement a program that would appeal to the average worker and possibly boost Bush's public appeal. He advocated pairing an investment tax credit with a payroll "new jobs" tax credit. The latter would have given companies a break on the payroll taxes they paid in exchange for hiring additional workers. The idea did not move forward. Not only was there a reluctance to admit that the economic recovery was slow but the administration also had just passed a budget agreement that included taxes; now the administration would be pushing a tax cut, and it would appear that it had not worked with Congress in good faith.

Joining Boskin in the effort to get the president focused realistically on the economy was Secretary of Commerce Bob Mosbacher. Behind the scenes Mosbacher argued that something had to be done about the recession, and he tried to get Bush past his aversion to "selling" his policies. In a Cabinet meeting early in the fall of 1991 Mosbacher laid out his concerns for Bush and the whole Cabinet. He argued that the president had to do something to reduce taxes or provide tax breaks to help stimulate the economy. In addition, Mosbacher volunteered that Bush had to talk about the economy more often; he needed to show, Mosbacher pointed out, that he was doing something about the situation. Mosbacher felt strongly about the issue and believed that he had made his case. Secretary of Housing and Urban Development Jack Kemp sided with Mosbacher, but the obstacles were too great. Sununu, Darman, and Brady opposed Mosbacher's idea that the government should take measures to stimulate the economy. Mosbacher continued his private lobbying of the president until Bush, somewhat reluctantly, relented and agreed. The Commerce Department provided some information for Bush to use in a speech that focused on the economy, which turned out to be the traditional Thanksgiving Day message.

The message was short on specifics but promised that more would be forthcoming in the State of the Union address. In keeping with Mosbacher's urging, Bush did seek to highlight his concern regarding the plight of Americans suffering the consequences of a slowed economy. "I do understand," he stated. "I am concerned. And I want to help. I know that for a person out of a job, the unemployment rate is 100 percent." In an effort to show Bush's empathy, the text also referenced two letters Bush had received from Americans who were experiencing hard economic times. However, Bush also made it clear "that hot rhetoric won't fill an empty stomach." While the line was aimed at political demagoguery on the economic issue, it also reflected Bush's aversion to high rhetoric and signaled that there was a limit to how far he would go down this road. Bush's view of rhetoric and its role in the policy process was best summed up when he told the American Legislative Exchange Council in 1992 that "real eloquence lies in action."

Brady, who had shared Boskin's cautionary approach in 1991, by 1992 had joined Darman in wanting to present an upbeat assessment of the economy. Both argued that the economy would right itself and that the government did not need to step in. In this atmosphere, the best that Bush's spokesmen could offer to the public was the exhortation, as one staffer dismissively categorized it, to "be happy." Boskin's frustration with these internecine struggles and the exaggerations about the economy, which he thought were quite damaging to the president, led him at one point to threaten to resign.

Bush's increasing troubles were evident to his press and communications staff even before the start of the campaign season. Invited to the president's private dining room off the Oval Office for lunch in the spring of 1991, Marlin Fitzwater and Dorrance Smith were faced with a particular dilemma. Bush was planning to go fishing, and Fitzwater was concerned about the image this activity might convey to the press: while the country was hurting economically, Bush was fishing. Compounding the image problem, Fitzwater worried, was Bush's tendency to don what he considered a "goofy-looking" fishing hat.

That day, Fitzwater and Smith discussed their mutual concerns by telephone and then went to lunch prepared to confront the president. Their resolve quickly dissipated in light of Bush's opening comments as they sat down at the table.

"I'm looking forward to going fishing," stated Bush, uncannily anticipating their concerns. "I don't care what anyone says." He loved fishing. He also hated being staged. His statement seemed to be definitive in both respects.

Both men knew Bush and his determination. Fitzwater sensed there would be no room for argument.

"Yes, sir, fishing is going to be great," said Fitzwater, willing to drop the subject.

Smith, however, was more determined.

"Do you think you will wear a hat?" asked Smith.

"Of course," stated Bush. "What's fishing without a hat?"

"Of course you wear a hat," seconded Fitzwater.

And so, a few days later, with the press in tow, Bush went fishing—wearing a silly hat.

The 1992 Campaign

In early December 1991 Bush's reelection campaign was entrusted to a triumvirate: Bob Teeter, Mosbacher, and Fred Malek, a businessman and former member of the Nixon administration. Teeter took the title of chairman while the other two were general manager and campaign manager, respectively. Personality differences quickly emerged, and it became clear that the campaign was off to a bumpy start as each of the three jockeyed for prominence. Some viewed the triumvirate as a three-headed monster lacking the discipline of the late Lee Atwater, the Republican political strategist who had helped engineer Bush's victory in 1988, and the political maturity of Jim Baker, Bush's closest political confidant. The campaign structure had been laid out under Sununu at a time when he was on his way out of the White House and thus was not able to oversee the organization or give it discipline. This problem was compounded under his successor, Sam Skinner, who could not mold the three into a cohesive unit.

The campaign team's inability to set even simple goals troubled Bush. On one occasion in early 1992, frustrated with continued scheduling indecisiveness, Bush summoned his White House scheduler, Kathy Super. "What's going on with the campaign and the schedule?" he asked, his tone suggesting something between a question and an accusation. He wanted to make sure he did not appear to be looking over the shoulders of his campaign managers. Then he got more forceful. "What am I doing next week? Why don't I know what I am doing?"

His frustration pointed to the general lack of coordination and planning that seemed to grip the campaign. Super understood his frustration. The campaign was being run by well-intentioned and loyal associates, yet cohesion and decisiveness were lacking. In some cases, the shortcomings were those of individuals blocked by the blinders of their own expertise.

As a pollster, Bob Teeter was mentally fixated on the next poll; his intense focus influenced the rest of the campaign. No single decision would be considered final, so there were constant changes. In one meeting with the speechwriters, Teeter displayed his chart outlining the campaign strategy. One notable blank was the block marked "theme." He wanted the speechwriters to fill in the blank. Before the astounded speechwriters could react, Teeter was off to another meeting. A few days later, at a morning meeting of senior staffers, Teeter audibly complained about the speechwriters.

David Demarest took exception. He felt compelled not only to defend his staff but also to note that it was not the task of the wordsmiths to devise policy and strategy; that responsibility lay with the campaign hierarchy. Chief of Staff Sam Skinner, who had by then replaced Sununu but was also encountering a hard time in getting the campaign strategy off the ground, voiced his own frustrations by supporting Demarest. He leaned toward Teeter and stated matter-of-factly, "I believe David is right on that."

Confronted by the frustrated president that day in his study, Super carefully chose how to respond to his frustration about the chaotic scheduling. She knew there was no easy, short answer to the president's questions and that it was not her place to grapple with fundamental shortcomings in the campaign. She knew what Bush was like when he was frustrated. Super had first met him in 1973 when he was chairman of the Republican National Committee. From 1978 to 1980 she served as an adviser while Bush was weighing a run for president, and during the 1980 campaign she managed the schedule for Barbara Bush and the Bush children. Subsequently, she had held a number of government positions before joining the White House staff in 1989.

Her goal at the moment was to allay the president's frustration about not knowing where he would be next week; she did not want to exacerbate it.

"Somewhere in the South," she responded, "probably Florida."

"Then I want to go to Pensacola," Bush declared firmly and definitively. The conversation ended as abruptly as it had started. It did not solve anything. Bush's statement of his desire appeared to satisfy him for the moment, giving a false impression, or more likely, a hope that things would now move in the right direction.

On another occasion, while the senior staff was assembling for their

7:30 A.M. meeting in the Roosevelt Room, exchanging pleasantries and humor, across the hall Bush and Quayle sat behind closed doors in the Oval Office sharing their frustration over the campaign. Quayle, in particular, complained about how the campaign was being run and about the lack of decision making that seemed to plague it. Bush, once again, sought to get some answers.

Bush found himself calling for Super to join them. With a concerned Quayle standing by his side, he faced Super.

"What is going on over there?" he asked with a nod of his head. There was no need for elaboration. Super knew he was referring to the campaign. It was on everyone's mind.

There was no anger or disappointment in his voice. He seemed tired, worn down by the questions he found himself repeating all too often. Bush and Quayle looked at her with hopeful eyes. Yet they already knew the answer. Bush looked at her with a drawn face, lips parted, his eyes reflecting concern. Quayle stood taut, the energy visible in his face and emanating from his body but seemingly with nowhere to go. They appeared as two men held hostage by some unseen force. Super dutifully reported what they already knew.

"There are never final decisions," she said, getting to the point quickly. "One can't rely on decisions," she added for emphasis.

The two men stood stoically. She knew the only way that things could be rectified was if the president took command of the situation. Then Super added, as if to move beyond the question and toward a resolution, "You could decide . . . ," Super began to offer, but her voice trailed off as Bush's response came quickly and predictably to what he apparently expected her to say.

"That's not the way I operate," Bush stated, almost dismissively, shaking his head. Quayle and Super knew that a nerve had been struck. "When I hire a staff, that's what they are there for," Bush continued. "I can't second guess them. I have to depend on them. I have to let them do their job." In the Navy, Bush had learned the importance of teamwork and the strength that comes with it; it was something he continued to believe in no matter how disjointed the staff became.

Super joined the rest of the senior staff in the Roosevelt Room. The campaign sputtered on. Despite Bush's public pronouncements to staff about his support of the campaign officials, some, such as Quayle, sensed his frustration and lack of confidence in the campaign.

That year, however, was an odd political year that unbalanced many a person's political compass. The Democratic standard bearer, Bill Clinton, was tarnished with images of draft dodging and womanizing, accusations that would have proved deadly in previous elections but now seemed to be inconsequential. The electorate's mood even stumped noted political pundits. The astute ABC reporter and commentator Sam Donaldson got a dose of political reality at a wedding that he attended. Donaldson, never shy for words, outlined for guests seated at his table the reasons why he believed Clinton would probably not be successful, zeroing in on the draft-dodging accusations. None of his tablemates, all younger than him and part of the post-Vietnam era of the all-volunteer military force, saw this as an issue. It was then that Donaldson realized the generational changes that had occurred and, with them, the different values and perspectives.

To its credit, the campaign had considerable concern about the economy; the staff realized that the only thing the public wanted to hear and talk about was the economy. It helped that individuals such as Mosbacher, who had championed the economic issue in the administration, joined the campaign organization. The differing views of the campaign staff and the White House staff regarding the economy added to the general disarray that was finally bridged when Baker left his post as secretary of state and took on the position of White House chief of staff to help run the campaign. He brought a sense of realism and a burst of energy and confidence into the campaign. In September 1992 he had Bush unveil an economic plan in an address to the Economic Club of Detroit. In what was termed an "agenda for American renewal," Bush outlined the economic challenges that the United States faced and the steps he favored to address them, including tax cuts, legal reform to limit lawsuits, and pension and health care reform. By then, however, Bush had fallen too far behind, and his catch-up politics fell short. Much of the damage, unfortunately, had been inflicted long before Baker came on board.

The confusion of the campaign was magnified at one stage by a decision not to have the president appear in photo opportunities with visiting foreign leaders. The campaign's fear was that this would show the president to be preoccupied with foreign policy and thus strike a sour note with the American public. This strategy was quickly dismissed by more sensible members of the White House staff. With Sununu's guidance, the White House decided to highlight the foreign policy accomplishments and downplay the domestic side in the belief that the former would be sufficient to carry the president to victory.

But there was an added reason for this strategy. Having broken his "no new taxes" pledge with the budget agreement of 1990, Bush was losing favor with many conservatives, who regarded his compromise deal as selling short the conservative agenda. Thus, campaign staff did not believe Bush should jeopardize his conservative base by pushing domestic initiatives that could find disfavor among various parts of that base. Furthermore, with a Democrat-controlled Congress it would be difficult for the president to pursue a successful domestic agenda, particularly in an election year, when partisan politics would be high on everyone's list. In such an environment, Bush could appear ineffectual in the public eye while the Democrats would have an incentive to stymie Bush on any initiative. Foreign policy was a success with which all Americans could identify. Thus, in June 1991, when the press was beginning to put the president's foreign policy successes behind him and starting to zero in on domestic issues, the White House turned a deaf ear.

During that month, Andy Card was warned by the Press Office of the impending public opinion shift, but his only retort was that Sununu believed that foreign policy would carry the president through. Meanwhile, others in the White House believed that there was plenty of time to set things right. The negative rumblings that the Press Office was hearing from the media were corroborated in correspondence and telephone calls to the White House, which were the basis of the public opinion reports that Shirley Green forwarded to Bush that summer. Green took her concerns to a senior staffer but was assured that "two or three domestic events" were being planned for later in the year. Green, however, did not feel reassured; she doubted that two or three events down the line would properly address the challenge the public was raising, and the vague plan certainly would not address the problem in a timely fashion. Wofford's Senate victory in November highlighted how the administration was misjudging the electorate.

By December 1991 Sununu was gone, but the campaign was already on the wrong track and losing touch with the public sentiment. Bush, who that spring had approval ratings as high as 91 percent in some polls, was losing ground quickly. By the fall he had slipped to 51 percent, still a good percentage, but the steep decline was indicative of the brewing trouble. Sununu, in addition to his chief of staff duties, also played two key political roles for Bush. Coming out of the conservative camp, Sununu was to serve as a bridge to the right wing of the party. Equally important, considering Bush's tough fight in the New Hampshire primary in 1988, the White House saw Sununu and the political organization that he had built in the state as important to preventing any potential challenger to Bush from gaining political traction there. Toward the end of 1991 Sununu was distracted by his impending resignation over the use of government transportation for private use, so Pat Buchanan was able to roam New Hampshire without anyone making an effort to undercut him. Buchanan ran a strong primary campaign in New Hampshire in February 1992. He garnered 40 percent of the vote, which was widely regarded as a moral victory and a sign of impending trouble for Bush.

Buchanan's exceptional showing in the primary, in turn, gave Ross Perot more traction and public exposure. Bush discounted Perot early on, believing that the latter would be marginal to the campaign. Perot actually dropped out of the campaign in the summer of 1992, as Bush thought he would, but on October 1 Perot was back in. Bush viewed Perot as nothing more than a gnat that had no bite. However, while Bush was increasingly dismissive of Perot, the latter kept growing in popularity. Perot's attacks on Bush gave the Democrats momentum while at the same time undermining Bush among Republicans and in conservative circles.

While there was no coherent plan or message for the campaign, Bush took no action to rectify the situation; he was fully expecting his advisers to set the right course. The disintegration of the campaign was even more baffling given two strengths Bush had. Despite Bush's own emphasis on personal relations, the campaign's senior advisers did not emphasize that tactic. And though Bush considered communicating through the chain of command to be very important, the campaign's senior staff had a tendency not to share information in its own hierarchy, thereby adding to the confusion and the inability to generate a coherent approach.

Some of the looseness of the campaign and lack of coordination could be attributed to Bush, however. He did not employ his own organizational skills to either supervise or direct the campaign. Having been Republican Party chairman of Harris County, Texas, and later chairman of the Republican National Committee, Bush was well aware of the benefits of tight organization and get-out-the-vote drives, yet he kept his distance from the nuts and bolts operations of the campaign. His hands-off approach was due partly to his view of the president's role in a campaign and partly to tradition. On the former, Bush believed the president's role was primarily to govern, and that is what he enjoyed most. On the latter, Bush thought of Labor Day as the start of the campaign, which had indeed once marked the traditional beginning of the effort, and he focused his campaign calendar on that date. In doing so, he turned a deaf ear to the media explosion and the new campaign techniques, such as Clinton's constantly operating "war room" that disgorged voluminous materials critical of Bush and his policies. Bush also did not bring his friend and confidant Jim Baker into the White House until mid-August 1992.

In the end, Bush was a victim of his own successes, much as Churchill had been after World War II. After leading the British successfully through the war, Churchill was turned out of office by an electorate that was looking toward the future. The electorate's collective memory is short; tantalized by Clinton's deft campaign of exploiting the economic recession the country had experienced, the American public hitched its wagon to Clinton's vision of building a better America domestically, something that Bush could not articulate.

Bush faced the dilemma that confronts many leaders. Put into a position of authority, leaders have a strong sense of dedication to their duty of serving the public and using their best judgment. Leaders may believe that everyone assumes they are performing well and doing what is right, and they may therefore also believe that the public should realize on its own that a leader has their best interests at heart. This scenario helps explain, in part, Bush's reluctance to engage in public selling of his policies and his reluctance to use the press as an intermediary with the public. Bush believed it was his record that mattered and by which he thought he should be judged; he invariably pointed to his record of accomplishments.

Bush's determination to run for reelection according to his own principles is important because it shows he never lost his urge to do what was right. In September 1992, with the campaign heating up toward a conclusion and Bush unable to find a way to gain the initiative, a number of campaign advisers urged Bush to make a public issue of the Democratic Congress's spending habits by exercising a line item veto of the proposed budget. The action would cast Bush as holding the line on spending. Teeter's polls showed that such a move would have public support. There was a caveat, however. The move would lead to a court challenge regarding the constitutionality of any such action. This, however, could serve to further highlight the determination of the president. Bush listened politely; he seemed to understand the political benefits that could accrue, but he was hesitant. As the conversation ended, Bush gave his decision: he noted that the first thing he promised as president was to uphold the Constitution and, unless he could be shown it was constitutionally correct, he would not use the line item gambit for political gain.

Bush had difficulty believing that he would lose to his Democratic opponent, Bill Clinton, a supposed draft dodger and alleged philanderer who, Bush believed, could bring only negative baggage to the office of president. However, there was always a chance that the polls predicting a Clinton victory could be wrong. Bush remembered the surprise election results of 1948; he had lost ten dollars in a bet that Thomas Dewey would defeat Harry Truman. There was to be no surprise ending in 1992, however. Bush received 37.4 percent of the vote compared to Clinton's 43 percent. The third-party candidacy of fellow Texan Ross Perot garnered 19 percent, which undoubtedly helped skew the election toward Clinton. Clinton carried the Electoral College vote, with 370 to Bush's 168.

In retrospect, Barbara Bush has a more sanguine view of the election. "After twelve years of Republicans, people were tired and wanted change," she says. "I accept that."

What she could not accept, however, was Bill Clinton. For Barbara Bush, as for George Bush, the office of the presidency is a trust and a moral beacon whose occupant should set a tone for the nation as well as serve as a personal role model. Barbara Bush, therefore, felt "heartsick" about Clinton occupying the office. She viewed him as "young but flawed." She credits three specific factors for Clinton's victory: "no war, he was young, and the economy." Not facing an external threat or war, the American people felt more comfortable changing leaders. Clinton's youth projected an aura of confidence and of moving into the future. The economy, in turn, was an issue because of the persistent perception that things were bad despite improving indicators.

Even though Bush had initial misgivings about Clinton, his respect for the office was stronger than his personal unease. On inauguration day, Bush told Clinton that he would not engage in any public analysis or criticism of the new administration; he did not want to undermine Clinton's authority nor be seen as a carping sore loser. Bush never wanted to put his successor in the same uncomfortable position that President Carter had placed him. During the debate in the lead-up to the Gulf War, Carter had written to the United Nations Security Council urging the members not to support Resolution 678, which authorized the use of "all necessary means" to ensure that Iraq abided by the will of the international community and set a deadline of January 15, 1991, for Iraq to comply. Carter urged continued negotiations. His letter, however, was tantamount to urging a vote against the United States, and it angered Bush. "I found it unconscionable," Bush now declares, "that a former president would do that to a sitting president."

Upon leaving office, Bush, therefore, assured Clinton that he would not have to worry about Bush second guessing or criticizing him. Throughout Clinton's tenure, Bush persisted in this silence except when he voiced concerns, for example, about Clinton's policies in Somalia. In Somalia, Bush believed, the humanitarian effort he had started had mushroomed under Clinton to become one of fending off the warlords.

The relationship between the two couples had from the start been proper. Between the 1992 election and the inauguration, the Bushes were accommodating to the Clintons in their efforts to move into the White House. Mrs. Bush, in particular, helped Hillary Clinton with access to the White House. The day that Bush's mother passed away in November 1992, Mrs. Clinton was at the White House.

That day, Mrs. Clinton had tea with Mrs. Bush in the residence and presented Mrs. Bush with a personalized silver bookmark. Mrs. Bush then took Mrs. Clinton on a tour of the residence. After a few moments, Mrs. Bush departed, leaving her guest to her work. An usher eventually came over to Mrs. Clinton, informing her that President Bush's mother had passed away. Mrs. Clinton quickly changed plans and left the White House, realizing that, at such a moment, the Bushes would need private time.

At the dedication of the Clinton Presidential Library in Little Rock on November 18, 2004, it was obvious that the passage of time had soothed the political wounds of the past. The steady rain and cold that cast a pall over the outdoor ceremony could not dampen the high spirits of the Bushes and the Clintons. Both Bush and his son, President George W. Bush, praised the forty-second president, bringing a warmth and a sense of satisfaction to the partisan crowd. Those close to the Clintons remarked how thoughtful and gracious former president Bush had been. Barbara Bush says she admires how the Clintons, in her view, did a wonderful job in maintaining a relatively normal life for their daughter, Chelsea, and keeping her out of the limelight and political turmoil of Washington politics.

When a devastating tsunami in the Indian Ocean ravaged southern Asia in December 2004, President George W. Bush named his father and Bill Clinton as the U.S. representatives for the relief effort. The two former presidents quickly solidified their growing relationship. The two made joint appearances, made joint public service announcements, and traveled together on an official visit to the stricken region. Bush found Clinton to be "very engaging, very accommodating." His admiration for Clinton is genuine and, for Clinton, Bush has become a new best friend. The relationship had progressed to the point that the two were exchanging telephone calls and notes and had become the subject of various cartoons. Clinton sent Bush one such cartoon, portraying them strolling hand in hand while a surprised George W. admonishes his father. Clinton had the cartoon enlarged and penned a note across the bottom: "George, Maybe we ought to cool it! Bill." The success of the duo's tsunami relief effort led President George W. Bush to name them as co-leaders of the Hurricane Katrina relief fund, and in September 2008 they teamed up on their own initiative to head the Bush-Clinton Coastal Recovery Fund to raise funds for victims of Hurricanes Gustav and Ike in Louisiana and Texas.

At the time of the election, however, all of this cooperation lay in the future. The days before the election of 1992 were a blend of optimism, concern, foreboding, and a high degree of anxiety, the air heavily weighted with the increasing realization that the election might not be a Bush victory. A few days before the election, Special Prosecutor Lawrence Walsh issued an indictment of Reagan's secretary of defense, Caspar Weinberger, in the Iran-Contra investigation. At the time of Walsh's announcement, Bush had closed the gap with Clinton to within approximately 1 or 2 percentage points. The indictment caused a media frenzy, leading to a sharp decline in Bush's support.[1]

Despite the pre-election unease in the president's circle, Bush arrived in Houston the day before the election for a grand welcoming rally at the Astroarena. Greeting Bush was a long list of celebrities, including Baseball Hall of Famer Ted Williams, comedian Bob Hope, golfer Arnold Palmer, and many of the president's country and western music friends.

The next morning, November 3, Bush voted early. He went for a jog in Memorial Park with his son George W. and some staffers. He was in great spirits, happy that the race was over. In the late morning, feeling restless, he headed out to a music store on Post Oak Road not far from the Houstonian Hotel, which served as his residence in Texas. Followed by his Secret Service detail and a handful of aides, including Don Rhodes and David Jones, Bush wandered through the store and bought two cassettes by the English singer Roger Whitaker. Jones had become involved with Bush in 1979 while working in Boston. Originally from Pennsylvania, Jones settled in Houston in 1980 and worked for a think tank. He later became a professional fundraiser, assisting on many of the causes supported by Bush.

Once back at the Houstonian, Bush headed out to the pool area, where, casually dressed, he sat with his cassette player and listened to his new music selections.

The victory celebration was planned for the Westin Galleria Hotel. Everything was in place. However, by late afternoon and early evening word was coming in that the election was not going the president's way. At that time White House chief of staff Jim Baker took the exit polls and went to see Bush. Bush was getting his hair cut in the Houstonian, and, as he sat in the barber's chair, he listened to Baker's gloomy assessment: it looked like Bush was going to lose. Bush took it well; it was a reality that he had hoped would not come, but he was steeled to deal with the outcome. He would not allow his emotions to overcome him. Even earlier, a stillness had come over the staff area, a harbinger of the news that was to come from Baker. In the late morning, the exit polls had showed Bush trailing Clinton, but even at that point Bush had a hard time believing that he would lose. With the growing tide of bad news, it was clear that the planned victory celebration would be a concession speech and the question of how it should be handled was being considered. Jones telephoned the president's oldest son, George W., who was serving as a campaign adviser to his father and was in the Houstonian.

Jones asked how the appearance should be handled and, specifically, who should introduce the president.

"It can't be me," stated George W., "because I'm going to be too emotional. If we win, I'll be too emotional. If we lose, I'll be too upset."

"Then who?" asked Jones.

"It's got to be Baker," George W. stated without hesitation.

"Okay," agreed Jones. "Who will ask Baker?"

"I'll do it," said George W., and he hung up the telephone.

He called back in a minute to report that Baker had agreed.

Backstage at the Westin a whirlwind of activity surrounded preparations for the president's appearance. The president and Mrs. Bush stood among a host of staff and friends in the holding area. In the highly emotional atmosphere, George and Barbara Bush stood strong, consoling everyone around them, reassuring them that "everything is going to be all right" and that "we are going to be fine." It was the strength of character that Bush draws upon in moments of adversity. No matter how much something may hurt personally, Bush, even though he tends toward tears in emotional moments, is able to evince the strength that is so important in bolstering those around him. This was such a moment, and Bush called on all his reserves to ease the pain of those around him. Only Baker appeared to be immune to the moment, being too distracted, hustling back and forth in a flurry of activity, making certain that everything was set just right for the president's appearance on the stage.

Baker's external demeanor, however, masked the emotion that was churning inside. For him it was not only a political loss but, more importantly, a setback for a dear friend, someone who had become an important part of his life. It was, therefore, with deep emotion and respect that Baker approached the friendly but emotional crowd. For Baker there was only one way to introduce Bush: "Ladies and gentlemen, the president of the United States!" To an audience chant of "Thank you, George!" Bush faced the crowd, wishing Clinton well, thanking his supporters, and, true to his spirit, urging the youth of America to participate in the political process of the nation. And then it was all over.

Back at the Houstonian, walking down the hallway, with Barbara trailing slightly behind, Bush headed toward their suite, mumbling under his breath. The emotion of the evening was catching up with him. He and Barbara entered the suite, and Bush, in a definitive statement of emotion and frustration, slammed the door behind them.

He wrote in his diary: "It's 12:15 in the morning, November 4th. The election is over—it's come and gone. It's hard to describe the emotions of something like this. But it's hurt, hurt, hurt. . . . Now into bed, prepared to face tomorrow. Be strong, be kind, be generous of spirit, be understanding and let people know how grateful you are. Don't get even. Comfort the ones I've hurt and let down. Say your prayers and ask for God's understanding and strength. Finish with a smile and some gusto, and do what's right and finish strong."

Postscript

STUDYING THE PRESIDENCY

S INCE WORLD War II, there have been various surveys and polls that
seek to rank the presidents. In these rankings there are a perennial few
who continue to lounge in the lower half of appreciation, while others
have consistently high ratings. Leading the list of those considered the greatest presidents are Abraham Lincoln, Franklin Roosevelt, George Washington, Theodore Roosevelt, and Harry Truman. Stuck at the bottom end are
James Buchanan, Andrew Johnson, Franklin Pierce, Warren Harding, and
Benjamin Harrison. Nestled between these two extremes are the majority of
presidents, with some slight shifting from time to time. Dwight Eisenhower,
for example, has moved up the scale in the surveys over time as his presidency
is reevaluated. Critics are quick to note that any rankings are subjective—
depending on the political leanings of the rater and the criteria chosen to rate
the presidents. One also cannot discount the influence of the historical times
in coloring the perspectives of presidential observers. Irrespective of these
caveats, the surveys continue and have become part of presidential legacies.
Bush is currently viewed as being in the middle of the presidential pack.

History shows that the great presidents have had the foresight and courage to do what was right for the country rather than for political expediency.
Abraham Lincoln's election to office tore the country apart with a civil war,
but he preserved the Union; FDR had the vision to move boldly on social
and economic programs to help overcome the Depression. Both were excori-
ated and mocked by their opposition during their respective tenures. Both,

however, have been placed in the pantheon of great presidents—in hindsight. History, therefore, is the ultimate and best judge of a presidency.

Bush's leadership has been criticized on issues such as vision and the slow economy. His failure to gain reelection only served to reinforce some of these early views. However, Bush himself recognizes the kindness that distance bestows on presidents. "I'd make a point that everybody looks better over time," noted Bush in a philosophical moment with journalists in 1989. "So history is basically kind to American presidents."

Presidents have no control over the times in which they live and govern, but they do have control over the mechanics of their leadership. Leadership qualities encompass a range of attributes: the ability to communicate well; the ability to form coalitions, particularly in Congress; interpersonal skills; and past experiences and knowledge. All of these have a bearing on how presidents handle a challenge and play a significant role in whether or not a president will be judged successful. Every president has had his own unique mixture of them, stronger in some, weaker in others.

Presidents exhibit these skills in various functions—as commander in chief, as chief executive, as chief diplomat, and as head of the political party, among others. As in the case of particular skills, here also a president may be stronger in one function than in another. Thus, presidents can be judged on three levels: how they tackled the historical issues their administrations faced; how they exercised their leadership arsenal; and, finally, how they applied those leadership skills to particular functions.

The international challenge that Bush faced with the collapse of communism was a situation that, if not handled properly, could have had dire consequences for the United States and the world. Through skillful handling of the international situation and the United States–Soviet bilateral relationship, Bush was able to bring a peaceful and highly successful end to the cold war. In addition, facing Iraq's aggression in Kuwait, Bush was able to assemble an international coalition that quickly ousted Saddam Hussein from Kuwait. The feat was all the more remarkable in that Bush was able to enlist the support of Iraq's patron, the Soviet Union, in this endeavor at the same time that he was pursuing policies, such as German reunification, that were undermining the Soviet Union.

The Gulf War also gave Bush an opportunity to excel in the role he most relished—that of commander in chief. Bush not only was able to supervise a successful military operation but also helped to restore the confidence and morale of the armed forces by the support he provided and by his definition of their mission. As for his leadership tools, Bush excelled at personal diplomacy and contacts. His style was to cajole and persuade on the strength of those personal relationships. Thus, his leadership was more effective in one-on-one and small group encounters and lacked the flair and rhetoric that is often associated with popular leaders.

Bush faced the criticism that he was a president without an agenda or vision. Much of this early evaluation was based on an assessment of the mechanics of leadership, such as communication skills, articulating an agenda, and dealing with institutions, rather than actual leadership. Historical assessments will likely show that Bush exhibited great leadership and that his personal leadership skills were instrumental to that success. His rank among the presidents of the United States will likely rise as the passage of time improves perspective.

NOTES

PREFACE AND ACKNOWLEDGMENTS

1. John Adams and his son, John Quincy Adams, had accomplished the feat back in the early years of the nation, serving in office 1797–1801 and 1825–29, respectively. George Bush held office 1989–93 while his son, George W. Bush, was president 2001–2009. In recognition of their feat, Bush took to referring to his son in jest as "Quincy."

CHAPTER 1. THE MAKING OF A LEADER

1. In 1999 legislation renamed the building the Dwight D. Eisenhower Executive Office Building, and it was rededicated in a ceremony in 2002.

2. The award is presented by the George Bush Presidential Library Foundation and recognizes an individual's or group's dedication to public service at the local, state, national, or international levels. It underscores President Bush's commitment to public service.

3. In 2007, the Points of Light Foundation merged with the HandsOn Network volunteer organization to form the Points of Light Institute. The term "foundation" is used in the text, since the references pre-date the name change.

4. A devastating tsunami hit southern Asia in December 2004. In 2005 Hurricane Katrina wreaked havoc in New Orleans and the surrounding area and Pakistan suffered a major earthquake.

CHAPTER 2. BUSH'S PRINCIPLES OF LEADERSHIP

1. In December 2005 the Chinese authorities allowed recognition of Hu's birthday, thus signaling a possible rehabilitation of his reputation.

CHAPTER 3. THE VISION THING

1. Teeter returned for the reelection campaign in 1992 but did not bring with him a vision or theme, which continued to elude the campaign.

2. The Iran-Contra scandal involved the covert sale of U.S. arms to Iran in exchange for the release of hostages in Lebanon held by pro-Iranian groups. The proceeds from the arms sales were used, in contravention to congressional stipulations,

to secretly arm the Nicaraguan Contras, who were fighting the leftist Sandinista government of Nicaragua.

CHAPTER 6. DELIVERING THE MESSAGE

1. Glasnost (openness) referred to Gorbachev's policy of government transparency and greater information for the public. Perestroika (restructuring) referred to the policy of social and economic changes that Gorbachev initiated with the aim of reforming the Soviet system.

CHAPTER 9. MANAGING THE ECONOMY AND THE CAMPAIGN OF 1992

1. In a parting move, on Christmas Eve, Bush granted a pardon to Weinberger both as a sign of Bush's belief in his innocence and as an indication that he believed there had been a politically motivated witch hunt.

INDEX

Abshire, David, 20, 168
Achille Lauro, 85
acid rain issues, 188, 189–90
Acland, Antony, 94, *fig. 2 gallery*
ADA (Americans with Disabilities Act), 162, 164, 190–92
Afghanistan, 139
"age of freedom," 139
"Aggie Spirit," 26
Ailes, Roger, 73, 124, 132
Air Force One, 78, 101–102, 117, 174
al-Bakr, Ahmed Hassan, 82
All the Best, George Bush (Bush, George H. W.), 112, 134
American flag desecration issue, 177–78
Americans with Disabilities Act (ADA), 162, 164, 190–92
Andover, Massachusetts, 6, 9
Andreotti, Giulio, 143
Annan, Kofi, 27
Arab-Israeli relations, 33, 140
Arab relations, 110
Archer, Bill, 173
Argentina, 103–104
Arizona, USS, Memorial, 124–25
arms reduction issues, 140, 148, 152–53, 157
Ashley, Lud, 167, 168, 174–75
Assad, Hafez al-, 101
Atwater, Lee, 73, 192, 199
A World Transformed (Bush, George H. W. and Scowcroft), 134

Baker, Howard, 2
Baker, Jim, *figs. 8, 12 gallery*
    background, 149–50
    and Bush's economic plan, 194
    as campaign chairman 1988, 124
    and Eduard Shevardnadze, 154
    and election day 1992, 209–10
    and foreign policy process, 81, 121–22
    and Gulf War, 44

    on making mistakes, 39
    and the media, 116
    move to chief of staff position, 202, 205
    and NSC advisory groups, 61, 86–87
    personal relationships, importance of, 86–87, 88
    personal relationship with Bush, 88, 149–50
    as prayer leader, 17
    scheduling issues, 81
    and Soviet Union, 148, 154
Baker, Mary Stuart, 149
Bakr, Ahmed Hassan al-, 82
balanced budget agreement issues, 178–79, 180–87. *See also* economy
Baltic states, 155, 156–57
Bandar, Prince, 110
banking scandal, House, 178
Basel Convention, 163
Bates, David, 17, 59–60
Beckwith, David, 7
behavior, Bush's rules of, 30–31
Belarus, 157
Bentsen, Lloyd, 13, 21
Berlin Wall, destruction of, 43–44, 119–20
Bierbauer, Charles, 104
Blair House, 24, 155
blogs, influence of, 114
boating, 108–109, 151
Boskin, Michael, 189, 195, 196–97, 198
Brady, Nick, 65, 88, 196, 198
Brady, Phil, 56–57, 100
Britain, 195
broccoli, Bush's dislike of, 22
Brock, Ann, 76–77
Bromfield, Louis, 10
Buchanan, James, 211
Buchanan, Pat, 179, 182, 204
Budge, Don, 7
budget (balanced) agreement issues, 178–79, 180–87. *See also* economy

Ford, Gerald, 150
foreign policy
    Bush's affinity for, 15–16, 134–36,
      142–48, 202
    Bush's world view, 136–42
    and dealing with Congress, 164, 172
    press issues, 121–22, 138–39
    and reelection campaign, 202–203
    Scowcroft's process, 81–82
    secrecy in, 86–87
    and speech diplomacy, 130–31
    Walker's Point diplomacy, 109–10
    (*See also* Gorbachev, Mikhail)
France, 195
freedom theme in world developments,
    139–41

Gates, Bob, 45, 61–62, 74, 87, 95, *fig. 7*
    gallery
Gehrig, Lou, 7
"General Bunny," 97
Geneva, Switzerland, 101
George Bush Award for Excellence in Public
    Service, 34
George Bush Presidential Library Center,
    26, ix
George Bush School of Government and
    Public Service, 26
Gephardt, Dick, 175, 176
Germany, 50, 119–20, 144, 157, 160, 195
Gibbons, Gene, 104, 127
Gingrich, Newt, 185–86
Giroldi, Moses, 122
glasnost, 119, 153
Glen, Alixe, 53–54
Golden Knights, 75
González, Henry B., 20
"Good Society," 50–51
Gorbachev, Mikhail
    and Boris Yeltsin, 156
    Bush's admiration for, 144
    Bush's friendship with, 26, 85–86,
      145–47
    Bush's support of, 119–20, 154–55,
      156–57, 159–60
    at Camp David, *fig. 3 gallery*
    1991 coup attempt against, 117, 157–59
    "drugstore cowboy" incident, 39
    signing of START, 155–56
    and "telephone diplomacy," 143

Gorbachev, Raisa, 146
Grady, Bob, 186–87, 188, 189
Graham, Rev. Billy, 17, 18
Gramm-Rudman-Hollings Act, 181–82
Graves' disease, 98–101
Gray, Al, 97
Gray, C. Boyden, 189, 191–92
"Great American Workout," 96
"Great Communicator," 112–13
Great Society, 50, 161
Greece, 56–57
Green, Shirley, 62–63, 72, 203
Gregg, Hugh, 5
Gulf War, 80
    "just war" concept, 18–19
    multilateral diplomacy, 137–38
    postwar diplomacy, 56–57
    and television, 115–17, 119
    troop deployment, 141
    UN Resolution 678, 83, 206–207

Haass, Richard, 45
Hagin, Joe, 71
Hamilton, Lee, 173
Hamtramck speech, 131, 153
HandsOn Network, 215*n*
Harding, Warren, 211
Harrison, Benjamin, 211
"Have Half" (nickname), 7
Havel, Vaclav, 153
health care initiatives, 165–67
health issues (Bush), 98–101, 102, 104–105
Hirohito, Emperor, 102
Home Ownership for People Everywhere
    (HOPE) Act, 162
Hope, Bob, 208
House banking scandal, 178
House post office scandal, 178
Houstonian Hotel, 208–209
human rights issues, 41, 116, 141
Hungary, 120, 153
Hunt, Terry, 104
hurricanes, 98, 208
Hussein, King, 110
Hussein, Saddam
    Arab states diplomacy issues, 110
    Bush's actions against, 81, 90–91
    and Bush's sense of humor, 6
    missle attack on Tel Aviv, 115
    morality of actions against, 18–19

World Transformed, A (Bush, George H. W.
and Scowcroft), 134
Wright, Jim, 171

Yarborough, Ralph, 13
Yeltsin, Boris, 117, 145, 156, 157–59, 158
Yeutter, Clayton, 65
Yugoslavia, 153

Zapata Off-Shore, 12
Zapata Petroleum, 12
Zionism and racism resolution, repeal of
United Nations, 140
Zoellick, Robert, 188